AN AMBASSADOR OF PEACE

Lord D'Abernon leaving the Presidency of the Reich on relinquishing the British Embassy at Berlin

Title:

AN AMBASSADOR OF PEACE,

LORD D'ABERNON'S DIARY

D'Abernon, Edgar Vincent,

VOL. I

FROM SPA (1920) TO RAPALLO (1922)

WITH HISTORICAL NOTES BY

MAURICE ALFRED GEROTHWOHL

Litt.D. (Dublin)

HODDER AND STOUGHTON
LIMITED   LONDON
MCMXXIX

The following will be published subsequently :

Vol. II
THE YEARS OF CRISIS

Vol. III
THE YEARS OF RECOVERY

Made and Printed in Great Britain.
Hazell, Watson & Viney, Ld., London and Aylesbury.

TO

THE FAIREST OF CRITICS

CONTENTS

INTRODUCTORY SURVEY

SOME PERSONAL APPRECIATIONS

DIARY

CHAPTER I

APPOINTMENT TO BERLIN—THE SPA CONFERENCE

CHAPTER II

FROM SPA TO BRUSSELS—EARLY DAYS IN BERLIN

CHAPTER III

CONFERENCES OF BRUSSELS AND PARIS

CHAPTER IX

FINANCIAL COLLAPSE IN GERMANY—CHAOS IN UPPER SILESIA

CHAPTER X

ANOTHER LONDON CONFERENCE—TOWARDS CANNES

CHAPTER XI

THE CANNES CONFERENCE

CHAPTER XII

SECRET INTRIGUES

CHAPTER XIII

TOWARDS GENOA

INTRODUCTORY SURVEY

General Scheme of the Book—The fundamental alternatives before Europe —German character—Opinions of England in Germany—Can Germany be trusted ?—American influence—The Russian danger—Defects of the Treaty of Versailles—Periods of decline and revival in Germany.

GENERAL SCHEME OF THE BOOK

LORD GREY of Fallodon has laid down the principle that it is of vital importance for the world that the causes which led to the Great War should be examined minutely in the light of the fullest knowledge obtainable ; he holds that it is therefore essential that adequate knowledge of political and diplomatic events in the period before the war should be made available. This doctrine has received general approval ; willing, and in some cases self-immolating, collaborators have come forward in many of the countries which participated in the war, and have, by the publication of memoirs, histories, and other compilations of unprecedented frankness, supplied, in a brief period after the events occurred, an abundant amount of detail for the guidance or confusion of future historians.

IF this rapid publicity offends against old canons of taste, there is nothing in it which is other than beneficial to the cause of peace, and to the maintenance of a high moral standard among sovereigns and statesmen. For the more rapidly follies and misdeeds become known, the less the temptation to commit them. Had William II realised that in his lifetime the text of the marginal notes he made on his Ambassadors' Reports would be published far and wide, it is hardly conceivable that he would not have refrained from committing them to paper. Had he been aware that so many intimate revelations by his attendant chamberlains would be given to the reading public within so short a time, he might have ordered his court and the policy of his Empire on different lines. Other in-

I

stances of a similar character will occur to the student of recent history.

To be of service in practical politics it is not sufficient that the recording angel should be accurate, his action must be prompt, and he must regard undue postponement in the production of his record as a dereliction of duty. Thus only can his ethical influence be exercised in an effective manner.

If the above considerations are valid in relation to the period immediately preceding the Great War, they are of still more convincing force in application to the post-war period. For here the lesson is not negative and minatory, but positive. It is not a recital of unfortunate events which led up to a great catastrophe. It is the narrative rather of a historical period in which immense progress has been made towards pacification, and during which the bitterness and animosity left by the war have been softened, international suspicion diminished, and the cause of co-operation between nations appreciably advanced.

Anyone who will contrast the condition of public opinion in Western Europe to-day with that which prevailed from 1920 to 1923 will realise how vast the progress has been. It would be rash to assert that permanent pacification has been ensured ; but a real improvement of the immediate situation has been achieved, while the prospect for the more distant future is far less menacing than it appeared a few years ago. A stronger claim might indeed be advanced, without overstatement.

The pages of the present volume have been set in order with a view to show the early phases through which negotiations passed between the Great Powers and Germany in the years before the Treaty of Locarno was signed and before Germany entered the League of Nations. They are principally concerned with the subjects of reparation, German disarmament, and with the German financial crisis. Professor Gerothwohl has undertaken the task of annotating the Diary, and of supplying the links necessary to a comprehension of the historical sequence of events. A more competent guide could not be desired, his grasp of the European situation at the period being probably unrivalled. It has been thought expedient to limit explanation to the bare minimum required for clarity, and to allow the Diary to speak as far as possible for itself. The views set down from day to day were occasionally falsified by the subsequent sequence of events, but it is only through their publication unaltered that an impression of sincerity can be given and the personal interest maintained.

How far the reader will find that the present volume fulfils its purpose and furnishes the necessary knowledge for a comprehension of the period is not for me to say, but it may be hoped that a clear idea will be gained of the essential object before English statesmanship, namely, the restoration of peace to Europe.

THE FUNDAMENTAL ALTERNATIVES BEFORE EUROPE

THE essential fact to be grasped in studying the then position in Europe, and in considering the manner in which it developed, is that there were, in the years following the signature of the Treaty of Versailles, two clear alternative policies.

EITHER Germany could be regarded as a permanent enemy, against whom the forces which were allied in the Great War must be kept ranged in serried ranks, armed cap-à-pie, and maintained in wakeful suspicion by a continuance of war propaganda and war recrimination, or an attempt had to be made to include Germany in the Western European group. This could only be achieved by diminishing mutual suspicion between ex-enemies through the establishment of efficient safeguards for reciprocal security. Security on both sides was the fundamental basis on which alone it might be possible to establish

I*

normal relations between former antagonists and to replace international rivalry in armament by international co-operation in industry, commerce, and finance.

No one believed that this objective of harmonious co-operation between countries lately engaged in so bitter a struggle could be obtained rapidly.   It was, at first, thought that years of patient effort and of delicate negotiation would be required.   A certain risk would be involved.   There would necessarily be moments when sceptics would declare that the whole policy had failed and that nothing but a reversion to the system of force, hatred, and suspicion could give efficacious results in a world like this in which we live.

In the event, once the right course had been set, progress was more rapid than could have been anticipated.   It was not more than eight months after the original German communication to the French Government proposing a reciprocal agreement regarding the security of the German-French frontier that the Treaty of Locarno was signed. Not more than eighteen months elapsed between the formal opening of negotiations regarding security and the entry of Germany into the League of Nations.   But if the period of negotiations was shorter than was expected, it was full of incident, and marked by almost providential escapes from hidden dangers.   Some of these may be indicated. Regarding others, it may be well for the present to preserve silence.

The first and gravest danger which threatened the project in its early days was inopportune, premature publicity. There is not the smallest doubt that if the German proposal of February 10, 1925, which initiated the official negotiations leading to Locarno, had become known to the public in the early months of that year, all chance of a successful issue would have disappeared.   In France the attack of the extreme elements of the Right on the Government would have precluded the possibility of further negotiation.

No Ministry could have outlived the storm which would have burst forth. In Germany the danger to Stresemann and those ministers and officials who were responsible for the German proposal would have been even more violent than the attacks made in France. There can be little question that Stresemann would have been turned out of office, and there is a strong probability that he would have been assassinated. Fortunately and wisely those who knew, and they were few in number, preserved a discreet silence. In diplomatic experience, no secret was ever more closely kept. The German proposal had a charmed life of secrecy. For five or six weeks the press knew little of what was going on. Whatever information leaked out was so inaccurate that a general contradiction was justified—and indeed made.

FALSE rumours appeared, and these were not without their utility. They accustomed the public to the idea that a negotiation regarding reciprocal security was either contemplated or had commenced. It therefore happened that when, after a considerable interval, some accurate details were published, there was no surprise at the principle of negotiation. Moreover, it was found that the real details were less unpalatable than the false rumours which preceded them. Exaggeration had for once been definitely helpful. Even under these circumstances the opposition in nationalist circles both in France and Germany was violent. In France the old cries were repeated that no German engagement would be adhered to, and that France was being duped into a false sense of security, and the only true protection lay not in conventions but in superior military force. In Germany the accusations made were that the proposed arrangement would amount to a renewed sanction of the most objectionable clauses in the Treaty of Versailles, and that it included the renunciation of German rights over Alsace-Lorraine. For many weeks it was doubtful whether sufficient support could be obtained in either country.

The clinching argument in favour of an understanding was less that it afforded solid ground for the hope of a better future than the obvious fact that the alternative policy, viz. one of armaments and unqualified force, was bound to perpetuate an atmosphere of sullen suspicion and animosity.

THOSE who advocated understanding were, moreover, influenced by the estimate they had formed of the fundamental strength of the German people.

GERMAN CHARACTER

THE military achievement of the German people in the Great War, when for four years, supported only by weak allies, they threatened to inflict defeat on the greatest military combination ever brought together in the world's history, is so remarkable, that the characteristics and principal features of the nation are worthy subjects of examination. To obtain a clear picture of their military achievement, the history of the war must be isolated from the period which preceded it, and considered independently of reflections on pre-war policy. Thus only is a fair idea likely to be formed of the military power of the people by whom the Allies were confronted.

So much has been written on the German character from the time of Tacitus to that of Madame de Staël that it argues some temerity to embark upon the task again.

THE country which Queen Victoria called in the 1840's " our dear little Germany " probably deserves these two epithets less than any in the dictionary. The greatest admirers of the German people can hardly apply the word " dear " ; their most virulent opponents cannot speak of them as " little." If superficially unattractive, they are fundamentally great. They are in the highest degree a peculiar people. To take outward appearance first : in this they are clearly distinguished from the nations which surround them in Central Europe. The dome-like heads, which are so much smaller than they look, the thick-set, round bodies, the peculiar development of the region which in a horse would be called the crest, their stiff, angular manners, are all in marked contrast with the suavity and grace of their neighbours, the French, the Austrians, the Bohemians, and the Poles. It has been said that the German figure is the only successful attempt yet made to square the circle—in that it is at once square and round. But whatever its contour, it denotes marked solidity and strength. The Germanic race is amongst the sturdiest in the world, the most capable of standing privation, a race of outstanding physical endurance. Their capacity for resisting fatigue and for enduring patiently long hours of monotonous toil and labour certainly exceeds that of Western Europeans.

MENTALLY and morally they are not less differentiated than physically. The current English conception of the German is that he is a machine which never stops working ; that he enjoys nothing so much as work. This is an exaggeration. But it is undoubted that the German has not only a physical capacity for long hours, but an innate inclination towards thoroughness, earnestness, and *Gründlichkeit*. He is more than a tireless plodder and an inveterate sap. Whatever he may have been before 1913, he has developed since the war a marked aptitude for physical enjoyment of all kinds, and displays to-day for athletics and sport an enthusiasm and aptitude which will soon make him a dangerous competitor for the highest honours. His physical strength combined with his love of method and his capacity for taking pains cannot fail to lead to great results. In the realm of amusement as distinguished from athletics German moralists assert that development has been too rapid. While his forms of self-indulgence may be different from those in vogue in this country, the German pursues his pleasures no less eagerly than his

English cousin, and holds to them no less tenaciously. The conception that the German willingly forgoes his leave if the call of business makes his absence from work undesirable is quite erroneous. Let the time for his annual period of rest and recuperation come round, nothing will induce him to remain at the desk. A grave crisis or even a great war may be on the horizon, he will take the train and proceed to some *Badeort* or sanatorium, ready to undergo a severe régime for the restoration of his health, and possibly roam through the woods in a state of nudity with a view to getting closer to nature.

SINCE the war, as has already been said, the Germans have taken to games much more vigorously than before. They were impressed with the benefit derived by the English from their addiction to sport, and by the rapidity with which a new officer-corps could be created from youths untrained except from the practice of team games at school. In tennis, in boxing, in football, they are making rapid strides ; golf evokes boundless enthusiasm. It is possible that the development of athletic games of a humane character may influence the national mind in affording an alternative to the only sport previously practised, centred as it was on the pursuit and destruction of animals.

WHEN not in training, the German takes advantage of his tough constitution and his strong health to indulge almost more than any other nation in the pleasures of the table. From the earliest times the Teutonic tribes have been great eaters and drinkers, and the present generation are not unworthy inheritors of the tradition, although their feasts do not now last three days, like those cited by the Roman writers. The extent to which alcohol is considered a necessary ingredient of social life is illustrated by the following anecdote of Madame de Staël and Goethe. When that talented but terrific lady was at Weimar in 1803, and on friendly terms with the literary circle which centred round the Grand Ducal court there, she complained at a dinner, in a tone of parnassian playfulness, that Goethe was only agreeable after he had drunk a bottle of champagne. Goethe replied : " Il faut donc que nous ayons bu parfois un petit coup ensemble."

THEIR capacity for work may be remarkable, but it is not more remarkable than their capacity for late hours heavily charged with meat and drink. Officials and business men will sit up till three and four in the morning night after night, either talking or playing cards or dancing, and will accompany these occupations with copious libations. Yet the next morning at 9 a.m., or earlier, they will be at their office ready to do justice to a day's task. With similar hours and a similar régime any member of a weaker race would be totally incapable of serious application.

ANOTHER peculiar feature of the German mind is a predilection for severe discipline and precise orders. A German subordinate appears to desire not to be treated with too great civility or kindness ; servants not only work better under quasi-military regulations, but far prefer curt and precise commands to anything less categorical. Gibbon says : " It was a fundamental principle in the Roman army that a good soldier should fear his officers more than the enemy." In the old German army, this Roman tradition was certainly maintained.

IT has been said that the best description of the German of to-day is the *Germania* of Tacitus, but this view can only be held by those who have not read Tacitus or who do not know Germany. Either the German characteristics of the first century have been modified fundamentally or Tacitus gave an inaccurate picture. He relates that among other peculiarities they are " intolerant of toil and labour ; flocks and herds are their only riches; gold and silver are withheld from them ; they do not enjoy the possession of these metals as others do ; jurisdiction is vested in the priests ; they fight with their tenderest pledges in the field ; they are incited to deeds of valour

by the shrieks of their wives and the cries of their children.
When routed they are incited to renew the charge by their
wives, who bare their breasts to the danger. They see
something sacred in the female sex, whose advice is always
heard and whose responses are considered oracular."

NONE of these peculiarities can be observed in Germany
to-day. Indeed, their salient characteristics are directly
opposite to those described above. Madame de Staël is
not much nearer the mark. She describes Germany as
a country without a capital, and consequently without any
centre dictating the laws of taste. This is no longer
true, since Berlin now dominates both politics and business. Patriotism, she says, is lacking in Germany, and so
are men of action ; the criticism to-day would be that
in 1914 patriotism was too impulsive and men of action
too influential. The rigidity of German etiquette has
been relaxed since her day, and it is no longer the case that
in German society everyone is kept in his place in the
hierarchy as if it were a post of duty.

REGARDING the German language, there is less to criticise
in her observations. The verb is still kept till the end of
the sentence, and preserves the mystery of the meaning of
the phrase in prolonged suspense. Whether this renders
brilliant conversation impossible, as Madame de Staël
asserts, may be doubtful, and is a point of taste. In some
minds, there is a certain charm in the elaborate involution
of what appears a reasonable order—reminiscent of the
Ciceronian phrase—but the complication is, perhaps, better
adapted to the rostrum than the salon.

THE German is exceptionally tolerant of pain. Not only
does he bear pain stoically, but he apparently feels it less
than men of other races. Medical students who have
studied in German hospitals testify that the capacity of
patients to endure suffering is far greater than in England
or France. German doctors and surgeons have become
so accustomed to this fact that they resort to anæsthetics

less than their English colleagues. Their contempt for squeamishness is extreme, perhaps excessive.

THE general belief in the superiority of German erudition is certainly well founded, but the high reputation which German scholars have earned is probably due in some measure to their complete indifference to wearying the reader. The extreme precision which they bring to their work and the exhaustive nature of their examination of problems proceed to some extent from technical probity, and an ambition to do full justice to the subject at the cost of prolixity and tedium. To make brilliant phrases, to prepare striking juxtapositions, is foreign to their preoccupation. Any such ambitions they would regard as frivolous and contemptible. Satire they positively dislike, and authorities on literature have declared that Heine is to-day intolerable to a healthy German mind on account of the persistent irony of his attitude towards life.

EXAGGERATED deference to professional opinion is possibly the explanation of Germany's greatest triumphs and of her great defeat. The technician, military, scientific, or professional, cares only for the opinion of his expert colleagues and despises the public. Conducive as this attitude may be to highly specialised efficiency in a particular branch, it opens the door to vast political errors and is apt to be accompanied by an incapacity to understand other nations. While it enabled the military leaders of Germany to create a war machine of astonishing efficiency and strength, it permitted the pre-war naval development, the invasion of Belgium, and the unrestricted submarine campaign.

AND the same professionalism may be held to explain, or at least to be consistent with, the two main weaknesses of the German people—the absence of political instinct and their peculiar addiction to envy and jealousy. The first is due to the dominance of the expert and the disregard of the public voice. Moreover, the fact adverted to above, that their minds are encyclopædic and exhaustive, stands in the way of a tactful sense of political expediency, and impedes their giving precedence to the argument which is suitable for the moment and which would clinch the debate. They prefer to hear all the arguments rather than to select the best. Preoccupied by the desire to write an exhaustive treatise on a problem, leaving nothing unexplored, nothing unsaid, they miss the sense of what the particular moment requires. A full statement appeals to them more than the most brilliant epitome.

PERHAPS the most important characteristic of the German mind, as compared with that of surrounding nations, is their peculiar capacity for bringing philosophy and science to bear on the problems of practical life. With other races, book-learning and all that is derived from scientific training have a tendency to remain in a separate compartment, divorced from the daily task. With the German, learning has been absorbed into the blood ; he remains through life something of a student, something of a professor. A modern writer cites a phrase overheard in a café as typical of the German view of life. One student said to another : " I, for myself, value a human being only inasmuch as his attitude towards the problems of the cosmos is an adequate attitude," and he goes on to observe that many Germans have a dual ambition to be at once Faust and Siegfried.

TURNING to the view that they are abnormally prone to jealousy and envy, do not these passions infest all professional coteries ? are they not avoided only through the absence of that technical competition which a close career induces ? In Germany, since everyone is more or less a technician and belongs to a definite school or a definite profession, personal jealousy is scarcely to be avoided. Whether avoidance is theoretically possible or not, it is certainly not achieved ; one has only to remember the distinguished statesmen who, since the war, have been assassinated or threatened in Germany to realise that exceptional brilliance and superior intelligence are dangerous attributes, and are apt to become targets for the assassin's bullet.

THE extreme professionalism of the German mind may be illustrated from personal experience. In early years after the war, one was constantly addressed by German ex-combatants as follows : " Throughout the war I only fought on the fronts against the English " ; this being honestly considered not as a reason for a feeling of hostility, but as an exceptionally sound foundation for future friendship with all Englishmen. German officers enjoyed nothing more than meeting ex-enemies against whom they had fought in a given battle, and discussing the technical aspects of the contest ; this usually meant a review of the many mistakes the leaders on both sides committed, and a cordial assurance that the bravery and endurance of the opponent were duly recognised and honoured.

SUCH a dispassionate professional attitude is difficult for an Englishman to understand. We incline to judge the situation as a whole, including notably what we consider the moral aspect. We allow our sympathies to exercise a dominant influence on our professional judgment. To the German the dry objective view seems to come as a result of professional training. There is little or no affectation about it, although as a nation they are certainly not unsentimental.

COMPARING Germany with the surrounding nations, the prevailing impression is that of thoroughness, earnestness, sturdiness, and strength. In many of their qualities they remind one of the Dorian tribes of Greece. Their immense belief in the power of the State, their confidence in the capacity of their own people to rule over weaker tribes, their reliance upon military discipline as a dominant force among nations, a certain contempt for the artistic and luxurious, their instinctive adherence to the view that the pursuit of wealth, while legitimate in the degenerate

times of to-day, is altogether on a lower level than service
to the State, particularly service in a military capacity—
all these are attributes of a virile and masterful race.   A
widespread German view on this matter may be illustrated
by the following saying of a Sophist from classical times:
" Let me always believe that he who commands thirty
legions is the wisest man in the world."   The German
possesses in addition to these characteristics a capacity
for business, both industrial and financial, such as has
rarely been surpassed.   Strength in this direction, so exceptional and rare in conjunction with military talent, is
the peculiarity which will always place Germany among
the most powerful nations of the world.

Possessing the qualities and powers which we have indicated, it is not surprising that the German regards himself as superior to most of his geographical neighbours.
It is vain to try to induce him to believe that either Poles
or Czechs are in any way comparable to his own country-
men, either as citizens or as soldiers.   Even the French,
for whose culture he has a great admiration, he regards as
essentially Ionic, partly because of the grace and agility
of the Gallic mind.   The English he considers politically
wise and incomprehensibly lucky, far wiser indeed than we
probably are, and far luckier than he thinks we deserve
to be.   Our success he attributes in the main to a political
instinct which enables the British Government, without
either logical argument or scientific analysis, to adopt
instinctively the most worldly-wise course in any conceivable emergency.   It would be superhuman not to
feel some envy at the possession by a rival nation of such
a useful endowment, obtained, as it seems to them, without
painful effort.   But there is little or no hostility to England
of a pronounced character, except indeed among naval
and to a lesser extent military officers, whose professional
careers have been suddenly curtailed by drastic reduction
of the Forces.

OPINIONS OF ENGLAND IN GERMANY

THE difficulty of giving a clear account of the feeling in Germany regarding England proceeds in part from the curious fact that those sections of opinion which are temperamentally most in sympathy with English life are politically the most adverse to the English policy of European pacification. The position is approximately as follows :

THE territorial classes in Germany are more English in mode of life and feeling than any similar class in any other European country or than any other class in Germany. Dine with a German country gentleman, and you will be amazed to find how exclusively the conversation is confined to sport. Not a word except of the chase, shooting, and bucolic interests. Discussion on art and literature is banned. The view of life is identical with that prevailing in the squirearchy of England in the more remote districts. ON the other hand, in liberal circles, which politically are favourable to the English policy of establishing an understanding between France and Germany, the temperamental and cultural affinity is far closer to Paris than it is to London : it is indeed almost hostile to London. The intellectual atmosphere is advanced, cosmopolitan, and humanistic ; the country gentleman view is derided as barbaric. Art, literature, music, and women are eagerly discussed and criticised. French painting of the modern school is keenly appreciated. French plays and French novels of a more advanced kind are read no less eagerly than in Paris.

THIS strange criss-cross between political opinion and temperamental affinity renders a clear view of the feeling of Germany towards England more difficult to gauge than it otherwise would be. The essential paradox is there, and the result of it is that if our policy of European pacification achieves success it will be by the assistance of those who are temperamentally against us ; while if it is wrecked it will be by the influence of the political section on the Right who have the most affinity with the English mode of life.

CAN GERMANY BE TRUSTED ?

THE question is often asked, Can Germany be trusted ? Is it possible to make an arrangement with the German Government, and to feel confident that it will be observed ? Are not bad faith and a propensity to military aggression such habits with the Germans that no treaty can be relied upon to restrain them ?   We were all taught to believe this during the war.   Can it be that it is no longer true ? THE question in the form above stated is hardly susceptible of a definite answer, and this for several reasons.   While my personal experience is extremely favourable to German respect for an engagement taken, and while I can assert that during the whole of the six years I was in Berlin I do not remember any definite promise which a German official or minister failed to carry through, this does not constitute an adequate reply to the inquiry, Can Germany be trusted ?   For the answer to the query will depend in the last resort upon German public opinion, and German public opinion is not entirely governed by a few officials in the Wilhelmstrasse, great as their influence may be. The views and prejudices of a considerable variety of different sections have to be considered.   These classes and these parties differ from one another even more fundamentally than in other countries, so that it is difficult to speak categorically of the national will.   Viewing the matter dispassionately, it would be rash to say that all classes and all parties are seriously desirous of peace, for it is clear that among the extreme Right, among the territorial aristocracy, and among the military caste there are influential groups who are in no way reconciled to the terms of the Treaty of Versailles.

On the other hand, it is no less true that there are large classes of the population to whom the idea of another war is intensely repugnant. The great mass of workmen organised under the Socialist Party, the majority of the Catholic Party organised under the Centre, a large proportion of the Democratic Party, are undoubtedly sincere in their detestation of war. Between these two wings lies the People's Party, where opinion is neither so military as it is on the Right nor so peaceful as it is on the Left and Centre. Taking a broad view, it may be said of the mass of the people that there is a considerable preponderance in favour of peace, this preponderance having increased substantially since the signature of the Treaty of Locarno.

I have said above that a definite answer to the question whether Germany can be trusted to maintain peace is hardly possible. It has been shown how divided opinion is ; and opinion is not merely divided, it is fluctuating. Moreover, much depends on the treatment accorded to Germany by foreign nations. Thus while to-day, three years after the signature of the Treaty of Locarno, it may safely be asserted that a considerable majority of the German people is resolutely in favour of peace, the same would not have been the case had the policy which inspired the Ruhr occupation been continued, and had Locarno not been signed.

The peace spirit in Germany requires nourishment. It must be shown that if there is faithful execution by Germany of treaty clauses and of reparation clauses the merit of this action is recognised by the countries of the war Allies. It must be shown that the desire for pacification is real, and that the benefit of pacification will be made reciprocal. Provided the spirit which prevailed at Locarno continues to guide the policy of the war Allies, I see no reason to apprehend any shifting of opinion in Germany such as will endanger the existence of a large majority in favour of the peaceful solution of international difficulties.

AMERICAN INFLUENCE

FAR above their regard for any European nation the German has a profound respect for the United States. Its size, its immense wealth, the business capacity of its citizens, impress the German with the deepest admiration, and he is, moreover, neither blind to the possibility of financial assistance which Germany may in future derive from the United States, nor unmindful of the assistance already given. The United States have lent Germany not less than £300,000,000 during the last few years.

IN all the more important developments in Germany during the post-war years, American influence has been decisive. Eliminate action taken on American advice, or in assumed agreement with American opinion, or in anticipation of American approval, and the whole course of policy would be altered.

THIS dominant power of American opinion on Germany may be explained in many ways and has many causes. The principal probably are : the plain geographical fact that the United States are non-European and therefore outside the sphere of old European rivalries ; that their wealth is stupendous, the United States disposing of a financial capacity far in excess of that of any European country ; that a marked affinity prevails between German and American life. The similarity of Berlin to an American city has impressed many travellers. The methods of American trade and finance are derived from Germany rather than from England, being based in the main on the traditions of Frankfurt and Hamburg.

ALL these influences would, however, have remained inoperative if the U.S.A. had not been represented during the critical post-war period by men of unusual authority, and peculiarly in touch and sympathy with German life. Dresel, Houghton, and Schurman had received a large part of their education in Germany and had acquired a mastery of the language. They were all men of easy access, of wise counsel, and of wide sympathies ; all were successful in establishing relations of intimate confidence with leading circles in Berlin, both political and financial. Many examples of their closeness to German life may be related. Let one suffice. Rathenau, the night before his assassination, spent the evening at the American Embassy in close conference with his bitter enemy and rival, Stinnes. At no other house in Berlin could this have occurred. Both men felt a peculiar confidence in Houghton ; both realised that he understood their views and sympathised with their patriotic aspirations ; both knew that he was discreet and reliable. His influence brought them closer together on this evening, which was to have so tragic a morrow, than they had been at any period of their careers.

THE close sympathy and instinctive understanding between Americans and Germans is difficult to analyse and explain. The German accepts an American argument far more readily than that of a European. He will find the Frenchman too logical and precise, the Englishman too vague and instinctive, the Italian too subtle and ingenious, the Russian too insincere. The American he at once finds practical and convincing. What the French would criticise as prolix and hypocritical he finds full, thorough, and yet adequately idealistic and sentimental. His own thoroughness reconciles him to the exhaustive methods usually applied to American autobiography, and he endures without an anæsthetic the tale of the corner block that was bought for five dollars by a newsboy or a druggist's assistant, and is now worth several millions of dollars.

THE RUSSIAN DANGER

APART from the fatal results which awaited Europe if an internecine policy of competitive armament were followed, it was apparent to those who took a world-view that

Western civilisation was menaced by an external danger which, coming into being during the war, threatened a cataclysm equalled only by the fall of the Roman Empire.

THIS danger arose from the sweeping success in 1917 of the revolution against the Czarist régime, and the establishment in Russia of a fanatical Communist Government, animated by hatred of all political organisations which stood in the way of a world-victory of the Soviet creed. The fundamental character of the change to be imposed by violence on the organisation of European civilisation was indeed such that it might have been anticipated that the Western nations would realise the pettiness of their own differences and compose them, in order to combine against the common danger. But such an anticipation would not have taken account of that weakness in human nature which is always prone to exaggerate the near, the local, and the national, to the exclusion of wide considerations and to the detriment of proportion and balance.

PUBLIC opinion both in France and Germany was so concentrated upon the Rhine frontier questions that it relegated the vastly more important problem of the defence of Europe against Asiatic communism to the category of the non-urgent. And yet there is little doubt that a blind persistence in the policy of maintaining the war grouping of the Allies against Germany would eventually have led to Germany being forced into close alliance with Russia. Admittedly there were difficulties in the way. Leading circles in Germany, both territorial and industrial, were strongly, even violently anti-communistic. Their sense of discipline and order, their Doric conception of life and manners, their strong caste feeling, are in categorical opposition to the doctrines of Lenin. But if the Western Allies continued to bully and to exercise pressure, there appeared to be no alternative for Germany other than the Russian connection. Already in 1923, at the time of the Ruhr occupation, a very shrewd observer in England had said that if he were directing the fortunes of Germany, the Russian alliance was the move with which he would parry excessive pressure by the Allies.

WHAT the ultimate consequences of such an alliance would have been it is difficult to estimate, but this is certain— a ruthless struggle in Western Europe and a vast accession to the forces of disorder in Asia. An Asiatic revolt under German direction against established institutions and supported by German industry and science may be considered an unnatural combination. But were it to come into being, the danger to European civilisation would be dire in the extreme.

MOREOVER, the risk of communism in Germany was generally underestimated. Under severe provocation it might have proved dangerous. There were critical moments in 1920 and 1923 when it constituted a real menace. It is sometimes held that, apart from the hostility of the military and territorial classes to advanced communism, the general tendency of the German mind among the middle and lower classes is proof against any Bolshevik infection. This view does not take sufficient account of the large number of the middle class in Germany who have racial ties with Bolshevik leaders, and still less of the intellectual influence this section exercises, which is far greater than its numerical proportion.

THIS fact reinforces the argument that in judging the Locarno policy in contrast with what may be termed the Ruhr occupation policy (or the policy of the Seven against Thebes), attention must not be confined to the Rhine frontier and the traditional antagonism between Gaul and Teuton. While these were vital elements of a problem of vast importance and of extreme difficulty, vision in the critical years between 1920 and 1924 had to cover a wider horizon and survey the probable effect of any given policy on events remote from the Rhine frontier. Notably it was essential to consider the East

2

and to form a judgment on possible combinations and reactions there.

On broad grounds of European interest the case was strong for all nations who regarded Western civilisation as a precious heritage.   It was even stronger when judged from the special standpoint of the British Empire.   Apart from the general danger resulting from the spread of communism, the anti-English bias in Russia throughout the nineteenth century had to be borne in mind.   The pressure of Bolshevik propaganda in combination with traditional political hostility might create a force of huge potentiality.

Resistance to communistic propaganda, the maintenance of peace in Europe, the avoidance of another Great War, the establishment of security for respective frontiers, the preservation of society on existing lines, were capital objects of English policy.   But there was more than this. England's stupendous and vital interests in Asia were menaced by a danger graver than any which existed in the time of the old Imperialistic régime in Russia. Hostility to England or jealousy of the intrusion of British civilisation into Asia was indeed of old standing.   For the last seventy years of the nineteenth century, rivalry between England and Russia had been a dominant fact in history. But the Bolsheviks disposed of two weapons which Imperial Russia lacked—class-revolt propaganda, appealing to the proletariat of the world, and the quasi-religious fanaticism of Lenin, which infused a vigour and zeal unknown to the officials and emissaries of the Czar.

In the presence of the menace of such forces no solution of the European problem could be tolerated by English statesmen which threatened the exclusion of Germany from the European combination and left her a prey to Russian wiles and Russian influence.   As has already been pointed out, the policy of a perpetual confederation of the war Allies against Germany would indeed have been unwise on purely European grounds.   But even if it had not been rejected on this basis, no statesman capable of taking a broad view of English world-interests could have hesitated to reject it.

THE security of the French frontier against German attack was indeed of vast importance to England, but this security must not be purchased at the cost of a prolongation of war animosities, if by doing so Germany was driven to support the already dangerous power of Russia in the East. The joint interest of the Allies was to discover some line of policy which would secure the French frontier without exposing Western Europe to the danger of German defection. IT might at first sight appear that the attitude of England, if based on these considerations, was tinged with selfishness and was ungenerous to our war Allies and particularly to France. But such an accusation would be superficial and would not resist close examination.

FOR the alliance of Germany with Russia, while primarily inimical to England in Asia, could hardly subsist without leaving Germany open to the penetration of Bolshevik propaganda, and if Germany was infected, could the rest of Europe—could France—remain immune ?

COMMUNISM had already shown its power over French troops at Odessa in 1919. The danger to France and to French civilisation if Germany became Bolshevik was no less great than to England. If therefore France from the standpoint of her Asiatic interests had less to fear than England from a Russo-German combination, she had even more reason than England to fear the infiltration of communistic ideas through Germany.

SUCH were some of the arguments which from the first made reflective men sceptical of any permanent benefit to Europe or to England from the policy of pure compulsion against Germany. It seemed necessary to find an alternative which would offer at once a better prospect of real pacification in Europe and which would be less dangerous to Asiatic stability and to European interests in Asia.

WHAT was the fundamental condition of pacification ?
Security for both France and Germany. Both must feel
safe. Both must have solid guarantees that their frontiers
were inviolate.

GERMANY must be brought into the association of Western
Powers on a basis of equality. The " Mad Dog of Europe "
theory must be abandoned, and the relations of Victor
and Vanquished resulting from the Great War must be
dismissed from the mind : the future must take precedence
of the past ; recrimination and suspicion must cease.

THE task of propagating these ideas was not easy. In
1922 and 1923, opinion in England and France had scarcely
advanced beyond the bitterness of the war period. Germany was still regarded as the permanent danger, the
ruthless destroyer of European peace, the constant military
menace which could only be held in check by the allied
combination of all the peaceful forces of Europe.

THE conceptions prevalent as to the respective strength
on the two sides were not only coloured by memories
of the war, but went further back, and were based on the
position as it was in 1914. It was vain to point out that
the distribution of military force had altered completely
since that time, that Germany was, in point of military
material, effectively disarmed, while France in a military
sense—with her allies of the Little Entente—dominated
the Continent.

IT was only by slow degrees that public opinion became
aware of the altered position.

DEFECTS OF THE TREATY OF VERSAILLES

THE main defects of the Treaty of Versailles, considered
as a permanent basis for the relationship between European
nations, were of a threefold character.

IN the first place, the Treaty was imposed upon Germany ;
the engagements taken under duress by Germany were
not considered binding by German public opinion.

IN the second place, Germany's responsibility for reparations was founded on the assertion that she was responsible for the war. This was denied, rightly or wrongly, by all German authorities and was not susceptible of impartial determination or of convincing proof. It was therefore a dangerous foundation for a contractual obligation.

THE third defect was that the Treaty of Versailles broke up the larger units of Central Europe into a considerable number of small States. This subdivision, based on racial differentiation, had two main political effects : a vast increase of the customs frontiers, constituting a grave impediment to international trade, and a multiplication of the centres of diplomatic activity.

THE irony of the situation under the latter head was accentuated by the fact that the policy was initiated and carried by the representative of the United States, a community where racial differences have been ruthlessly smothered under an overriding national merger. Czecho-Slovaks, Yugo-Slavs, Poles, and Bulgarians emigrating to the United States are at once absorbed and unified into a vast American entity, and are induced or compelled to abandon all those racial and linguistic aspirations which President Wilson obtained for them in Europe with such eloquence and insistence.

IF the above view respecting the practical defects of the Treaty of Versailles is at all correct, it becomes clear that some endeavour had to be made to supplement that treaty by a new agreement. The general basis established at Versailles could only be maintained if certain adjustments and alterations were introduced—changes which without impairing the central structure would ease the practical working of the more onerous clauses. A minute and cast-iron interpretation of several articles signed at Versailles carried out in the Versailles spirit, would bring about the destruction of the whole fabric. Only by introducing a certain elasticity could the general basis be maintained.

THIS consideration afforded a further argument for pressing on the negotiations which led to Locarno. So far from regarding Locarno as an infringement of Versailles and a departure from its essential stipulations, it would be more correct to consider the Locarno pact as a supplementary interpretation adjusting the original document to later circumstances and rendering it better suited to resist the destructive force of time.

PERIODS OF DECLINE AND REVIVAL IN GERMANY

THE years 1920–6 may be divided into two distinct periods. The first, from 1920 to 1923, was characterised by extreme demands for reparation, which were refused, by repeated conferences, by menaces, by sanctions, and by short-lived settlements. The picture is one of confusion and exasperation.

THE second period commenced in the autumn of 1923. By then the failure to obtain a settlement of the reparation problem, and the political situation which resulted from failure, had produced in Germany a financial catastrophe of extreme gravity. The crisis was eventually overcome, but not till it had threatened the whole fabric of financial and industrial life. Precisely how shipwreck was averted will be told in subsequent pages. Suffice it to say here that the main cause of salvation was a measure, in the efficacy of which no expert believed, and which derived its force more from the credulity of the public than from any sound principle. But sound in principle or not, it achieved its object, and a period of recovery followed, during which a vast and continuous improvement has taken place both in the financial and political situation.

DURING the period of difficulty and decline which came to a climax in 1923, the efforts of the Western Allies to obtain from Germany a satisfactory solution of the reparation problem remained futile. They were bound to do so, in that the necessary basis, namely, the reorganisation of German finance, had not been secured. It was vain to attempt to build a house without a solid foundation. That foundation could only be a sound financial system in Germany. The result of the fallacious expedients and compromises which were adopted was that each temporary settlement worked for a few months and then broke down. Each breakdown was followed by recrimination, and charges of bad will were brought against Germany by the Allies. While these were undoubtedly exaggerated, it cannot be said that they were entirely without justification.

THE fact that the methods pursued by the Allies could not but result in a real reduction of Germany's financial ability was so clear that many observers held the view that authorities in Paris were themselves uncertain whether they desired reparation payments on a substantial scale from a recuperated Germany, or whether they preferred the financial ruin of the debtor even if it entailed non-payment. If Germany was discomfited financially, France would dominate militarily, politically, and diplomatically. That might be a prize greater than the payment of reparation.

WHILE the real aims of the French Government were by no means clear, it was almost equally difficult to understand the policy of Germany. In the numerous conferences which took place in 1920, 1921, and 1922, the German negotiators did not give the impression of any exaggerated anxiety to put their own finances in order, nor did they appear to make a serious effort to meet the reparation claim of the Allies, as established by the Treaty of Versailles. They left on observers the suspicion that no genuine endeavour would be made by Germany to restore stability to the currency or equilibrium to the budget until the final settlement of the reparation problem had been reached on terms satisfactory to the German financiers.

As regards the attitude of England, it may be claimed that our efforts to obtain financial satisfaction and to receive reparations were almost too ingenuous, too free of political preoccupation. Perhaps London did not realise adequately that the indispensable condition of payment by Germany was stability in German finance and currency. Had we grasped this fundamental condition with sufficient clearness, it would have been pressed on our Allies with greater vigour and persistency. Weak compliance with a policy we believed financially sterile, if not politically dangerous, was not an attitude worthy of England's best traditions.

UNDER the circumstances pictured above it is inevitable that the diplomatic history of the years 1920–3 is not very satisfactory reading. Conference followed conference, threat followed threat, sanction was piled on sanction, but as the foundation was absent on which alone permanent result could be built, neither conference, threat, nor sanction produced a solution. An enumeration of the many conferences which took place, following one another at short intervals, makes a dismal story. First came the Spa Conference of July 1920. This led to no solution. In December 1920 a Conference of Experts met at Brussels, but its recommendations were negatived by the meeting of the Supreme Council which met in Paris early in 1921. As the decisions of this Council were rejected by the German Government, another meeting of the Supreme Council was held in London three months later.

THE story of the abortive discussions which followed in quick succession is briefly told in the present volume. They lasted throughout 1921 and 1922, conference following conference, failure succeeding to failure.

IN the spring of 1923 the chance of a satisfactory solution appeared less than at any previous period, for on January 11 French and Belgian troops had advanced into the Ruhr and had practically abolished German sovereignty there. This brought about passive resistance, which involved so severe a strain on German finance that, as long as it lasted, there was no possibility of any increased payment to foreign nations. Things reached such a pass that it became obvious to all that further wrangling over reparations and a further postponement of some reasonable settlement would lead inevitably to a financial catastrophe in which countries other than Germany might become involved. Financial opinion in the great monetary centres became alarmed, and early in 1924 American influence was exercised effectively in bringing about a solution. The Reparation Commission appointed two Committees of Experts, the one " to consider the means of balancing the German Budget and the measures to be taken to stabilise the currency of Germany," and the other " to inquire into the amount of German exported capital and to consider the means of bringing about its return to Germany." The United States were represented on both these Committees. Her representatives took an active part in bringing about a compromise. But even American practical sense, and the clear recognition of what was impossible, did less to achieve a settlement of the reparation problem than an unexpected event in France, viz. the fall of the Poincaré Government, which occurred on May 11, 1924. A fortnight before this event Poincaré had published a memorandum on the solution of the reparation question on the old legal lines. It was clear that he had not receded to any considerable extent from his original attitude of steel intransigence. It seemed probable that his stubborn will, supported by a legal mind of unrivalled precision, would still control the situation, and that the English Government, while advocating a reasonable course, would yield to French pressure and co-operate in measures to which they were fundamentally hostile.

Lord Curzon's Notes on the subject of the Ruhr occupation were indeed a clear and eloquent indication that England heartily disapproved of the measure. But they

had little effect upon events.   There is indeed no doubt that
had Poincaré remained in power, the London Conference,
which sat from July 16 to August 16, 1924, and which
adopted and brought into force the Dawes Plan, would
not have achieved a successful solution.   The attitude of
Herriot, who succeeded Poincaré as Prime Minister, was in
marked contrast to that of his predecessor.

IT will be seen in subsequent pages that during the years
from 1920 to 1924 no less than twelve different conferences
of Prime Ministers or Ministers of Finance were held on
the one subject of reparation.

As already stated, while these conferences were sitting,
German finance was going from bad to worse.   In the
autumn of 1920, when the first Brussels Conference of
Experts came together, exchange stood at 254 marks to
the £ sterling.   In January 1923, at the time of the Conference in Paris, which preceded the Ruhr occupation, the
mark had fallen to 83,000 to the £ sterling.   Nine months
afterwards, when the Ruhr occupation had resulted in the
complete discomfiture of German finance, the paper mark
had fallen to the almost incredible level of 18 billion
to the £ sterling.   In other words, the mark in October
1923 was worth in gold one-fortieth million part of its value
in 1914, at the outbreak of war.

UNTIL the crisis had reached the catastrophic stage, the
inexorable truth that German finance must be restored had
not been adequately realised either in Western Europe
or indeed in Germany itself.   There were many there to
whom the Ciceronian taunt might be applied, " They
thought that the State might founder and their own
fish-ponds remain safe."   It is indeed open to question
whether, even if the Allies had themselves adopted a wiser
and more moderate line, the German Government would
in the early years have been able to pass the necessary
legislation to re-establish German finance.   Until the
autumn of 1923 there was no general conviction in Ger-

many that a stable exchange was an indispensable condition of financial recovery. When this view was urged on German authorities during the years 1921, 1922, and 1923, the only result was that those who pressed for immediate stabilisation were condemned as currency cranks who held an altogether exaggerated opinion of the dangers of inflation. How little German financial opinion was prepared to adopt sound views of currency may be seen in the fact that when the German Government had been persuaded to bring together in Berlin a conference of international experts in December 1922, no attention whatever was paid to the recommendations made by these experts, although those recommendations contained the germ of the scheme of reform by which salvation was finally attained.

THE story of the collapse of German currency in 1923 and its recovery in 1924–5 is fairly well known. The violence of the crisis, the rapidity of the fall in the mark, the extent to which the mark lost its value (having fallen in gold value to one-millionth of a millionth of its face value), the complete failure of German financial authorities to realise that currency stabilisation was a necessary preliminary to sound finance, and the not less remarkable failure of the Allied Powers interested in reparation to act upon the same truth in a practical manner—these are all matters of history that can only be glanced at here. Those interested in currency problems may find an account in greater detail in the paper which I read on November 16, 1926, before the Royal Statistical Society.

IT is the custom in some circles in Western Europe to regard the whole currency devaluation crisis as an act of supreme financial skill and rascality on the part of Germany's financial advisers. I find it difficult to subscribe to this view. In my judgment, there was a genuine ignorance of a remarkable character both among official financiers and private bankers as to the inevitable effect of large issues of currency notes. One cannot credit Havenstein, President of the German Reichsbank, and Rathenau with deliberate misrepresentation of their own views in the speeches that they made during the inflation period. Havenstein's most ingenuous statement in August 1923 that next week the Reichsbank would supply the public with necessary currency in such quantity that one week would add fifty per cent. to the total amount of currency in circulation can hardly have been made by so honourable an official in a spirit of irony or with intent to deceive. Rathenau was never tired of asserting that the depreciation of the mark was due to the adverse balance of German foreign trade, and had no practical connection with the increase of currency issues. Here, again, I cannot believe in a deliberate deception. Stinnes may have had a clearer understanding of the truth. But even in this case a clear conception of the ultimate and inevitable result was not shown, for the financial inflation he is alleged to have advocated led in the last resort to the destruction of that fortune of his which was deemed—and probably was—at one moment so gigantic.

THE net result of the events of the inflation period were to relieve the German State of the greater portion of the burden of its external and internal debt. There was virtually complete repudiation. The State was relieved of debt to the extent of £5,000,000,000 sterling, equal to more than half the total National Debt of England to-day. Private debtors, owing money on mortgages, on debentures, and on other forms of security are estimated to have been relieved of an equal burden, the total repudiation amounting to not less than £500,000,000 a year. What was the effect on the community? Unquestionably grave suffering to the middle classes and to all who depended for their living upon invested funds. But this gigantic default did not have the result which might have been expected in destroying credit and paralysing the saving instinct. Since 1925, the year in which German currency again assumed a normal course, saving in Germany has proceeded at fully the pre-war rate, taking into account the changes of territory and of public fortune which have occurred. The sacrifice imposed on those who previously held German State funds or mortgages in Germany has not had any apparent effect in alienating the public confidence in new German securities. There was a moment during the currency crisis when it was alleged that a flight from the mark was taking place, and the public were so impressed with the instability of money tokens that they hastened to turn them into goods. This tendency, if indeed it really exerted a great influence during the currency inflation, most certainly does not operate at the present time. The State has regained the confidence of the investor, and the amount of currency in circulation is normal.

THERE is something of ironical justice in the fact that the classes in Germany who in the end suffered the most heavy losses from inflation were those who were the most favourable to it in the early stages. They imagined that loans contracted on a given date and repayable six months later in paper would be repaid by them on very advantageous terms, provided large note issues continued to be made. They not unnaturally held that a currency dispensation which facilitated such a pleasant business could not be wholly vile or radically unsound. As long as currency depreciation remained within moderate limits their calculation was sound ; but the final result was that, when the ultimate crash came, all the profits which had been acquired through this astute calculation vanished in the catastrophe, and the excessive issues which they had favoured led to the confiscation of so large a portion of their holdings that their temporary gains were more than swept away.

REFERENCE might here be made to another element in the problem. One of the most dangerous heresies regarding foreign exchange is the supposition that it is fundamentally dependent upon and is governed by the balance of trade. This easy explanation, which finds no support in any parallelism between the larger curves of exchange and trade balance, has been so widely adopted that it is responsible for much that is erroneous, and indeed disastrous, in the financial policy of countries involved in currency difficulties.

In Germany general belief in this theory diverted alike theorists and financiers from the search for the true explanation of the phenomena, and probably deferred stabilisation for nearly two years.

The restoration of stability to the German currency is in the main the work of two men, namely, Dr. Luther, who became Minister of Finance in the autumn of 1923, and Dr. Schacht, who was appointed Governor of the Reichsbank at the same time, and still continues to discharge the duties of that onerous post with unlimited courage and independence. Germany owes a vast debt of gratitude to the financial severity and the civic courage of these two statesmen.

The German example points to the general conclusion that recovery from a position of catastrophic exchange and inflation requires certain conditions. These are as indicated below :

(1) Strict limitation of the amount of currency, implying and involving a resolute avoidance of budget deficits.

(2) A formal proclamation of limitation of such a nature as to inspire belief. Further,

> (a) A definitely fixed and unalterable level of exchange maintained by a national bank or other organisation endued with adequate funds and adequate fixity of purpose.

> (b) A new form of currency replacing the old discredited currency, public confidence being more easily accorded to a new issue than restored to one already discredited.

(*c*) An imaginative element stimulating public confidence in the new issue.

There is another reflection which impartiality compels me to make. Looking back on the events of 1923 at an interval of several years, one is tempted to ask whether the Ruhr occupation, which precipitated the final crisis of German finance by destroying temporarily the most active part of German industry, was in the long run as great a misfortune as was thought at the time in Germany. If French action precipitated and aggravated a catastrophe, did it not also bring nearer the day of recovery? Was not an acute crisis a necessary step on the path of restoration? Without the complete collapse which followed this violent disturbance of industrial life in Germany, is it not possible that the wrangle over reparations would have dragged on through many years? The havoc wrought by the Ruhr occupation and the collapse which ensued in the whole German financial organisation may have been necessary to bring the world to its senses. Without it, statesmen might not have realised the folly of the course they were then pursuing. If not a case of *irae amantium*, the reaction was not dissimilar.

I have completed a brief survey of the main questions before statesmen in the post-war period in so far as my views on them are relevant to the pages of Diary now published.

I now add a few personal sketches of the leading men by whom great decisions had to be taken. While the list is intentionally restricted to those for whom I feel a special admiration, I have been at pains to avoid the danger attendant on such a selection, viz. a lapse into indiscriminating and unrelieved panegyric.

SOME PERSONAL APPRECIATIONS

Lloyd George—Rathenau—Aristide Briand—A. J. Balfour—General Weygand—The Marquess Curzon.

LLOYD GEORGE

IF the results attained by the numerous Conferences on Reparation between 1920 and 1922 were disappointing, no one who was present at them would attribute blame to the leading English representative. It was indeed a constant pleasure to watch Lloyd George and listen to him. His facility of speech, his wit and readiness in reply, his rapidity of decision, were alike admirable. Not less admirable were his constant good-humour and his inexhaustible appetite for new work. No matter what the hour, he was ready to take on a new discussion, to receive information, to give a decision. Provided indeed that the information was given verbally, for no one rebelled more against reading official memoranda, or had less patience with involved and complicated reports.

His mental alertness and his readiness in finding appropriate words to support argument protected him from the usual weakness of English negotiators—a proclivity to concur in the views of others, partly from good-nature and partly from indolence, or again in some other cases from a deliberateness of mind which defers decision.

For Lloyd George it was more natural, and perhaps more agreeable, to differ than to assent ; it was more easy to decide than to defer decision. He was sometimes quick to a fault, never tardy. On occasion he was deliberately aggressive—a rare attitude for an English negotiator. Experience had taught him that no international conference reaches its goal without at least one serious crisis ; he therefore precipitated the crisis early in the proceedings in order to get through with it.

THE changeableness with which Lloyd George is usually

charged was never shown in the course of the Conferences on Reparation. On the contrary, the line or the policy taken from the first was adhered to steadfastly throughout. He was, indeed, extremely obstinate.

THIS policy was for England to adopt a reasonable, broad-minded, and even generous attitude to our ex-enemy, provided that Germany displayed goodwill and showed promise of good faith. It was evident throughout that Lloyd George would go as far in this direction as the forces behind him allowed. The limiting factor was not so much what he thought right as what—as a Minister dependent on a Parliamentary majority—he thought it safe to put before the House of Commons and the public.

HE was, perhaps, too conscious of the fact that to go in advance of public opinion might imperil his own influence and destroy his power for good. While a prudent sense of expediency and a genuine solicitude for pacification alike suggested the wisdom of waiting until the healing influence of time had brought public opinion to a saner view of the diplomatic, political, and military position, a stronger lead to the public might nevertheless have been given by the Prime Minister.

SECURITY was the goal ; without it, there was no hope of any appeasement between France and Germany.

FROM an early stage it was clear that security could only be negotiated on the basis of reciprocity. Lloyd George probably realised this as soon as anybody. He deemed it inexpedient to press it.

IT is often said that Lloyd George was too mercurial to be a safe companion for tiger shooting. The accusation, if not totally unjust, is far too general. Moreover, it ignores the essential cause of Lloyd George's mutability in regard to persons, viz. his obstinate immutability in respect to things. His conduct when tiger shooting would depend entirely on the classification he gave to the tiger. If it appeared to him that the animal was of the aristocratic

3

type, no one could be more keen and eager, none more ardent and bold. If, on the other hand, Celtic imagination could endow the object of pursuit with some remote affinity with the underdog, it would be prudent for his companion not to expect meticulous fidelity. An invincible devotion to what he conceived to be the oppressed would overcome any conventional or contractual obligation of comradeship.

THIS overpowering bias against the privileged is the explanation of much in Lloyd George's career which has caused astonishment and provoked criticism. Admirable in itself as the sentiment may be, it was pushed by him to the verge of obsession.

BUT despite his prejudices, and their detrimental working on his political action, he will be recognised by history as the minister whose unprecedented supremacy in the English political arena during 1917 and 1918 contributed powerfully to bring the Great War to a victorious conclusion.

WHATEVER may be thought of the wisdom of the Versailles Treaty, judged from a European standpoint, there can be no question as to the achievement of Lloyd George as an English advocate. The handing over of the German Fleet, the restrictions as to its future size, the mandates established over former German colonies, the recognition of the right of the British Dominions to adequate representation on international councils and at Geneva—all these were essential and fundamental objects of British policy, and all were attained. This constituted an outstanding achievement of skill, tact, energy, and advocacy.

RATHENAU

RATHENAU was once described as a prophet in a tail-coat, and the description conveys something of the theoretical outlook which he professed, together with the polish and slightly theatrical brilliancy of a modern Sidonia. With less taste he was termed " Le Christ en frac." Above all, he possessed a fascination which impressed contemporaries with an undeniable superiority. I shall never forget the enthusiasm with which Wirth, then Chancellor, announced to me that he had persuaded Rathenau to accept the post of Foreign Minister. He said, almost textually, " Do not let us discuss current affairs to-day. There is a great, a most important event : Rathenau has joined the Ministry."

IN the result, the benefit to Germany and the world of this combination was less great than Wirth, with his boyish enthusiasm, anticipated. Rathenau was assassinated a few months later, and the Ministry fell without solving any of the major problems before the country.

FORTUNE was malevolent in this, if not misguided, for the Wirth-Rathenau combination had possibilities of great achievement. Rathenau enjoyed immense prestige abroad ; he was regarded, perhaps, as rather demoniacal than saintly ; but he was eloquent in three languages, he was subtle. There was no Teutonic obstinacy or dourness about him : if he assented, it was with grace ; if he differed, it was with urbanity. His arguments were ingenious, even when unsound, and it was easier to feel that his conclusions were wrong than to confute them. It might have been said of him as of Mephistopheles—

> " Er ist nicht hässlich, er ist nicht lahm,
> Er ist ein lieber charmanter Mann."

But, again like Mephistopheles, he had one dominant weakness, an egregious vanity—a determination, if he could not rule in heaven, to shine on earth.

THE story of the Genoa Conference and of the Treaty of Rapallo has often been told. But it has never been told rightly. The inner workings, which inspired events, have remained unknown. In last analysis, it was a conflict of three vanities—Lloyd George, Rathenau, and Poincaré. The last-named was determined the Conference should not

succeed—that Lloyd George should not attain his purpose
of conciliating Germany, of bringing Russia into the
European conclave.   Lloyd George was sincere in his
belief in Russian possibilities, and was prepared, rightly or
wrongly, to make sacrifices to obtain Russian co-operation.
He might have found in Rathenau an ardent convert to
this policy, and the two in combination might have carried
the day—and altered history for better or worse.   But
vanity came in.   Lloyd George had met Poincaré a few
weeks before at Boulogne.   Lloyd George had been conciliatory.   Poincaré had been truculent.   Commenting
on this matter in the Reichstag, Rathenau said that Lloyd
George had been defeated by Poincaré.   This was not
true ;   had it been ten times true, it would have been a
grave blunder on the eve of Genoa to say it.   Lloyd
George read this speech ;   naturally he resented it—resented
it all the more that he had been in friendly touch with
Rathenau.   When the two arrived at Genoa, Lloyd George
avoided giving Rathenau an interview, even if he did not
refuse to receive him.

RATHENAU's vanity was wounded, his suspicions were
aroused.   If he was not received by Lloyd George, it
must be that deep plots were being hatched between Allies
and Russians.   Germany would be isolated.   Rathenau
would appear ridiculous, and return to Berlin as a German
delegate who had been neglected, outwitted, and befooled.
The Russians, with their accustomed skill, played on these
feelings.   Rathenau and the rest of the German delegates
were stampeded ;   the Rapallo Treaty was signed.   *Vanitas
vanitatum, et omnia vanitas.*

WHAT posterity will think of Rathenau's philosophical
and economic writings is still uncertain.   It was a startling
phenomenon to see a young and elegant millionaire
launching out in the field of speculative thought, with
complete command of the weapons of controversy.   The
style was too obscure, the matter too difficult for the general

public. They took him on trust as a meteoric genius, and they were possibly right.

THERE is a floating suspicion in many minds that he was not very sound, but this impression, in my case at least, is based on two inadequate grounds : first, that he was abnormally brilliant ; secondly, that on two quite minor subjects of theoretical controversy—currency and trade balance—he held theories opposed to my own, and these subjects happen to be among those about which I am less sure than usual that I know nothing.

ARISTIDE BRIAND

AMONG the statesmen of Europe who have played leading parts since the war, none has attained—and none deserves —a higher fame than Aristide Briand. This pre-eminent position and reputation he has achieved despite characteristics which are usually a bar to contemporary popularity. Briand is fundamentally a sceptic, but so kindly, so generous, so compassionate a sceptic, that one is tempted to ask whether sympathy with the sufferings of mankind was ever manifested in clearer relief by the professed votaries of demonstrative philanthropy. No prejudice has led to graver mistakes in the judgment of history than the erroneous belief that human kindness is denied to those with a bias towards irony and agnosticism.

IN Briand's case, this is pre-eminently true. The common verdict on him would be that one who smiles so critically and disbelieves so much can at best be estimable.

SOME of Briand's followers lapse into excess in their admiration of him. One of them proposed that the principal rôle in The King of Kings belonged by right to him, on the ground that his attitude towards life was—taken broadly —less at variance with the Gospel story than that of any contemporary politician or artist. In the episode of the tribute money, of the woman taken in adultery, in the

story of Mary Magdalene, and in many other occasions,
Briand—in impersonating the part—would have had in
no way to depart from his natural self.

COMPARISONS are odious, and we prefer not to follow
the enthusiastic into exaggeration.   It is enough to claim
that no leading statesman of our time has shown a kindlier
generosity and a broader view of life.

THERE is another test of his admirable qualities.   What
man more than he—except perhaps Stresemann—has
run equal political risks for the advance of Europe towards
pacification ?   Who has been bolder in advocating a policy
of reconciliation, more prudent in refusing to be diverted
from this policy by secondary issues ?   It is said that
philosophy has no martyrs.   But Briand has endured
much for his conviction that Europe can be pacified.   He
might be deemed the St. Sebastian of pacification but for
the perpetual smile and the perpetual cigarette.

A. J. BALFOUR

IT is usual to associate Balfour's early political career
with the Fourth Party, and to connect him with Randolph
Churchill, Gorst, and Drummond Wolff.   But this association, which is suggestive of ruthless and rather rough political
activity, gives a false impression of the more delicate sides
of Balfour's character and of the ruling bias of his nature.
A more correct impression may be found if he is regarded
not as a member of an aggressive political cave, but as the
leader of a brilliant intellectual and literary set.

THERE never was any question as to the leadership of
that group called the " Souls," which astonished and fas-
cinated London in the nineties and before.   Balfour
stood far above the rest ; he was the inevitable chief,
though the group included Curzon, Wyndham, and
Cust.   What did Balfour's superiority consist in ?   In
a supreme dialectic.   It was impossible to argue any
subject with him without being left with the impression

that one's own view was clumsy and erroneous, that one's statement of it had been more clumsy than the view itself. He made it appear that his opponent had seen only half the problem and that what really mattered had been over-looked.

THE best way to give a true idea of Balfour's intellectual quality is perhaps by analogy and contrast. Compare him with other men who have been the leaders of their generation, with men who, like him, have been Prime Ministers of England. I have known no less than eleven of these eminent statesmen, and for vision, detachment, and adroitness Balfour was unequalled. Unlike Glad-stone, he was hampered by no passionate convictions; unlike Rosebery, he was not hypersensitive; compared with Campbell-Bannerman, he had a much finer intellect; compared with Asquith, he was more Greek and less Roman, and perhaps less a party man, strong though his party feeling was. The usual comparison is with his uncle, Lord Salisbury. While the two had marked qualities in common, the younger man was more of a philosopher and less of an aristocrat; he had a wider outlook, a finer dialectic, and a more impartial survey of mankind.

IN default of any close similarity with a contemporary, one is forced to recur to the classical world, and no analogy is so close as that with the Athenian philosopher Demonax, who lived in the first century of the Christian era. Of him, it was said that he never had an enemy, and that by his strange personal charm he attained such popularity and reverence that in his old age he could enter any Athenian house uninvited. The same could be said of Balfour. An anecdote of Demonax is characteristic of both men. When criticised by Epictetus for not marrying and thus founding a line of philosophers, he replied by asking the celibate philosopher to give him one of his daughters.[1]

[1] Dill, *Roman Society*, p. 366.

BALFOUR's mind was like a rapier of finest steel, flashing through the opponent's guard with lightning rapidity and unerring aim, inflicting wounds that were controversially fatal, less because they were heavy than because the vital spot was touched. If it is thought that the above description implies instability or want of conviction, such an impression is erroneous. There was no suspicion of either.

HIS general theory of life appeared to be that happiness is close to us, in freedom from bondage to imagined good, and in emancipation from the things of sense. No one less than he sought happiness in regions where happiness is not to be found.

THE completeness of his original survey was such that no argument produced by an opponent could impress by its novelty. As regards an alleged want of conviction, the reality of belief was much stronger than the superficial appearance. There were profound convictions on a limited number of subjects, and these were proof against the assaults of time or argument. Admittedly, fundamental convictions were few in number, but even outside these Balfour was tenacious rather than changeable. With such rapidity of mind, this was unexpected. While he might admit the force of arguments against his own view, he did not change his opinion, partly because he was never at a loss for counter-arguments to strengthen his original position. In discussion, one was indeed constantly reminded of a fort surrounded by barbed wire—a fort, moreover, where reserve troops were always ready to succour any threatened point in the defence.

FOR many of his contemporaries the problem about Balfour was to discover the inside man. What did he really think ? What did he really feel ? Was his judgment as sound as his arguments were ingenious ? Was he himself convinced by his own arguments ? Was there an instinctive subconscious mind which reached conclusions independently of dialectic or ratiocination ? Was the extreme delicacy of his apparent attitude really a reflection of his inner being, or merely a superficial cloak which covered a more robust or coarser self ?

ALL these are problems which have remained insoluble during his life, and will probably remain insoluble for posterity. For even his most intimate diary—if such exists—will only extend and strengthen the defence against indiscreet prying into the soul's sanctuary.

THE picture I have drawn of this extraordinary man will be incomplete and erroneous if it has not suggested a mind of the highest quality, an attitude towards life attained only by the truly philosophic, a charm, both for men of taste and women of refinement, which has rarely been equalled or approached.

LIKE Dion Chrysostom, he held that detachment of spirit can be attained without withdrawing from the mundane arena and the clatter of political life. And his whole career proves that what he held as a philosopher he could practise as a politician.

GENERAL WEYGAND

IN the last years of the war those who attended the War Conferences of the Allies were deeply impressed with the speed and precision with which decisions taken on the inspiration of Maréchal Foch were carried out. They became accustomed to the view that this punctuality of execution was largely due to the ability and zeal of an alert officer who was the constant companion and faithful adviser of the Maréchal. While the conception and the plan of action was that of Foch, and while it was through his energy and conviction that the plan was adopted, its execution was attributed in large measure to Weygand, and

many think, in furtherance of victory, execution was not
less important than conception.

My acquaintance with General Weygand dates from a later
period—the time when serious alarm was felt lest the
Soviet invasion of Poland should result in a communistic
menace to the whole of Central Europe.   The Polish
Army had advanced rashly and precipitately into the heart
of Russia.   This was done against the military and political
advice of the Allies, and led, as a much more celebrated
invasion of Russia had led before, to the necessity of a
disastrous retreat.   The Polish forces in June, July, and
August 1920 were driven back in disorder from Russian
territory which they had occupied, and did not stop in
their flight until they passed far within their own frontiers.
There was practically no resistance to the Russian advance
until the spires of Warsaw were within sight of the advancing
Muscovite.   Urgent appeals were made by the Polish
authorities for support from France and England, but it
was more easy to recognise the danger than to decide how
to ward it off.   The Governments of Paris and London
might be willing and anxious to send munitions and even
to send troops.   How could they be conveyed to Poland ?
The path across Germany was practically blocked.   There
were many obstacles in the route via Danzig.   Goods
dispatched through Czecho-Slovakia were by no means
certain of arrival owing to the close relations between
the Czechs and the Russians.   In view of all these difficulties
the English and French Governments determined to replace
the physical by the moral, to send a Mission to Warsaw
composed of military and civil elements, to advise as to the
best means of meeting the danger and affording the support
required.

It may fairly be claimed that no politico-military mission
ever worked more harmoniously together than the Anglo-
French delegates who were sent in July 1920 to assist
in defending Warsaw against the Bolshevik attack.

THEY were united in zeal for the defence of Poland ; there was the closest international co-operation; only one preoccupation filled their minds, viz. to bring the Mission to a successful and victorious issue.

AND in the result, no success could have been more complete. In July, when we arrived in Warsaw, there was confusion, if not consternation ; the probability that Warsaw would fall within a few weeks was in the proportion of ten to one. In August, when the Franco-English Mission withdrew, the Bolshevik attack had been shattered; the Muscovite aggressor was routed and was retreating in disorder to the security of his own territory.

ALMOST all dangers which are successfully warded off are subsequently regarded by sceptics as having been imaginary or exaggerated. The danger to Europe in August 1920 belongs to this category. The menace to European civilisation which the Bolshevik advance constituted has been grossly underrated. The work of the Anglo-French Mission has shared a like fate.

A POLISH enthusiast, if asked what occurred, would reply that the genius of Pilsudski achieved a miracle, and that the resilience and resource of the Slav nature brought off an improbability to which the Western Mission contributed little.

THIS view may be popular in patriotic Polish circles. I am sceptical about it myself, believing rather that the military success was due in a large measure to the sober methodical method of Weygand in organising Polish resistance, and that the confidence inspired by the presence of a Mission, representing the vast forces of Western Europe, had a powerful influence on the morale of the defence.

IF this judgment is correct, it becomes interesting to inquire what manner of man was Weygand. The reply is clear—the ideal soldier, precise, hardworking, firm in opinion yet modest, brave yet prudent, believing intensely in discipline, method, and organisation, but neither stereotyped nor deficient in resource. A man of excellent judgment both in civil no less than in military affairs, ambitious but devoted, the most faithful subordinate, the most competent leader.

THE MARQUESS CURZON

" O fortunatam natam, me consule, Roman."

THE Marquess Curzon was born grandiloquent ; his flow of language was no acquired talent, but innate and bred in the bone. There was an air of profuse magnificence in his diction. He lisped in Gibbon, for the Gibbon came. Had he spoken simply, it would have been affectation. Fine phrases were the natural outcome of his view of life. Everything was seen in the grand manner.

POMP and ceremony were for him the natural attributes of a dignified career—not the accompaniment, but the essence. While the ostentation was not vulgar, there was no understanding of the simple and the intimate ; the cool, sequestered vale of life had no call for grandiose souls like his.

CURZON's unique achievement was to combine this pomposity with humour. No one was naturally more pompous, but no one had a keener appreciation of the ludicrous side of things. This went so far that he saw the laughable aspect of everything except of his own attitude towards life. This remained unaltered to the end. He was born and he died in the faith of an aristocrat of the English eighteenth century : an aristocrat of so superb a type that it is met with rarely except in romance ; unremitting and indefatigable in the service of his country ; never sparing himself and still less sparing others ; exacting both towards subordinates and friends ; domineering but good-natured ;

and, in spite of great physical suffering, serene, cheerful, and humorous.

UNDER many of the definitions of genius which pass current, Curzon has an almost superlative right to claim it. For if it is a capacity for taking pains, no one took greater pains than he.

IF it consists in the union in a high degree of qualities not usually found in conjunction, no one could assert a right to possess these with a title better than his. What could be in sharper contradiction than his pride and his laboriousness, than his pomposity and his humour ?

IF, again, genius is defined as the possession of one aptitude in the highest degree, he might found his claim on the dignity and grace of his oratory.

NATURE rarely allows to the eloquent and facile the genuine gift of penetration and understanding. They manage well enough without it. Judged by this standard, Curzon had an abnormal endowment, for he added a real comprehension of many subjects to a fabulous facility in expatiating upon them.

THE best and most attached of friends, he regarded his circle as an extension of himself, and entitled, therefore, to infinite consideration, affection, and respect.

IN speech, his facility and felicity were astounding : always in the grand manner ; the phrases admirable in form, never descending to the colloquial or the commonplace, without much wit, but with a pervading humour which never deserted him. In his occasional speeches the transition from the purple patch to the impromptu was scarcely noticeable, so admirable and so stately was the phraseology of the improvisation. One of his friends said of him that he gave orders to a footman in language which would not have disgraced Cicero addressing the Roman Senate, and he occasionally called to servants not by name but by the title of their station, saying, " Housemaid, throw wide the casement," " Footman, add fuel to the flame."

EVERYTHING he attempted was conceived on a magnificent scale : his hospitality was profuse, but concentrated on great entertainments. Not the usual slipshod intimacy of a few friends dropping in to luncheon or coming in to play a quiet rubber after dinner. Such enjoyments had no attraction for him. They interfered with work—they lacked style—they had neither dignity nor grandeur.

No one would lavish more loving care on large entertainments than Curzon. Every item was thought out : every arrangement for comfort and convenience was elaborately drawn up and written down, not by proxy, but by the host himself ; no detail was too paltry for his meticulous care, and neither wife nor secretary was allowed to mar or to dilute the majestic virility of the entertainment.

NEVER before were united in the same person so dominant a love of the pompous and stately with such an appreciation of the slight absurdity there is in all pomp and pretension—how nearly they approach the futile. Curzon would have admitted the absurdity ; he would have denied the futility. The grand manner, he thought, impressed the world.

CURZON's power of work and his love of work were alike remarkable. None of the adventitious modern aids like shorthand and the dictaphone. Most letters written in his own hand, many of them after midnight. The story is authentic of the Secretary of the National Gallery Commission, who asked whether Curzon could receive him to discuss a draft report which had to be drawn up. Curzon replied : " Come any day after midnight." It is less known that when the Secretary did present himself at 1 a.m., Curzon had written out a draft report with his own hand. And with certain alterations his draft was adopted by the Committee, and now forms the Main Charter of the National and Tate Galleries. After twelve years' experience, this document constitutes an epitome of all that administrative wisdom and an instructed taste could suggest.

IT is also little known that in his last fatal illness, a few days before his death, he wrote an elaborate will, without any aid from lawyer or secretary, in a style reminiscent of a Cæsar.

THERE was something imperial about Curzon, and nothing about him was more imperial than his enjoyment of vanity. Moralists may condemn this passion ; ascetics may eschew it ; there can be no question as to the reality of the satisfaction it procures to its votaries.

VANITY has, however, one serious defect. A grave affront may be fatal. This was the case with Curzon. He never recovered from the catastrophic disappointment of the missed Premiership of 1923. This blow was succeeded by the intense mortification of Austen Chamberlain's appointment to the Foreign Office in 1924. What was the position ? Curzon had led the House of Lords with brilliancy for several years ; he was a past-master in the kind of occasional oratory required of a Prime Minister, indeed, he already spoke like a Prime Minister when still an undergraduate. He had a long record of distinguished service to the State. He was in the highest degree representative. It was not without justification that he considered himself the probable successor to Bonar Law as Premier.

BONAR LAW resigned in May 1923, and Baldwin was appointed Premier ; Chamberlain became Foreign Minister in November 1924. Curzon died in March 1925. The surgeon's explanation of death was an internal hæmorrhage, the deeper cause was a double charge of mortification and disappointment. He had long considered himself a potential Prime Minister and irreplaceable at the Foreign Office. After half a century of hope and forty-five years of unceasing toil, the highest prize seemed to be within his grasp. For causes which were to him incomprehensible it passed to another, and abasement in the ministerial hierarchy replaced the expected advance. In a world where such injustice was possible, where Fate was so malignant, there could be no joy, no contentment in living.

> " The prize was lost.   He for a moment tried
> To live without it—liked it not—and died."

HAD an epitaph to be found, it should be :

> " Immense orgueil : justifié."

CHAPTER I

APPOINTMENT TO BERLIN—THE SPA CONFERENCE

Lord Curzon's offer—Reception by President of Reich—The Spa atmosphere —German attitude—Lloyd George and General von Seeckt—Signing of disarmament protocol—Coal discussions—Hugo Stinnes's violent outburst—Millerand's dignified retort—German obstinacy—Allied Marshals called in—Dr. Simons—Lord D'Abernon's review of German finance.

LONDON, *June* 25, 1920.—After luncheon to-day in Carlton House Terrace Lord Curzon asked me to come into his room and said that he had authority from the Prime Minister to ascertain if I would undertake the post of Ambassador to Berlin. He suggested that an announcement should be made that the Mission was only temporary ; a period of less than two years, however, would appear uncivil to Germany.

WOULD the work interest me ? I replied : " As a temporary Mission I should like to undertake it, but I have no desire for permanent diplomatic work."

HE then said that the Mission would be like that of Mr. Goschen to Constantinople in the sense that I should be Ambassador Extraordinary and Minister Plenipotentiary, but that it would be understood that the Mission was in character somewhat different from the usual diplomatic appointment.

LORD CURZON went on to say that at the present juncture technical and specialised qualifications were required— notably a close familiarity with economic and financial subjects and wide experience in dealing on friendly terms with various classes of men. He thought the case for a special appointment overwhelming.

DID I know German well ? I replied : " No ; I am able to read German, but have no knowledge sufficient to carry on a discussion in that language." He said : " I think I ought to tell the Prime Minister that before making you

4   53

the final offer of the post, as he may have counted upon your being able to discuss in German." (Later in the day he telephoned to say the Prime Minister did not consider this absence of knowledge of German sufficient detriment to outweigh other special qualifications.)

AT a later interview, before leaving England, I asked the Secretary of State for Foreign Affairs : " Is the policy of the Government to be severe as regards military precautions, but at the same time to take a broad view of economic questions, provided that military requirements in the matter of security are fully satisfied ? " Lord Curzon said : " That appears to me to give the Government policy quite correctly."

> ON taking up the appointment, Lord D'Abernon spent only four days in Berlin (July 1–5) before proceeding to the Spa Conference. On July 2 he was received by President Ebert.[1]

Speech to the German President on presenting letters of credence, July 2, 1920

MONSIEUR LE REICHSPRÄSIDENT,
HIS Majesty's Government have charged me with the honourable duty of establishing full diplomatic relations with the German Republic.

I HAVE assumed this task in the hope that beneficial intercourse in many spheres between two great communities may thus be facilitated.

THE situation which the Governments of the world have to face to-day is one of unexampled difficulty. The world crisis can only successfully be met by general co-operation and by frank recognition of the truth that the good of each is the good of all. The essential foundation for us of this

---

[1] PASSAGES from Diary are printed full width; the indented passages are explanatory historical notes.

co-operation is the firm and affectionate maintenance of CHAP. present alliances and the strict execution of the obligations of the Treaty of Peace.

ECONOMIC reconstitution is the most imperative need of the world, and this can only be accomplished in an atmosphere of confidence.   Provided confidence is re-established by loyal acts of good faith, nations are entitled to expect from one another, not only latitude to develop, but assistance in development.   Narrow and short-sighted selfishness in this regard are altogether foreign to the traditions of my country and are no less opposed to the policy of His Majesty's Government.

IT is well known that in former days the doors of the Temple of Janus stood either open or shut.   There was no intermediate condition.   In the execution of my mission I shall constantly remember that peace has been signed.

I TRUST that in the difficult and honourable task which I have undertaken I may count on Your Excellency's goodwill and powerful co-operation.

[TRANSLATION]

Reply of the German President

MONSIEUR L'AMBASSADEUR,

I HAVE the honour to receive from Your Excellency's hands the letter of His Britannic Majesty by which you are accredited as Ambassador to me, and I am highly pleased that full diplomatic relations between Germany and Great Britain are thus re-established.

THE words which you have addressed to me find an appreciative echo in myself, and, I am convinced, in the whole German people.   The situation which the Governments of all countries have to face to-day is indeed one of unexampled difficulty.   You are quite right in considering that the only means of overcoming this world-crisis is a co-operation of nations based on the conviction that the good of one cannot be separated from the good of all.   I welcome the words in which you have given eloquent expression to this thought as an auspicious introduction to your activity in our midst.

THE German Government and the German people are united in the earnest resolve to meet the obligations they have undertaken, to the utmost of their forces, within the limits of possibility.   We sincerely wish that goodwill on both sides may succeed in dispelling the atmosphere of distrust which still partly survives, and in replacing it by mutual confidence and true sentiments of peace for the good of all peoples.

IT gives me great pleasure, Monsieur l'Ambassadeur, to bid you welcome on behalf of the Government of the German Republic.

THE SPA CONFERENCE, JULY 5–16, 1920

THE Spa Conference opened on July 5, M. Delacroix, the Belgian Premier, presiding.   The Conference had been preceded by a two days' meeting (July 2 and 3) of the Allied delegates in Brussels, where the chief business had been the apportionment of reparation receipts between the Powers primarily concerned. A previous and private understanding between Great Britain, France, and Serbia caused stormy discussions, as under it only 12½ or, at the outside, 14 per cent. of the total indemnity would have been available for distribution among Italy, Belgium, Japan, Rumania, Greece, and Portugal.   The Belgians were annoyed, as also was Count Sforza, the Italian Foreign Minister. On July 3, after King Albert had intervened in support of his Ministers' contentions, the French Premier, M. Millerand, and Mr. Lloyd George intimated that they agreed to reduce their countries' claims from 55 and 25 respectively to 52 and 22, Belgium accepting 8 per cent. and retaining her priority in respect of the first £100,000,000 payable by January.   It was decided that on this basis a

detailed plan should be worked out by the Allied
experts at Spa.

FROM July 5 to July 9 the Spa Conference occupied
itself mainly with the completion of Germany's
disarmament, Mr. Lloyd George conducting the
proceedings on behalf of the Allies. From the rather
discursive explanations by the German civilian ministers and the more precise data furnished by the
Reichswehr Commander, General von Seeckt, it
transpired that Germany had still twice the number
of Regular troops allowed her under the Versailles
Treaty, viz. 200,000 instead of 100,000, 6,000
machine guns instead of 2,000, 6,000 trench mortars
instead of 250, and from five to six times as many guns
as the statutory number.

MOREOVER, it was admitted by General von Seeckt
that there were no fewer than 2,000,000 rifles still
unaccounted for in the hands of the population. The
German Delegation asked for a respite of fifteen
months, until October 1921, in which to comply
with the treaty clauses under this head, but were
finally given until October 1, 1920, to reduce the
Reichswehr establishment from 200,000 to 150,000,
and until January 1 to bring it down to 100,000.
On July 9 the German delegates subscribed to a
special protocol embodying this and other conditions.
The protocol stipulated that, failing the full and
timely compliance by Germany with these demands
of the Allies, the latter would be entitled to enlarge
the occupation area, by incorporating within it the
Ruhr or any other district. From disarmament
the Conference then turned its attention to reparation
coal, the deliveries of which by the Reich had fallen
badly behind the quantities prescribed under the
treaty (39,000,000 tons) and the revised total fixed
by the Reparation Commission (21,000,000 tons).
A bad impression was created by the offensive speech
delivered by Herr Stinnes, the coal magnate, on July
10, which Dr. Simons, the German Foreign Minister,
hastened to disavow. But when, on July 11, Dr.

Simons submitted a most inadequate offer by the German Government regarding reparation in each kind, there ensued a crisis which caused the suspension of the main Conference for two days (July 14 and 15). The Allied Marshals (Foch and Wilson), General Maglieuse the Chief of the Belgian General Staff, and the Commander-in-Chief of the Occupation Army, Degoutte, were sent for, and instructed to prepare plans for the military coercion of Germany. This threat induced the German Delegation, on July 16, to sign a special Coal Protocol, but with one reservation concerning the claim of the Allies to apply territorial sanctions in the event of another German default.

OTHER questions dealt with by the Spa Conference comprised the trial of war criminals ; the objections of the Sultan's Government to the Treaty of Sèvres, which were overruled ; the reference to the Ambassadors' Conference of the delimitation of the Teschen area as between Poland and Czecho-Slovakia ; and Poland's appeal to the Allies for support against the invading Soviet army. This appeal was presented by the Polish Premier, M. Grabski, and the Polish Chief of Staff, General Rozwadowski.

SPA, *July 5*, 1920.—The picturesque is usually the uncomfortable. Spa is no exception to the rule, but it is less the deficiencies of the place than the excess of official visitors. The Delegations of the different nations are so swollen by experts on all subjects, that it would be difficult even in a much larger place than Spa to house everybody with decent comfort and without sending the minor lights too far afield. The Conference itself takes place in a beautiful Louis XVI villa called " La Fraineuse," a house where many German councils of war were held during 1917–18. M. Millerand, as the first French delegate, occupies not only the mansion but the bed so long occupied by William II ; since yesterday, the distinguished colleagues of the French Minister and their staffs have been shown round the steel and concrete shelter which afforded very efficient

and frequent protection to the German Kaiser against
Allied air raiders.

THE other Delegations are variously housed : some in the
centre of the town, like the English ; others on the peri-
phery. Count Sforza, the picturesque Italian Foreign
Minister, has been given an appropriate background in a
battlemented château with turrets, accessible only by
means of a drawbridge suspended over an artificial moat.
As a reputed descendant of the tyrants of Milan, he is
thoroughly at home in these medieval surroundings. He
mingles, however, modern methods with medievalism, for
whereas British and French Ministers have bound themselves to the strictest reticence in their dealings with the
press, Count Sforza addresses on the open boulevard massed
bands of Italian journalists and gives them discreet accounts
of inter-Allied conversations.

AMONGST those lodged far from the centre of the town is
the German Delegation, composed of Chancellor Fehrenbach
and Dr. Simons, assisted by a numerous staff. The rustic
inn which they inhabit is a long way from the town and
very secluded, but this isolation is deliberate and has been
adopted to avoid the danger of disagreeable episodes which
might occur if the German delegates showed themselves
too freely. The anti-German feeling among the population
is still most bitter.

SPA, *July* 5, 1920.—The Conference made a bad start
to-day. This is hardly surprising, for the German delegates have not been more than a few days in office and have
had little time to study their briefs. The consequence was
that when they were closely questioned regarding disarmament, their answers were unsatisfactory, and went to show
that the national thoroughness which the Germans affect is
not merely predilection but a physical necessity ; without
thorough preparation they are apparently lost. It was
unfortunate for them that the first issue raised at the Con-

ference was the highly technical one of Germany's present state of disarmament ; so technical was it that the leading German delegates, after endeavouring to answer without prompting, were obliged to call experts to their assistance, since they professed inability to deal with the problem from their own knowledge.

IT is curious to observe the attitude of the Germans towards the Allies. As might be expected, they are extremely sensitive and prone to see offence where none is intended. For instance, on their arrival at Spa the Germans immediately left cards on all the other Delegations. These cards were not returned at once by the English Delegation ; there was a press of work at the time ; cards were a pure formality ; besides, the war had rendered such trivialities unimportant. In any case no discourtesy was intended ; yet on account of this omission a grave misunderstanding nearly arose, as, according to the European code of etiquette, the return of a visiting card is an obligation of the most sacred nature. Accuse a man of crime : if you are punctilious on the visiting-card question, he will take no offence. Be careless in this matter, and abject flattery from you will be unavailing to atone for your neglect. Critics often complain that English diplomatists have not enough knowledge of the world or adequate contact with the rough and tumble of life. This may be true, but in the minor arts of etiquette and courtesy they have the advantage of modern politicians. Both might be improved : the politicians by six months abroad, the diplomatists by six months in the silver ring at English race-meetings. The one would gain a knowledge of Europe, the latter a knowledge of the world. In the eighteenth century it was said that the English were the only race whom bad manners suit.

SPA, *July 6*, 1920.—To-day, Herr Gessler,[1] the German

[1] GESSLER, Dr. Otto Carl.—Dr. Gessler, who succeeded Noske as Minister of National Defence in 1920, caused some little disturbance at the Con-

Minister of War, and General von Seeckt,[1] the Commander of the Reichswehr, arrived, accompanied by a
staff small in number but gigantic in stature. He was
immediately called to the Conference, and made a dramatic
appearance. A rather haughty demeanour and extreme
military stiffness—these were in striking contrast with
the rather dejected appearance of the German civilians.
Von Seeckt is an austere man, with a severe death's-head
face and an ultra-correct ceremonious manner. He was
supported by two subordinate blond giants. The three
wore the sober uniform of the new German Army, with iron
crosses and other war medals. The effect produced by
this appearance was different on different minds. Lloyd
George, who has little sympathy with military pomp and
paraphernalia, thought the appearance in uniform a signal
instance of military arrogance and tactlessness. Allied

ference at Spa by his statement that Germany had not disarmed according
to the Versailles conditions ; his remarks, which were lengthy and vague,
created a less favourable impression of his abilities than might be given
by his subsequent career.

HE was born at Würtemberg in 1875, and won some fame as a lawyer.
For five years, from 1905 to 1910, he was a judge at Munich. When war
broke out he was burgomaster at Ratibor, and from 1914 to 1919 was
entrusted with the care of Nuremberg.

GESSLER modified his democratic principles in 1926, when be became
Reich Minister in the Cabinet of the Right ; this position he resigned in
1928.

[1] VON SEECKT, General.—The professional head of the Reichswehr down to
1927. Essentially military, prim, stiff, and courtly. During the late war
was two years with the Austrian Army, one year with the Bulgarians, and one
year with the Turks, acting as Chief of the Staff to Field-Marshal von Macken-
sen. Enjoys an excellent reputation as an officer and is said to keep clear of
politics. Is the real organiser of Germany's present army, having raised
this limited force of 100,000 to a remarkable pitch of personal and technical
efficiency. Von Seeckt always chose the Reichswehr officers himself with
the utmost care, on their professional merits, and regardless of their political
opinions. He showed in 1922 and 1923 that he was equally prepared to
suppress " Putsches," whether from the Right or from the Left. He was
dismissed by the Reichswehr Minister, Herr Gessler, in 1926, for allowing
the ex-Crown Prince's son, Prince Wilhelm, to attend the summer
manœuvres as a supernumerary lieutenant in the Reichswehr. He had
previously been raised to the rank of Colonel-General.

soldiers, on the other hand, took the opposite view, and held that the German officers, in thus putting up a proud face in adversity, were behaving with dignity and military decorum.   Personally, I thought von Seeckt carried through a difficult part like an officer and a gentleman.

SPA, *July* 6, 1920.—Lloyd George and George Curzon are fine representatives.   Impudence and Dignity, some foreign critic called them.   But the impudence is so extraordinarily quick and intelligent and decided, the dignity so grand in manner and imposing, that no country could wish for anything better.   Lloyd George speaks only in English, and will not allow any English delegate to do otherwise ; he insists on everything being translated into English before he will deign to understand it, or even try to comprehend.   The only French he understands, so it is said, is that spoken by Lord Grey of Fallodon ; both grammar and pronunciation must be Northumbrian.

CURZON's French is fluent, and he would possibly like to air his verbal facility in a new dress but for Lloyd George's ban.   The latter has very wisely broken through the previous European practice of considering French the language of international discussion.   It places us and some other nations at too great a disadvantage, especially ourselves, as we are shy and self-conscious in addition to not knowing French too well.   The mere fact that all the drafting has to be done by the French is in itself a danger. No foreigner that I have ever met can write French perfectly, and very few can speak it without applying a portion of their intelligence to the task ; and in political discussion the whole available brain-power is wanted for the argument, so that none can be diverted to the vehicle.   Lloyd George would have been wise if he had insisted on some neutral city as the home of the Reparation Commission and of the Ambassadors' Conference.   What the situation required

was impartiality and technical knowledge of local conditions
in Germany. The last place to obtain either was Paris.
London in 1919 would possibly have been almost as bad.

Spa, *July* 7, 1920.—A rather painful scene took place at
to-day's meeting. Lloyd George was pressing the German delegates to carry out disarmament without delay,
and above all to disarm the irregular bodies who so com-
plicate the German position. Dr. Fehrenbach exclaimed
with apparent sincerity : " I am an old man who will soon
be appearing before the Great Judge ; believe me, therefore, I beg of you, when I say I am perfectly honest in my
desire and in my undertaking to execute the treaty, but
I cannot achieve the impossible."

Spa, *July* 10, 1920.—The special protocol relating to the
disarmament of the Reich was signed to-day, but Herr
Gessler, the German Minister of War, refrained from signing. This did not make a good impression.
A DRAMATIC scene occurred at the close of the proceedings.
General von Seeckt emerged from the Council Chamber
after the signature which carried with it the obliteration
of the great German Army of the previous régime. As the
General's car had not arrived, he stood, a lone and tragic
figure, outside the entrance to the Conference villa on the
marble steps, exposed to the gaze of several hundreds of
spectators, civil and military. He remained as impassive
as a statue, calmly surveying the audience through his
glass. The only sign of emotion which certainly raged
within him was the spasmodic way in which he chewed
the stump of a cigar. Otherwise, no indication of nervous
storm.

Spa, *July* 12, 1920.—The previous meetings of the Conference have been sensational enough, but to-day all records
were surpassed. The sensation was caused by Herr

Stinnes,[1] the great coal magnate, who made a most violent outburst at the Supreme Council. I do not know why the official German delegates had asked that Stinnes should be heard ; they must have known the danger. No sooner had the President invited Herr Stinnes to address the Conference, than he rose and read a carefully prepared speech. The studied deliberateness with which he spoke added to the offensiveness of the phraseology. He said : " I rise because I want to look everybody in the face. M. Millerand announced yesterday that we Germans were accorded the right to speak as a matter of courtesy. I claim to speak as a matter of right. Whoever is not afflicted with the disease of victory . . ." At this point Stinnes was stopped by the President. Dr. Simons interfered gently with the remark that Herr Stinnes had no official status. Later on, when referring to the Allied threat to occupy the Ruhr, Stinnes broke out again, and declared in a roaring voice : " If black troops—those worthy instruments of Allied policy—are used for this purpose, the feelings of every white man will recoil, nor will the Allies get any coal."

THE Allied delegates were pale with anger and surprise ; the Belgian President, M. Delacroix, sharply called the German coal king to order. It was subsequently explained by Dr. Simons, with a view to allaying excitement, that Stinnes was in the habit of addressing board meetings in similar tones. M. Hymans, the Belgian Foreign Minister, remarked on this : " What would have happened to us with such a man, if he had been in the position of the conqueror ? "

STINNES played a part, also, in a subsequent incident.

[1] STINNES, Hugo.—Born 1870. A millionaire with a genius for coal and steel. Deviated into politics, concerning which he was far less gifted. He exercised, however, a considerable influence upon German politics and the German Government, owing to his wealth and to his various newspapers and press agencies. His actual wealth was possibly exaggerated. He was, besides, much involved in world-wide speculations.

During a pause in the Conference, Stinnes was seen
haranguing the German Delegation in loud tones, with violent and even wild gestures. It was in vain they sought to calm him. We learned subsequently that the object of his harangue was to persuade the official delegates that he should draft a memorandum on the subject of coal, declaring that Germany was unable to export more than 12,000,000 tons a year. Throughout the meeting to-day M. Millerand was dignified and moderate, saying, as he rose to answer the German arguments on coal, that his remarks were addressed to the official German Delegation (of which Stinnes was not a member).

A TURNING-POINT in European history was reached this afternoon, when M. Millerand described Germany as a " necessary and useful member of the European family." Some of the minor French delegates were astounded at his boldness and breadth. For the first time, that afternoon the German delegates were invited to join the Allies at tea. The cup of international reconciliation was drunk cordially, and proceedings at the Conference will probably gain thereby.

SPA, *July* 13, 1920.—There is not much to say about the negotiations here, outside the reports in the press, which seem fairly full and accurate.

IT looks as if the discussion about coal deliveries to be made by Germany would end in a compromise, round about 1,800,000 tons a month.

A SPECIAL Committee discussed the indemnity question for the first time this morning. The German delegates had been expected to mention a figure, but finessed and said they could not give one without consultation with Berlin ; then they alleged that no figure could be given except with a great many reserves—the retention of Upper Silesia, etc. The Committee adjourned until later in the day, in order to give the Germans time to consult their

Government and produce a figure for a minimum annuity. It remains to be seen what the result may be.

THE general tone of the Prime Minister and of Lord Curzon regarding Germany is extremely reasonable. They are anxious above all to co-operate most cordially with the French, but clearly realise that Germany must be allowed to get on her legs economically.

SPA, *July* 14, 1920.—The sky has suddenly clouded over.

THE German delegates—possibly on unfavourable news from Berlin—unexpectedly declared that they would make no further concessions regarding coal, and raised the question of Upper Silesia in connection with it. They also withdrew their promise to present a written statement regarding the indemnity, stating that no offer could be made, as a settlement regarding coal was so improbable.

LLOYD GEORGE had anticipated that no meeting would take place during the day, so was away on an excursion. He was suddenly called back. Foch and Wilson were sent for, the implication being that the occupation of the Ruhr must be considered at once.

I BELIEVE the Germans regard the occupation of the Ruhr as a fixed determination of the French. They believe that no efforts on their part can avail to ward off this blow, so think it best to get it over at once.

To my mind, the occupation of the Ruhr would be deplorable. I doubt if it would improve the coal position. It would certainly endanger the whole " Europe " position.

PERHAPS the best course of negotiations would be for the Germans to make a mixed proposal, including both coal and indemnity. It is doubtful if coal can be settled as a separate proposition.

THE Germans allege that not only the coal magnates, but also the miners, hold that a greater delivery to France is not possible.

VARIOUS subsidiary schemes are under consideration, the objects being :

(*a*) To improve the price paid to Germany for coal, in the view that it is against human nature to work hard to produce coal which will be sold below its real value ;

(*b*) To promote the food-supply of Germany and especially to improve the food of the miners.

THE second of these proposals was mooted in consequence of a delegation of German miners, representing three groups (Social Democrats, Independent Socialists, and Catholic Trade Unions), accompanied by a Councillor of the German Ministry of Labour. They made a very good impression on the Allied delegates, Herr Hué, their leader, proving both intelligent and eloquent, when he addressed the Supreme Council.

SPA, *July* 15, 1920.—Stinnes again appeared in the lime-light. While the Conference was in session, news was received that the gendarmes had arrested a sinister-looking individual in the woods adjoining the villa, suspecting him of lurking there with a view to the commission of some crime or assault. Some of the secretaries of the Conference rushed out on hearing this news, and discovered, to their astonishment, that the man who had been arrested was the great industrialist, who was struggling with three Belgian gendarmes, expostulating furiously. It was explained that *cet individu* had been caught wandering in the gardens, and had been arrested on account of his menacing appearance and terrible mien. The identity of the prisoner was soon established, and he left the villa for his hotel. His temper has probably not been improved by the incident, but it would be difficult to make him more aggressive than he was yesterday, when unprovoked.

SPA, *July* 15, 1920.—Foch and Wilson have arrived. IT is so far uncertain what military action will be taken. WILSON regards the present attitude of Germany as a skilful attempt to put a rift into the relations between England and France on the point where our interests are least identical. If this is correct, it was a mistake to negotiate coal by itself. I still believe that the best chance of a satisfactory solution is to discuss it in conjunction with indemnity and economic restoration—all of them form an indissoluble whole.

SPA, *July* 16, 1920.—There has been no more interesting personality at the Conference than the Italian delegate, Count Sforza. Most carefully non-committal and somewhat changeable. Yesterday, Sforza declared that the present temper of his country would not warrant him in making an offer of Italian military participation in the projected occupation of the Ruhr. To-day, mainly owing to strong pressure from Lloyd George, he modified his attitude, and agreed that one battalion of Italian troops should take part in the operation, as a proof of the unity of the Allies against German resistance and bad will.

ONE reason for Italian reluctance to take a prominent part in any measures of pressure against Germany is probably the fact that they are not too well pleased with the Allied agreement for the apportionment of reparations. Sforza wittily termed this agreement " an inequitable division of our disappointments," and he appears to consider that Italy has been treated as " the Cinderella of reparations." It is true that Italy has been offered as a compensation the solace of a higher percentage of the Austrian, Hungarian, and Bulgarian indemnities. But this does not afford much solid food for satisfaction, as Austria, in Sforza's words, has been " conquered too completely." The truth is that Sforza is somewhat too medieval and knightly to feel quite at home in wrangling with Treasury experts and in sordid squabbles over percentages. For him diplomacy is nowadays too mathematical to be quite a gentleman's profession—" Ce n'est plus affaire de gentilhomme."

DURING the closing stages of the Spa Conference,
the Supreme Council received a hurried visit from
M. Grabski, the Polish Premier, accompanied by the
Chief of the Polish General Staff, General Rozwadowski. They came to appeal for Allied support
against the Bolshevik advance on Warsaw—the
result of a successful counter-offensive launched by
the Soviet armies after the capture of Kiev by a bold
but unwise Polish cavalry drive during the previous
spring. The Supreme Council, after hearing M.
Grabski's appeal, undertook to intervene diplomatically
on behalf of Poland. Accordingly, Lord Curzon
cabled a warning and proposals to the Soviet Government, fixing a provisional ethnographical frontier between Poland and Soviet Russia, called after him the
" Curzon Line." The Russian armies were to halt at
a point 50 kilometres east of that line.

AT the same time the Supreme Council—and in
particular Mr. Lloyd George—impressed upon the
Polish Government the need of moderation in any
armistice or peace negotiations that might take place.
Soviet diplomacy as usual procrastinated and, while
professing readiness to discuss armistice and peace
terms with the Poles, continually found some excuse
for postponing actual discussion, as the Russian
armies drew nearer and nearer to the Polish capital
in a wide converging movement.

MEANWHILE, Mr. Lloyd George, after a long consultation with M. Millerand, the French Premier,
decided to appoint an Anglo-French Mission to bring
moral and technical support to the distressed Poles.
On the British side, Lord D'Abernon was appointed
special delegate for this purpose, accompanied by
Major-General Sir Percy Radcliffe, Director of
Military Operations at the War Office. The French
representatives were M. Jusserand and General
Weygand, Marshal Foch's Chief of Staff. On
July 22 the Allied Mission left Paris for Warsaw
via Prague, in the latter place interviewing President
Masaryk, whom they found by no means favourable

5

to the Poles but insistent on strict neutrality. The Mission arrived at Warsaw on July 25 and found everything there in a state of chaos, politically and from the military standpoint. The ministers were at loggerheads with President Pilsudski, who kept all powers in his hands and exercised absolute control over the army, ignoring the counsels of the French Military Mission. The Russian armies were fast enveloping Warsaw from three sides, and the defences were inadequate in some parts and wholly lacking in others.

LORD D'ABERNON set himself, before all else, to secure that General Weygand's brilliant gifts as a strategist and tactician should be utilised to the full by the Polish Army chiefs. The obstacles, both personal and political, to be overcome were most formidable, but by plain speaking and persistency the British envoy secured that General Weygand, whilst refusing to assume in titular fashion the leadership of the Polish General Staff, should advise Marshal Pilsudski and his lieutenants as to the defence of the capital. As a sequel to this agreement, the Polish Government, on August 6, issued a proclamation to the Polish nation exhorting them to resist the enemy to the utmost. On the twelfth of that month the Bolsheviks had almost reached the eastern suburbs of Warsaw, when the Poles, animated by a new spirit and encouraged by the clear-sightedness and coolness of General Weygand as their chief adviser, made a splendid rally, striking a remarkable counter-blow on August 14. The effects of this counter-blow were stupefying. On the Russian side, army after army broke and fled. By August 23 the Poles were able to claim a capture of 200 guns and 35,000 prisoners, the latter figure being raised to over 100,000 a week later. Warsaw had been saved, thanks to the moral support of the Anglo-French Mission, to the powerful stimulus they exercised on the national spirit and to the military genius of General Weygand. Lord D'Abernon, on leaving Warsaw, received a

cable of congratulation from Lord Curzon and a
message of personal appreciation from Mr. Lloyd
George.

AFTER his return to England, Lord D'Abernon was
laid up for some weeks with dysentery contracted
in Warsaw, but recovered in time to take up the
Embassy at Berlin on October 21.

WARSAW, *July* 30, 1920.—My preparations for the journey
to Warsaw have been complicated by a demand from
London that I should submit a report on the financial
situation of Germany, with a view to the discussions which
are to take place at Geneva.   I have so short an acquaintance with German conditions that my views are not
definitely formed, but I have come clearly to the conclusion that Germany is so near bankruptcy that this
menace is the governing fact to be remembered in all
economic and financial discussions.   Recovery is only
possible through great skill on the part of her financial
authorities, aided by careful nursing of economic factors
on the part of all interested.   The only chance of obtaining
from Germany any large annuity towards reparation is
intelligent assistance, enabling her to revive her agriculture
and her industry.   Blind demands for payment either in
kind or in cash, without reference to the practical possibilities of the moment, without intelligent consideration
of the psychology of the taxpayer, and without reference
to the effect of an excessive immediate burden on the
economic recovery of the country, are certain to mean a
breakdown.   The first consideration for the pilot is to
avoid the shoal of bankruptcy ; it matters much less if
he takes a course a little wide of the shortest.

IT should be recognised from the beginning as a basic
fact that, without a radical change in Germany's present
financial situation, there is not the faintest chance of
Germany being able to pay the full amount of reparation
for which she is responsible under the treaty, which may

be estimated at from £11,000,000,000 to £12,000,000,000. An improvement so radical as to enable her to raise this amount may or may not be ultimately possible, but it is certainly impossible without the most careful administration and without time.

IT follows that it is useless to press a hard or precise interpretation of any individual claim, since the result will be not to increase the total sum obtained from Germany, but merely to transfer payments from Germany from one heading to another ; thus an increased contribution under heading (*a*) would merely diminish the amount available under heading (*b*).

IT may therefore be said, and this is an important point, that nothing is to be gained by riding any individual claim too hard. The real desiderata at Geneva appear consequently to be :

1. A MINIMUM annuity at once.

2. A POSTPONEMENT of the discussion for fixing the total amount of the final indemnity until the situation has developed.

I SHOULD even doubt whether an endeavour to fix a sliding scale or bareme, under which the minimum annuity would increase in proportion with either German production or German exports or German revenue, is now desirable. My chief reasons for this view are :

THE extreme confusion of German currency. Until this is stabilised no serious forecast can be made of the financial future of Germany. It is impossible to exaggerate the importance of this factor.

A SECOND reason why any serious forecast is impossible now is the fact that during the war no increase of taxation was imposed in Germany. A very stringent scheme of taxation has been elaborated during the last six months, and is now being applied. We must see how this increased taxation is paid before forming an opinion as to the possibility of its maintenance or its increase. It is, therefore, impossible for anyone, even with the fullest information, to estimate now the payment Germany could bear in future years. Any excessive demands or even undue precision in demands will gain nothing, and will injure, if they do not kill, the prospects of the future. Apart from this, as a matter of tactics, it may be observed that the Germans themselves have greater interest in fixing a definite sum than the Allies have in imposing it. They must, in their own interest, come forward with a proposal. Is not a proposal from their side a better basis for negotiation than a demand from ours ?

THERE is another reason against a premature attempt to fix the final figure of indemnity. The views of the French and German Governments are, for the moment, too far apart for any compromise to be possible or for any broker, however ingenious, to bring them together. I can imagine no figure which, adopted to-day, would not so shock public opinion in one country or the other as to break down negotiations.

THE Boulogne scheme represented a great advance, in that it constituted a considerable reduction of the previous French estimates. On the other hand, it did good in Germany, where its chief outlines were known, in that it showed the German ministers how far their ideas went short of those of the Entente. But, as a matter of fact, the Boulogne figures represented a level of demand which is quite unattainable at present, unless the reparation in kind represented by coal and other deliveries is calculated at a very high figure. The minimum annual payment agreed to at Boulogne was 3 milliards of marks, gold, per annum. This represents, at the present exchange, approximately 24 milliards of marks, paper. The total estimated revenue of the German State on the basis of the new taxation is approximately 31 milliards (ordinary budget), and her minimum internal expenditure necessary to her existence as a State at approximately the same amount.

As the German budget barely balances, without leaving anything for indemnity, the payment of this annual sum in cash would mean nearly doubling all German taxation. Now, it is quite doubtful whether the new scheme of taxation (calculated to produce 31 milliards) can be smoothly worked. It is altogether impossible to conceive that twice the new rate of taxation could be imposed without producing a revolution.

THERE is a further question, the advisability of a loan based on a minimum annuity, which was discussed at Spa, in the belief that a loan was urgently required by France and would be cordially welcomed by Germany. The French financial authorities, however, appeared less keen than we anticipated about a loan, while the German unofficial financial authorities said that, as far as they were concerned, they were indifferent whether a loan was issued or not. The only real point of vital interest to them was the possibility of balancing expenditure with revenue, and thus ceasing to depend upon the printing press. Whether this view was sincere or not I cannot say. It seems rather to conflict with other statements which have been made regarding the necessity of more food and more raw material. But, even if a loan is not urgent, I should still advocate an endeavour to obtain at Geneva a promise of an annual minimum payment, as a payment on account of future indemnity and as a basis on which further financial arrangements could be made.

IN conclusion, the view which the Entente should, in my opinion, keep constantly before them, is that Germany's present financial position is very precarious ; but that, on a long view, the economic position shows signs of the possibility of future improvement.

THE above gives my views on the position as seen from Berlin, but the whole future is threatened by the Bolshevik invasion of Poland. If the Bolshevik armies capture Warsaw, there will be such an outbreak of Communism

throughout Germany that no financial recovery there will
be possible for months or years to come. The reality of
the danger to the whole of Central Europe if Warsaw is
captured is enormously underrated in London and, to a
minor degree, in Paris, but the French have a clearer
conception of the menace than have politicians in London.

CHAPTER II

FROM SPA TO BRUSSELS—EARLY DAYS IN BERLIN

A talk with Tardieu—Berlin personalities: the French Ambassador—
Chancellor Fehrenbach—German diplomats, old and new—A coming
man, Dr. Wirth—The Italian Ambassador—The Papal Nuncio—Herr
Deutsch—Prince and Princess von Bülow—Herr von Kahr—Herr
Loebe.

Berlin, *October* 21, 1920.—Arrived in Berlin this morning, after three days in Paris.

Saw no political people in Paris, having kept deliberately clear of them.

The only exception was Tardieu,[1] whom I met at luncheon at the British Embassy. He is one of the principal writers in the French press who favour France exacting the full indemnity according to the strict letter of the treaty, so I thought it well to tell him, quite frankly, what the results of such a policy would, in my judgment, be. I made it clear that England was not less interested in obtaining adequate reparation than France was, Tardieu having intimated that we did not care whether Germany paid or not. Our small portion of the cake was as sweet to us as their larger portion was to them—only we think that on the lines now advocated by certain sections in Paris there is great risk of there being no division of cake at all. The true position is that we—England and France—are both deben-

---

[1] Tardieu, André.—The Treaty of Versailles owes a great deal of its construction to Tardieu; and a good deal of its championship and avoidance of revision to the *Echo National*, founded by Clemenceau and Tardieu in order to wage fierce war on the opponents of the Treaty.

Born in 1876, Tardieu made his reputation as a writer and politician. For twelve years before the war he was foreign editor of *Le Temps*. Towards the end of the war, in which he took an active part, he was sent as High Commissioner to the United States.

Tardieu was associated in policy and actions always with Clemenceau, for whom he worked and wrote always with tireless industry and loyalty. Between 1919 and 1924 he refused to take any active part in the Government in order to maintain this attitude. He emerged from inactivity as Minister of Public Works in the Poincaré Cabinet.

ture holders in the German Company, and if we wish the
interest on our debentures to be paid, we must wish for
and assist the prosperity of the Company. " Yes," said
Tardieu, " I agree to that, but are not the debenture
holders being defrauded in favour of the shareholders ? "
to which I replied : " Look at the facts ; make an impartial
examination and tell me what the position is. The German Government appear so unable to meet their expenditure with current revenue that they continue to issue
large amounts of bank notes. As long as this position
continues it is useless to talk about any indemnity, or
reparation, or dividend, for anybody. Germany must
first pay her own expenses, either by increased revenue or
reduced expenditure. The continuation of the present
policy of meeting the deficit by means of the printing
press must lead to bankruptcy at no distant date. No
serious reparation will be paid unless currency is put
right. It is no good talking away from the essential
condition. An intelligent and impartial investigation or
the financial position is necessary. My information is
that the economic position in Germany is slightly better
than three months ago, but the financial position is much
worse." Tardieu had very little to say in reply, and he
certainly gave the impression of realising that the unrestricted and unbridled Shylockism advocated by some
nationalists could not be justified financially, and could
only be defended on the basis of ulterior political aims.
Tardieu appears to be extraordinarily intelligent and quick.
This is somewhat marred by a preternatural glibness.

Berlin, *October* 21, 1920.—Spent the day yesterday at
Cologne, and went to the races.
Cologne streets and shops suggest considerable prosperity
and activity. There was quite a crowd at the races,
mostly men, and all quite as well dressed as at any ordinary
English race-meeting. Most race-crowds look as if they

ought to be sent off to Botany Bay at sight, but the Cologne crowd was certainly no worse than that in other countries.

BERLIN, *October* 22, 1920.—A long conversation with Dr. Simons at the Foreign Office on the principal questions of current interest. His general attitude was reasonable, and he appeared disposed to fall in with our views as far as possible on all the points discussed.

REGARDING disarmament, Dr. Simons said that the demands of the Ententefor the dismemberment of various Einwohner-wehr and Orgesch organisations was equivalent to deliver-ing up the orderly section of the population to their greatest foes. Without organisation the burgher element cannot resist the Reds, who are a real danger. He gave it as his opinion that the Bolsheviks were endeavouring to create in Germany a feeling of violent antipathy to France and of resistance to the execution of the Peace Treaty. France would thus be brought to attack Germany, Germany would be broken up and accessible to Bolshevism. The Bolsheviks would then be able to destroy the Polish army. France, being engaged in a war with Germany, could not help the Poles, and the latter could do nothing without English and French support. Germany was in reality the barrier against Bolshevism and disorder.

I POINTED out that Poland was usually regarded as the barrier, and that they had achieved recently a notable victory. Dr. Simons replied : " We are the real barrier. Poland is far too weak ; without Western assistance she can do very little."

BERLIN, *October* 26, 1920.—The French Ambassador—M. Charles Laurent—is a man of exceptional intelligence and spirit. I discussed with him to-day the proposed financial conferences at Brussels and Geneva. He takes the view that the important thing is to get the financial specialists to meet at Brussels and go into the real facts. Quite indifferent as to whether the financial delegates belong to the

Reparation Commission or not. It seems, indeed, that Dubois, President of the Reparation Commission, who we thought was responsible for pressing the right of the Commission in this matter, has been in reality the other way and has urged that the financial delegates at Brussels should be chosen from outside the Commission. Dubois's idea apparently is that anyone who has been appointed Judge by the treaty cannot as a private individual come off the Bench and discuss with laymen.

LAURENT holds that it is useless to trouble now about what will happen after the Conference at Brussels, as Brussels should shed much more light on the whole position. The extreme claims brought forward by the press on both sides must not be taken too seriously. France would never agree to abandon the treaty or to modify it, but in its details and execution there are modes and attenuations. " We have all to reckon with what is possible."

REGARDING the relations between France and Germany, a month ago Simons had proposed to him that private conversations should take place between the two countries, in order to arrive at a better understanding. Paris, after ten days' delay, agreed in principle but made reservations. The projected conversations had, however, never taken place. He himself thought that nothing but advantage could result from business-like discussions.

SIMONS he thought an intelligent man with whom one could talk, but, of course, the German Government was very weak. Even if you are on good terms with them, the German habit of chicane spoils negotiation. Laurent said : " You will find them chicane regarding everything. You can never get broad views on any point ; all sorts of absurd legal technicalities will be raised."

BERLIN, *October* 26, 1920.—This afternoon I called on the German Chancellor—Fehrenbach. Our conversation, though friendly, was formal and without special point.

His failure at Spa has largely diminished his influence and position here.

NOTWITHSTANDING this loss of face, combined with an abscess in the cheek, he remains as benevolent and benign as ever. I believe he is a thoroughly honest old fellow who would always exercise such influence as he may possess in the right direction in any grave emergency.

FOR my own part, whenever I see him I understand the official who said : "He ought to sit as the model for the father of the Prodigal Son—he is so welcoming, benevolent, and paternal."

BERLIN, *October* 28, 1920.—Had an opportunity yesterday of dining with two members of the old Foreign Office.

THEIR general attitude was one of unmitigated gloom : Germany was in the trough of the sea—nothing was improving. The Government, though honest and sincere, was lamentably weak and the financial situation was deplorable. All their banker friends were sending money out of Germany, a process which no amount of restriction could prevent. Non-payment of taxes was no longer a crime but a patriotic duty. During the winter there would be terrible unemployment and probably a good deal of social disturbance.

FRANCE was all-powerful and had vowed the disintegration of Germany. There was no good in trying to prevent the occupation of the Ruhr. Inspired by Foch, France had determined to effect this, and also to detach South Germany from the Reich and thus make a direct means of communication with Poland.

ENGLAND had certainly shown a more benevolent attitude towards Germany, but when it came to the pinch she would probably defer to the wishes of France.

THEY said much more on the same note of wail, but I pointed out that the picture they drew was very much overcharged with shadow. The food situation was better than a year ago, and German industry, if not prosperous, was improving, while German competition in the world markets was bound to be successful, owing to low cost of production. But they continued to argue that the position was catastrophic.

THEY gave interesting information regarding Turkey's entry into the war. So far from there having been a binding alliance with Turkey [1] which obliged the latter to support Germany, Germany had the greatest difficulty in getting Turkey to take the decisive step, and only succeeded in doing so by paying large sums to Enver and Talaat. Enver had received bribes on five different occasions and had always succeeded in extracting gold. Talaat had received £80,000 in gold the first time, but the second time had been induced to accept paper money. However, he was so sceptical regarding its value that he spent the next two days in going round to the big jewellers in Berlin and buying precious stones as being safer than German paper. Enver had not told Talaat of the money he had received, and there had been a great quarrel between them until matters were equalised. Enver was a terrible scoundrel, but a very vigorous enemy who would give England lots of trouble in Central Asia.

THE attitude of these members of the old Foreign Office regarding the Kaiser was curious. They maintained, as do all the Imperial Party, that the Kaiser was more a fool than a criminal. His great idea in creating a large German

---

[1] BUT see the Memoirs of Djemal Pasha (the then Minister of Marine). These speak of an alliance between Germany and Turkey, signed in June 1914. A good authority here declares this was only a vague *projet de traité*. I suspect it was more.

THE actual text of a treaty alleged to have been signed on August 2, 1914, has been published by the German Foreign Office. It was a signed engagement that if Russia intervened during the war between Austria-Hungary and Serbia, and thereby a *casus fœderis* was established for Germany, a *casus fœderis* would also come into force for Turkey. There is a good deal of obscurity about the transaction, for, though the treaty was signed, it seems not to have been considered to come into effect. It is uncertain whether it was recognised.

navy was to swagger about in admiral's uniform—to pace the quarter-deck with Beresford. This silly vanity had been exploited by von Tirpitz—he was the real author of Germany's downfall. But for the naval policy, an understanding would have been achieved with England. So far back as 1878 Bismarck had proposed a friendly understanding to Beaconsfield ; again in 1882 and 1887 he brought forward the idea. On subsequent occasions an agreement had nearly been reached, but von Bülow had prevented the signature.

THEY then went on to talk about Poland. Both declared that no German Ministry could be friendly with a Power which possessed what was clearly German territory—such as Danzig and Graudenz. They did not mention Posen. The Poles had always been the same : if you want a perfect description of Polish policy, read the letters of Catherine the Great to Grimm.

I VENTURED to observe that these Poles—so disliked and so contemned—had rendered Germany great service in driving back the Bolsheviks last August. Had Warsaw fallen, Bolshevism would have extended to Danzig, Czecho-Slovakia, to the Ruhr, and to a great part of Saxony. They quite agreed, but one of them said : " I would rather see Germany Bolshevik than in its present condition under the heel of France. After all, Bolshevism would only be a passing phase." But the other dissented from this view, saying : " Galling as it is to accept a service from Poland, it is probably better that the Bolsheviks were defeated."

THE mild anti-Bolshevik attitude of these partisans of Imperialism, contrasted with the firm and vigorous anti-Bolshevik attitude of the present German Government and of the Majority Socialists, is not without interest.

BERLIN, *October* 29, 1920.—Dr. Wirth,[1] the Minister

[1] WIRTH.—Born 1879. Minister of Finance in 1920 and Chancellor in May 1921. Showed great courage and unremitting industry in his efforts to

of Finance, lunched here to-day. One of the younger
ministers, he was a Professor of Mathematics before the
war, and served on almost every front during the war,
partly as a private soldier. A healthy, outspoken, and out-
door type of German. He has advanced democratic ideas
and makes a favourable impression by his frankness and
sincerity.

WIRTH told me that at the Spa Conference he had been in
favour of offering a definite figure towards reparation,
such figure to be increased on a sliding scale parallel
with German prosperity. But this view had been overruled by the Government. He was still anxious for an
early settlement of the amount of reparation to be exacted
from Germany, although he recognised that there was some
political danger in Germany's making an offer far inferior
to the expectations of French public opinion.

HE complained bitterly of Germany being kept perpetually
under the menace of a Ruhr invasion, saying he was
convinced that German labour would stop working if the
Ruhr were occupied. France was so militaristic that she
neglected the most obvious economic facts and her own
interests. She was infinitely more militaristic than Germany ever had been. The attraction of military glory was
understandable, but France pushed this pursuit to absurd
lengths.

THE excessive cost of the French and English armies of
occupation was another subject on which he dilated.

ON the general position, Wirth appeared fairly optimistic,
provided the German workers could be made to see the

carry out the programme of fulfilment of the Allied ultimatum of May
1921. When in office attached great importance to cultivating friendly
relations with Great Britain. His oratory is characterised by a marked
South German accent, and is often hard to follow, but contains excellent
matter. Wirth is the embodiment of the better elements in modern German
democracy. He is honest and straightforward, with a touch of real Catholic
devoutness, and with a hearty, rough-and-ready manner which endears him
to all except the extreme political parties.

real advantage of Germany fulfilling her treaty obligations, and provided production could be increased to full
blast. I asked how this could be done. He replied :
" It is largely a question of nourishment. We shall
require from one and a half to two million tons of imported cereals, for the German harvest has been so poor.
The bad effect of the harvest has been increased by the
fact that the peasants are beginning to distrust paper
money and refuse to sell their produce, preferring to
store it. The amount required from abroad may thus
have to be increased by another million tons."
WIRTH complained that English public opinion seemed
to think there was nobody in Germany but Prussians and
militarists, whereas the South German Democrats, of whom
he was one, were not without considerable weight and
authority.
To summarise my impression of the conversation :
Wirth seems anxious to come to some practical compromise regarding reparation, and will, I think, take a
reasonable attitude at the proposed Brussels Conference,
either directly or through his representatives. His first
offer will probably be less than he would have proposed in
July, as he considers the financial situation has deteriorated
since then.
I IMPRESSED upon Wirth the importance, in my judgment,
of giving the real naked facts of the German financial
situation, at Brussels, without dressing them in declarations about the iniquity and injustice of the Versailles Treaty.
The amount of payment possible should be based upon
authentic figures and close examination of revenue possibilities—not from verbal assertions of general incapacity
to pay. Such assertions would create the impression of
unwillingness rather than of genuine inability.

BERLIN, *November* 3, 1920.—The Italian Embassy is one
of the few meeting-grounds between the Diplomatic Corps

and leading Germans. The Italian Ambassador (de
Martino [1]) is in close touch with all the more important people both in and out of the Government. He has the reputation of being pro-German, but I should think his sympathies were fairly impartial and guided more by ambition than by prejudice. The de Martinos have made their house a most agreeable centre.

BERLIN, *November* 3, 1920.—An Allied diplomat called on me this morning and discussed the question of Paragraph 18, Annexe 2, Part 8 of the Treaty of Versailles.
HE said he regretted that the English Government had taken any action which might prejudice the rights of the Entente in respect of reparation and the sanctions on which reparation depended. I replied that, in my personal judgment, the whole incident had attained an absurdly exaggerated importance in the press, a fact largely due to the deplorable habit of not reading texts with sufficient care. Anyone who studied Paragraph 18 could see that it did hardly any of the things it was supposed to do. The original German apprehension regarding seizure of bank balances was not justified and could not be read into the text. Paragraph 18 did not authorise the seizure of bank balances any more than it justified barratry, indecent assault, or murder. What the English Government had done was to remove a quite imaginary apprehension by the abandonment of a purely

---

[1] DE MARTINO, Cavaliere Nobile.—First obtained his diplomatic eminence as Secretary-General to the Italian Foreign Office. Reared in the pre-war Giolittian tradition, but with a natural bias towards Nationalism. Took a leading part in the Versailles Peace Conference of 1919 and the London Conference of 1920 under Signor Nitti. Appointed Italian Chargé d'Affaires, and subsequently Ambassador in Berlin. Transferred to London in 1921, where he negotiated the Albanian Agreement of November 1921, but failed to lay the basis of an Anglo-Italian Entente. On Signor Mussolini's advent to power, Martino was replaced as Ambassador in London by the Marchese della Torretta. He was first sent to Tokio and finally to Washington, where he scored a big success in connection with the Italian-American Debt-funding Agreement.

imaginary right. It would be impossible to contend that Paragraph 18 gave any specific right to seize bank balances or private property. As our renunciation appeared to be confined to this right, which is, as I have shown, non-existent, we could not have prejudiced the Allied case in regard to reparation. The French press had assumed that we had abandoned an important and effective means of pressure on Germany in case of voluntary default. In truth we have abandoned no real right which we possessed nor anything in our possession which was likely to prove in any degree efficient against the German Government.

BERLIN, *November* 3, 1920.—The natural affinities of the German people seem to run north and south along meridians of longitude and not along parallels of latitude. The streets of Berlin are full of enormous posters vaunting the merits of Italy in winter and of Scandinavia in summer. Nothing about France ; nothing about Poland. They regard Western Europe on the one hand and Russia on the other as being nearly as different in nature from themselves as an Englishman is from a savage. Quite apart from the political convenience of the moment, I imagine that, temperamentally, Sweden and Italy will continue to gravitate towards Berlin.

POSSIBLY character is governed more by longitude than by latitude. So one should talk of the ability of the tenth meridian east of Greenwich and the well-known inefficiency and listlessness of the twentieth.

THIS may be more true than the supposed fire of the southern beauty and the frigidity of her northern sister.

BERLIN, *November* 7, 1920.—Dr. Simons's critics say he is not strong enough to put the Foreign Office in order, and that the number of officials and employees is now about 8,000 compared with 1,600 in the great Bismarck days. They say Simons cannot maintain discipline and the office is run largely by subordinates.

THE Right and the aristocratic party are rather frightened
at the electric strike and still more at the threatened disbandment of the Orgesch organisations.   They say that
safety in the provinces depends on these organisations, and
that if they disappear, the large houses and estates will
be pillaged.   A current story for which there is fair authority is that the Communist Party in Germany have organised
about eight army corps and can dispose of a force of about
150,000 men and 260 guns.   It is practically impossible
to verify this.   Speaking generally, I think the Right
unduly alarmed ; but on the other hand, I consider the French
demand for the total disarmament of all Einwohnerwehr
and similar organisations almost insane.   It is like cutting
the branch of the tree on which you are sitting.

THE French do not appear to understand that the military
danger-point is past and that the real danger in Germany
is communist disorder.   The acuteness of this danger
depends largely upon the military prestige of the Soviet.
It vanished temporarily with the Soviet disaster at Warsaw,
but re-emerged with the Soviet success over Wrangel.[1]

BERLIN, *November* 7, 1920.—A typical member of the old
Bavarian régime came to see me to-day.   Very royalist

---

[1] WRANGEL, General.—Baron Peter Nicholaievich Wrangel came of a line
of Baltic Barons of Swedish descent, and was born in St. Petersburg in 1879.
Having received his scientific education at the Mining Institute in St.
Petersburg, he served for a year in the Horse Guards, and then settled
in Siberia as a mining engineer.   He served with distinction in the Russo-
Japanese War, and later in the Great War was given the command of a
Cossack division.   After the outbreak of revolution in Russia, Wrangel
served successively under Generals Kaledin and Denikin against the
Bolsheviks, and distinguished himself particularly by the defence of Tsaritsyn.
After the defeat of Denikin, Wrangel was appointed in April 1920 Commander of the Russian volunteer army, which he successfully reorganised.
FOR a time, Wrangel repulsed all attacks, but ultimately had to yield to the
pressure of the well-equipped Bolshevik armies.   Under the supervision
of General Wrangel, Sevastopol was evacuated in November 1920 ; the
refugees, of whom 70,000 were soldiers, were given shelter in Yugo-Slavia
and Egypt.

or loyalist, he constantly excused himself for serving the present Government.

THE most interesting thing he said was that many royalists now regarded the Hohenzollerns as impossible. If there was to be a restoration, it would have to be some other family ; possibly Prince Rupprecht of Bavaria, who might come to the throne first in Bavaria and later in Germany. Prince Rupprecht, though a very able man, was the reverse of a pretender or intriguer.

MY visitor's language regarding the Kaiser was contemptuous : he wore trousers, but he was not a man ! Very timid, very false—just a play-actor. During the war the Kaiser's immediate entourage had a list of forbidden subjects on which it was not safe to speak. Hindenburg and Bülow were the first two subjects on this list. Bülow had fallen from power because he had first of all lectured the Kaiser severely, and had then organised a Royal Family demonstration in the Kaiser's favour. At this demonstration all the Princes in Germany had expressed devotion. This so emboldened the Kaiser that he turned Bülow out and would never hear him spoken of.

BERLIN, *November* 7, 1920.—One of the best-informed people here is the Papal Nuncio. Young and very intelligent. He recalls to memory the epitaph :

> " Bland, passionate, and deeply religious
> He was second cousin to the Earl of Cork
> And of such is the Kingdom of Heaven."

BY name Pacelli—a name like George Sand's friend, but in appearance very different—more like the Pope of the Napoleon epoch who was painted by Lawrence. He says that the religious revival in Bavaria and in other Central European countries is remarkable.

BERLIN, *November* 8, 1920.—I have been long enough in Berlin and seen enough of the new school of officials—

as well as of the old—to form a definite opinion regarding
them. My first conclusion is that there is a real and
fundamental difference between the two schools—not
superficial or due to change of circumstances, but innate.
My second conclusion is that I much prefer the new
to the old. Although perhaps somewhat chastened by
adversity, the members of the old school are not much
altered—they remain overbearing, bullying, and tyrannical,
and give the impression of unabashed unreliability. The
new school representatives, Simons, Wirth, Sthamer,
impress one as sincere, straightforward men who accept
the new situation and endeavour to do the best they can
with it. They are in no sense servile, but sensible and
business-like. They have perhaps an excessive tendency
to take minor legal points, but that does not do much
harm. All appear to be equally adverse to the return of
the old régime and to Communism.

BERLIN, *November* 8, 1920.—The best opinion here seems
to be that the chances of disorder during the coming
winter are decidedly less than twelve months ago. The
country has settled down to work to a considerable extent ;
the Government, though not strong, is stronger than it
was. Party animosities no longer absorb the entire activity
of party organisations as they did at the beginning of the
year. There is thus somewhat more room left for the
restoration of German national feeling.

THE real danger lies in the financial problem. The lot
of the lower middle classes and of those with fixed incomes
is extremely hard. In some cases their incomes have not
increased at all, while the cost of living has gone up from
eight to ten times.

REGARDING the wages of the working classes, though these
have not increased in full proportion to the rise in the cost
of living, they have been raised incomparably more than
salaries. Working-class conditions are certainly not good,

but general discontent appears less prevalent than earlier in the year.

WITHOUT doubt, the failure of the Soviet armies in the Battle of Warsaw a few months ago greatly discouraged the extreme parties here, while the unfavourable reports brought back from Russia by German workmen who had lived there have prevented the extreme sections of labour from gaining the recruits they expected. Personally I regard the chances of grave labour disturbances in Germany as largely dependent upon the gain or loss of prestige by the Soviet Government. I believe, indeed, that tranquillity is even more dependent on this issue than upon the causes more usually alleged—a hard winter or food prices.

BERLIN, *November* 9, 1920.—Luncheon yesterday with Dr. Wirth, Minister of Finance, to meet his principal officials. Luncheon took place at the Hotel Bristol. Broadly speaking, everything in Berlin in the way of entertainment takes place in one or other of the four big hotels. The party consisted of the principal officials of the Ministry of Finance, and particularly those who were connected with the taxation schemes and with the proposed Conferences at Brussels and Geneva. Discussing Brussels, Dr. Schroeder, who had been at Spa and at the Brussels Financial Conference, and had but recently returned from Paris, rather surprised everybody by saying that he would prefer the meeting to take place in Paris rather than at Brussels. The Germans might be exposed to bad treatment in Brussels, whereas in a larger town like Paris nothing untoward need be feared. Others mentioned Frankfurt as a possible meeting-place, saying that telephonic communication with Berlin would be much easier from Frankfurt, and that the German delegates could thus get quicker information.

BERLIN, *November* 9, 1920.—Deutsch, one of the founders

of the Allgemeine Electricitäts Gesellschaft, came to luncheon to-day. A sturdy little Jew, who started the business
in 1882 with three employees. Now 60,000 men are
employed. Deutsch says that the men produce infinitely
less per day than before the war. With a larger number
of workmen than in 1913 they only turn out 40 per cent.
of their previous output. This he attributes partly to bad
food, partly to the eight-hours day. The A.E.G. have
enormous orders on their books for foreign countries,
including France, Belgium, and England. He claimed
that everything interesting in electrical production was
done by them, and that they were far in advance of foreign
practice. Deutsch is a near relation of Sir George Lewis,
and his wife is a sister of Otto Kahn, of Kuhn, Loeb & Co.
of New York.

His ideas regarding trade with Russia are very much on
the same lines as those of Lloyd George. The first thing
is to repair the Russian locomotives. The only way to restore
German commercial prosperity is for her to develop her
Russian business—this he would like to see done in conjunction with England and France, but it would also be
necessary to bring in America in order to obtain the capital
required.

BERLIN, *November* 14, 1920.—Met Prince and Princess
Bülow at luncheon at the Italian Embassy. (I had looked
forward to the meeting with considerable interest, as
Bülow's speeches when he was Chancellor appeared to me
unusually adroit and brilliant.) He has, however, more
of the official about him than I had expected, and less of
the man of the world. He talks French admirably, but
relapses into German in moments of excitement. As the
amiable Princess is also most voluble and lapses into
Italian when she has anything particular to say, there is a
good deal to remind one of the Tower of Babel.

MUCH talk about Bismarck, who, it was said, was in

private affairs very much a Prussian country gentleman. He had the simplest ideas of finance, his main objective being to invest money in rounding off his estates. He bought land from the peasants at excessive prices. Although advised in all his investments by Bleichroeder, he left quite a small fortune, much less than the public would have expected from one who had been Chancellor for twenty-eight years.

Bülow speaks of the present Government without criticism and with admiration for their genuine honesty.

He speaks of Germany as " this unfortunate country," and in terms which would satisfy those who attach importance to the fact that the Germans should acknowledge themselves the beaten party.

A remarkable man with superior endowments, but without much understanding of England or the English character.

Berlin, *November* 23, 1920.—In the matter of disarmament, it is, in my judgment, essential to proceed vigorously with the destruction of the larger war material, including aeroplanes, submarines, guns, mine-throwers, etc. Without in any way abandoning the demand for the surrender of rifles and small arms, I should advise a somewhat less energetic and categorical attitude than in regard to the larger material. The German disarmament authority says that he can get hold of large quantities of rifles now in the hands of Communists, but I rather doubt whether this is so in fact, and I should fear to disarm the orderly sections of the people, leaving arms in the hands of the extreme Socialists and Spartacists.

Regarding the Einwohnerwehr and Orgesch organisations, it is difficult to decide whether these make for order or for future trouble. They are at bottom monarchical and military, although they deny it. But I consider the danger from the Left far exceeds the danger from the Right, and in the event of a new outbreak of Communism in Germany, it can be regarded as certain that these organisa- tions would powerfully serve the cause of order.

IT is alleged that at one time some French agents rather encouraged the Bavarians to maintain the Einwohnerwehr, but that was at a time when they thought Bavaria would separate from the Reich. Now, the same agents have swung round and are among the loudest in demanding prompt and categorical action.

BERLIN, *November* 23, 1920.—It is clear that all parties in Germany would regard the occupation of the Ruhr as an act of violence dictated by the desire to break up Germany. Serious labour troubles would probably result, and the orderly process of restoration in Germany would be violently disturbed. For these reasons I am strongly against the occupation of the Ruhr, or the creation of any situation which would lead to or justify it.

FURTHER, if the Ruhr were occupied, our most powerful means of bringing compulsion to bear on Germany would cease to exist. The menace of the occupation undoubtedly keeps the German Government up to the mark, if it does not keep the mark up.

BERLIN, *November* 23, 1920.—The Italian Ambassador (de Martino) called this evening to say that his appointment to London was now official. It had been the ambition of his life to go there, and he felt convinced that he would be able to render good service to the friendly relations between the Allies. He implied that the love of his life had been England.

[IN the event, de Martino only remained two years in London, being soon transferred to Tokio. De Martino was not as popular in England as he deserved to be, but London taste in foreign diplomats is by no means sound. They prefer *l'homme du monde* with personal charm and Court affinities to either the philosopher or the statesman.

Cambon was the latter in a high sense, but London never really appreciated him, and he only became mildly popular after twenty years' incomparable service.]

BERLIN, *November* 23, 1920.—It is an unfortunate fact that whenever Dr. Simons speaks in public he gets into trouble. It would seem that he loses his head in the presence of a large audience. This tendency is the last one would expect in a lawyer, and the last to be desired in a Foreign Secretary. I greatly fear that it may make his long tenure of the Ministry difficult. Already he is being severely attacked.

BUT notwithstanding this, my opinion that Simons is preferable to any probable successor remains unchanged.

BERLIN, *November* 25, 1920.—Herr von Kahr, the Bavarian Prime Minister, whom I saw yesterday, says : " The real analogy to the Einwohnerwehr is a fire brigade. If a fire—political or otherwise—broke out, the Einwohnerwehr would put it out." It is a fire brigade " manned by the best elements of the population, even up to the age of seventy. One of the great advantages of the Einwohnerwehr is that it leads to a mixture of classes and tends to break down class barriers.

" THE force is essentially temporary ; it was created to meet a grave danger, and would be reduced as the danger diminished, abolished when the danger disappeared. Bavaria has been through terrible times in the spring of last year when under the dominion of the Bolsheviks. Houses were plundered, women were insulted, and those who resisted were shot. No sensible Bavarian would run the risk of allowing such conditions to recur. It is quite unjust to assert that only men with monarchical proclivities are admitted to the E.W. ; all are admitted without distinction of party, provided they are friends of order. Of course, if a man was known to his neighbours to have taken part in Soviet excesses with a red band round his arm, he would not be admitted to the force.

" So far from being organised on military lines, the force elect their own officers, they have no uniforms or barracks, and do no drill. It is more like a club than a regiment. There is no militarism in the idea. So far as Bavaria is concerned, the country is tired of war, particularly the peasants."

I ASKED von Kahr whether it was not possible, in the present circumstances, when things in Germany were settling down and the elements of order getting stronger, to reduce the numbers or to give up some of the rifles. He replied : " The reduction of the Bavarian Army is now in full progress, and the reorganisation of the police is still in its infancy. We have great difficulty in getting good men. Thus the present moment is one of an extremely difficult character. Moreover, the defeat of Wrangel has enormously increased the chances of a Soviet invasion of Poland, and if Poland is invaded again the chances will certainly spread farther west. The Soviets in Bavaria are in close touch with Moscow, through Berlin and through Vienna. The Soviet has also recently established a large organisation in Vienna."

BERLIN, *November* 30, 1920.—One of the most influential financiers in Germany before the war—the ex-chairman of a great bank—gave me further details regarding events preceding the declaration of war in 1914. He had been in the thick of it. If any financier had known what was coming he would certainly have been the man, and yet his daughter only escaped from Scotland, on the declaration of war, by the last boat. All that had been said about a Council of War in July, at which big financiers were present, was absolute nonsense. It was true that the Austrians had sent a deputation, headed by Prince Thurn und Taxis, and that this deputation, accompanied by the

Austrian Ambassador, Szechenyi, had been received by the Emperor. They had drawn a thrilling picture of Serbian intrigue in the murder of the heir-apparent to the Austrian throne—of the tottering condition of the Austrian Empire—and it had appealed to the Emperor in his rôle as a chivalrous medieval knight. He had, therefore, assumed the attitude of a Nibelungen hero and had sworn that Germany would stand by her friend. The Austrians had known how to appeal to the weak side of the Emperor's vanity. They had been so pleased with their success that they had had a big dinner the same evening at the Kaiserhof, and had talked very freely. An intelligent waiter was in the room. As for the German Foreign Office, they had been a set of idiots. Jagow [1] had thought there was so little danger in the situation that he had gone off to get married. Zimmermann [2] was a kind of swaggering student of the type that always had a pot of beer by him and who dreamed only of breaking people's heads. If the Kaiser was—to use a Chinese

[1] von Jagow, Gottlieb.—Von Jagow, Foreign Secretary at the outbreak of the war, was associated with Bethmann-Hollweg's policy of an Anglo-German agreement. The ultimate aim of this policy was an approach to France, through England. The superimposition of militarism on diplomacy was as unwelcome to von Jagow as to the Chancellor.

Von Jagow was born in Berlin in 1863 ; he was an able if undistinguished diplomatist, gaining his experience at various Legations, but chiefly at Rome, where he became Ambassador in 1913.

His appointment as Foreign Secretary was probably largely due, not to ability, but to the personal intervention of the Emperor. Von Jagow was a member of the exclusive Bonn Borussians, and his urbanity and loyalty to imperialism made him an ideal Secretary for an Imperialist Germany.

Von Jagow had professed publicly, on the eve of war, his belief in the revival of Anglo-German relations, and the actual declaration found him as much opposed as was Bethmann-Hollweg.

Industrious and conscientious, von Jagow lacked the initiative and personality of his predecessor, Kiderlen-Waechter ; politics were to him rather an industrious occupation than achievement of brilliant statesmanship.

[2] Zimmermann.—The " Zimmermann Note " of 1917 revealed the amazing lengths to which German diplomacy under Herr Zimmermann would go. Zimmermann succeeded von Jagow as Foreign Secretary after a long probation as Permanent Under-Secretary. The publication of Germany's inten-

expression—" a big A1 damn fool," Bethmann-Hollweg
was almost worse and was quite inferior to his task.   The
truth was, German leaders had worked Germany into a
corner, and once there they did not know how to get
out.

THE military authorities in all parts of the world were
always in favour of war—" look at Lord Fisher's declarations in England, and Beresford's ! " The German
headquarters had, furthermore, been frightened by accounts
from travellers who had come through Siberia that mobilisation was already going on in the spring of 1914, and that
troops were being hurried to Russia's western frontier.

IF Bethmann-Hollweg [1] had had any brains, even at the
end of July, he would have said to England : " We will
make a free alliance," or he would have said to Russia :
" What you do at Constantinople doesn't concern us."
In either of these cases there would have been no war.

tion to enforce a ruthless submarine warfare, as the " Note " indicated,
brought discredit on German diplomacy.

Zimmermann's early life was spent in Consular service in China, and it was
not till 1902 that he entered the ranks of real diplomacy, when he was
appointed to the Foreign Office in Berlin.

IN spite of his incredibly belligerent " Note," Zimmermann's reputation
before the war was that of a courteous diplomatist. He was, however,
more sympathetic towards militarism than most of the Foreign Office, and
in the crisis of 1917, when at all costs the United States must be kept neutral,
Zimmermann seized the only apparently effective means of ensuring this.

[1] VON BETHMANN-HOLLWEG, Dr. Theobald.—Von Bethmann-Hollweg
sounded the keynote of his policy in 1909, when he succeeded Prince
Bülow as Imperial Chancellor : he warned the Reichstag to avoid party
quarrels, and embarked on his own long career of compromise.

FOR five years he worked in Europe to promote peaceful relations, and more
particularly to prevent any coalition against Germany. His ideals, his
sincerity, and his honesty were greater always than his abilities and his
resolve. In 1914 and 1915 he protested against the violation of Belgium's
neutrality and the submarine warfare, but still retained his office. His
greatest achievement, in the early years of the war, probably lay in his
inducement of all parties to present a united front to the attacks on Germany,
but his own profession of belief in a League of Nations, uttered as early as
1915, made him an unnecessary and unpopular figure in German politics.

His long diplomatic career—he was fifty-three when he became Chancellor
—developed his philosophy and integrity of character.

BERLIN, *December* 1, 1920.—Dined quietly last night with Loebe.[1] An interesting man with a great future. He has only been in Imperial politics a year and a half—since the Revolution—but he is now Speaker of the Reichstag, where, by universal consent, he has discharged his duties with skill and authority. His father was a carpenter, and he himself began life as an itinerant vendor of books, tramping about Italy and Switzerland. Under the late régime he spent eighteen months in prison for a press offence, as editor of a provincial Socialist paper. He says that the happiest time of his life was in prison, as he had been able to complete his education, and he was not bothered by the prison food, which was better than food he was used to at home. The prison director was kind and artistic, and had only taken to prison work because he had failed as an operatic singer.

LOEBE is somewhat pessimistic in his outlook, particularly with regard to the financial position. " Of course, we Germans cannot expect to be liked. We have done enough in the last five years to prevent that. All we can claim is impartiality from an objective standpoint. I am grateful if that is the attitude adopted, and I welcome the signs of it from England. The real danger in Germany comes now from the bad conditions of nourishment. If conditions become worse during the winter and if the Bolsheviks capture Poland, you may have grave difficulties here.

" I KNOW from the case of my own children how badly the people are fed. You cannot get milk, and an egg costs $2\frac{1}{2}$ marks. The financial condition of the middle classes, the small employers, etc., is even worse than that of the working class, to which I belong. Only to-day we had a

---

[1] LOEBE.—Born 1875. Has risen from an itinerant bookseller to the position of President of the Reichstag. Owing to his statesmanlike and impartial attitude, he enjoys the respect of all political parties. His views are those of a progressive Liberal. He has had a sound moderating influence on both domestic and foreign policy, but has, somewhat prematurely, espoused the cause of Austro-German reunion.

memo from the lower officials in South Germany saying
that if their pay was not increased they would wreck the
till. Working-class wages have roughly been increased
eight to ten times compared with pre-war ; smaller salaries
have only been increased two to four times. This makes
an impossible situation when the cost of living has gone up
tenfold."

CHAPTER III

CONFERENCES OF BRUSSELS AND PARIS

A talk with Belgian Ministers—Reparation discussions with Bergmann—
Occupation costs—Jaspar's idea for Anglo-Belgian co-operation—
Visit to Millerand—A visit from General Weygand—Suggestions for
Allied-German reparation compromise—Doumer's Memorandum—
Mythical milliards—Negotiations with Doumer and Loucheur.

BRUSSELS REPARATION CONFERENCE

PARTLY as the outcome of the Brussels World Finance Conference, a joint meeting of Allied and German Reparation Experts was held in the Belgian capital on December 16–22, 1920, in order to consider the Reich's capacity for payment from a really objective standpoint. The German Delegation, headed once more by Dr. Bergmann, readily supplied their Allied colleagues with facts and figures relating to both the financial and the economic position of Germany. It had been agreed that the Experts should resume their joint labours on January 10, 1921 ; but before this second meeting could take place, the Allied Governments decided on holding a further plenary session of the Supreme Council in Paris and instructed their Experts to draft, for the basis of the Brussels meeting, their recommendations for a fresh Reparation Commission. Accordingly, on January 14, the Allied Experts submitted a voluminous and elaborate report, with annexes.

BRUSSELS, *December* 13, 1920.—Arrived here last night from Berlin and dined at the Embassy with George Grahame.
THE views of the Belgian Government about the approaching Conference appear to coincide very closely with our own. Theunis agrees that the great difficulty will be to get French public opinion to understand Germany's limited ability

to make large immediate payments, or even to guarantee
any very large sums for the future, until her economic
recovery has developed further and financial collapse has
been averted.

MY view of the best method of conducting the proceedings of the Conference is as follows :

THE Germans first of all to state their general attitude towards reparation, and what their proposals are.

KEEP the discussion very strictly on business-like lines ; check any oratorical excursions on either side on the damage done to the devastated regions, or Germany's inability to pay, etc.

THE Conference then to explore both the present condition and the possibilities of the German budget.

BRUSSELS, *December* 16, 1920.—In conversation with a leading German financial delegate this evening I said I was anxious to make a great effort to get Germany up to the Boulogne figures (269 milliard gold marks, payable by annuities of 3 milliards during the first years).

THE German delegate said : " In Berlin they have not contemplated any figure of the kind, and I do not think they will accept it. At any rate, they would have to be educated up to it at some length, otherwise I am convinced they will consider the basis as altogether inacceptable."

I REPLIED : " We have brought the French down to much more reasonable views than they originally held ; you must bring Germany up to meet us. The French are now in a very sensible frame of mind, and I am not sure that you would not be missing a great opportunity if you omitted to bring matters to a conclusion here."

HE then said : " Well, on that basis I can do nothing, but I quite admit that I am gratified to find how reasonable the French are. Payment of a considerable money annuity by us depends to a great extent on the reduction

7

of the cost of the Armies of Occupation. What is saved there is freed for reparation."

BRUSSELS, *December* 17, 1920.—The general upshot of Bergmann's speech this morning is that Germany expects to be able to pay, and will pay, a fair amount of money reparation, in addition to reparation in kind, provided that she is helped to restore stability to her exchange and equilibrium in her budget. As, without equilibrium in the budget and stability in the exchange, no German promise to pay could be held to or would be worth anything, these two conditions add little or nothing to the inherent underlying assumptions.

His declarations regarding the restoration of the devastated provinces were entirely satisfactory, and went far beyond French and Belgian expectations.

BRUSSELS, *December* 18, 1920.—It is apparent that Bergmann is a good deal cramped by some of the experts who are with him. They think that he is too conciliatory in his attitude. He seems satisfied with the practical direction in which the discussion has developed, but says it would be easier to settle things in Paris about January 2, as he could by then have brought round some of the hostile members of the Government.

HAVING been entrusted by the Conference with the task of negotiating regarding cash reparations, I thought the best plan of opening the discussion was to tell Bergmann approximately the result of the Boulogne discussion. I said : " We had great difficulty in bringing the French down to this level, but they have now fortunately accepted it. Therefore, if Germany can make an offer on these lines, acceptance could be assured. There would be obvious advantage in not having to begin the whole discussion over again with Paris."

BERGMANN replied : " But these figures are quite impossible. At the present moment I do not see that Germany can possibly pay anything in cash without making her exchange even worse, and you know how bad it already is. Equilibrium in the German budget and stability in the German exchange are conditions precedent."

IN answer I said : " These two conditions do not appear extravagant, as any promise to pay by a Germany whose budget was not balanced and whose exchange was not stable would have a quite insignificant value. Subject to these conditions, why can you not agree to the Boulogne figures ? It is clearly understood that the reparation in kind you are now paying—about 1½ milliards of gold marks a year—would be counted in deduction ; indeed, I feel convinced that the Entente would count them in deduction on a fair if not a liberal estimate.

" As to the costs of the Armies of Occupation, these would be in addition, but I do not think that the Entente would refuse to discuss the possibility of reducing the costs to a fair level. The progress of disarmament in Germany gives Germany a good argument on this subject. The further you push disarmament, the better your case on this subject will be."

WE argued to and fro on these lines for some time, with no very definite result.

BERGMANN said, on leaving : " I wish I could get the Entente to see that meeting, to some extent, the German demands with respect to ships, sequestered property, etc., would greatly encourage us to increase our endeavours regarding the block figure of reparations. We have applied to the Reparation Commission, to the Council of Ambassadors, to the Supreme Council, time after time on all these points, and we always get turned down. Do make some small concessions in order to facilitate my task and encourage the German Government to come out more boldly about reparations."

I REPLIED to Bergmann : " When a request is refused, two

people are responsible—the man who refuses and the man who has asked in the wrong way ; or perhaps I might say the man who asked but who led the other to suppose that a request granted would not be taken in the right spirit. The Entente may be wrong in some cases, but the responsibility is at least equally great with Germany. At the same time, I am anxious to do anything in my power to arrive at a sensible and practical settlement."

My own impression is that the Germans have a pretty good case for pleading hard treatment on a considerable number of points. A conciliatory attitude on these points, which are of minor importance, might indeed bring about an arrangement of the larger issues.

BRUSSELS, *December* 20, 1920.—The difficulty of obtaining any exact idea of the cost of the Armies of Occupation is so great that the Germans do not know what they are paying, and we appear to be quite unable to tell them what they ought to pay.

SUETONIUS says of Tiberius Cæsar that " while other people found it difficult to carry out what they promised, he found it difficult to promise what he was already performing." The Germans would be surprised at the comparison. But they are now paying reparation under forty-five different heads—partly in kind, partly in paper, partly in cash—and so little do they know what is going on (and we are not much wiser than they) that they would be quite unwilling to undertake to pay what, in fact, they are already paying.

No technical authority ever gives you a figure about the costs of the Armies of Occupation without saying two minutes afterwards : " Remember, the figure I gave you does not include . . ."

AND the excluded is greater than the contained.

BRUSSELS, *December* 22, 1920.—Luncheon at the Embassy,

where I met M. Jaspar, Minister for Foreign Affairs, and M. Francqui, a Belgian financial leader.

JASPAR raised the question of a commercial alliance between Belgium and England, saying he was very strongly in favour of this.   He said : " With England, a commercial alliance should be easy.   I believe Belgium would offer great advantages to England—we could give them great facilities at Antwerp, and make it something like a bridge-head in Europe."

HE thinks a commercial treaty would be much easier and much more practical than anything in the nature of a military alliance.   He even spoke of the possibility for Belgium of adopting sterling currency.

I ASKED if he had any draft conditions which would enable one to form a clearer idea of the proposal.   He said : " No, but it would be quite easy to prepare them."

IT is worth remembering that, when Sir Herbert Samuel was Commissioner in Belgium, there was talk of a similar project.   Considering the novelty of the proposal when put forward by Samuel, it appeared to me that the refusal of the Board of Trade was mild and almost friendly.

WHAT precisely Belgium would ask in exchange for her action in relation to Antwerp, I do not know, but it appears to me that the benefits in view are so considerable, that the scheme should not be discarded off-hand.

PARIS CONFERENCE, JANUARY 24–30, 1921

THE Supreme Council, at which Great Britain, France, Italy, Japan, and Belgium were all represented, but not Germany, was presided over by M. Briand, who had succeeded M. Leygues in the French Premiership. M. Doumer, the French Finance Minister, produced an amazing schedule of payments to be made by Germany.   This the Conference rejected.   At the same time it also ignored the moderate recommendations made by the Allied Experts as the outcome of the Brussels Conference, and actually formulated demands exceeding those of the Boulogne Conference. This new proposal, adopted by the Conference on January 28, was communicated to Germany on the following day.

THE Allies also indited a very stiff and detailed Note to Germany concerning her outstanding defaults in respect of the disarmament clauses of the Versailles Treaty. The substance of this Note, which it had been agreed to regard as secret, was revealed by an indiscretion in the French press. Other matters dealt with at this session of the Supreme Council were the monthly deliveries in coal designed to supersede those prescribed under the Spa Coal Protocol ; the trial of war criminals ; the financial and economic reconstruction of Austria ; the status of the newly founded independent Republics of Esthonia and Latvia ; and an invitation to Greece and Turkey to be represented at an early conference, to be held in London, for a readjustment of certain territorial and political clauses of the Treaty of Sèvres.

PARIS, *December* 28, 1920.—Lunched yesterday at the Elysée and had an opportunity of some conversation with President Millerand regarding reparation and disarmament.

MILLERAND began by saying : " You have done excellent work at Brussels ; the Conference appears to be working on sound lines, and I sincerely hope that you will arrive at a practical result soon. If you reach this before the end of January you will render a great service. People think that France is unreasonable. That is not at all the case: we are quite open to a speedy arrangement on sensible lines. If you propose something practical, you will find us ready to agree."

I REPLIED that my idea was to base the arrangement as closely as possible on Boulogne, but that he must not imagine that he would get full Boulogne terms ; some considerable

reduction on these would have to be made—it might be
10 per cent. or 20 per cent. or more. Without assenting
to this, the President appeared to be not surprised and did
not in any way protest.

HE agreed with my suggestion that it was essential to
give the German delegates something to take home—
something they could show their Government and their
public that they had gained in the shape of concessions.
There were certain points on which we were pretty clearly
in the wrong, notably the expenses of the Army of Occupation. Apart from extravagance, it was a scandal that after
ten days at Brussels we had been quite unable to ascertain
the amount due from Germany on account of the Armies
of Occupation, unable also to form a correct estimate of
the future cost of the Armies. I added that it was obviously
wrong in principle for the party who determined the amount
of expenditure not to be interested in economy, the bill being
payable by the other side. Under such conditions not
even an angel would be economical.

TURNING from the subject of reparation, I stated my
opinion that the military danger from Germany no longer
existed. It might exist four or five or ten years later ;
it did not exist to-day nor in the immediate future. In the
process of disarmament, a vast number of guns, aeroplanes, and submarines had been destroyed.

MY general impression from Millerand's attitude and
from his conversation is that he is pleased with the first
stage of the Brussels negotiations and is anxious for an
agreement to be arrived at. It would not be fair to
assume that he will assent to any specific terms, but his
general attitude was distinctly friendly to a reasonable
compromise.

PARIS, *December* 28, 1920.—Bergmann called yesterday and
met Delacroix and Bradbury.

HIS great idea is to raise a loan for the purpose of stabilising

the German exchange.   He quite loses sight of the main
cause of the low value of the mark—the excessive number,
and the increasing number, of notes in circulation.

DELACROIX also favours the raising of a loan by Germany,
such loan to be guaranteed by sequestrated property and
hypothecation of the customs revenue, and to be tax free
in all countries.

MY own idea is that any loan operation should be left aside
for a second act.   If a loan is mentioned, it should only be
a kind of funding loan relieving Germany of cash payments
during the first years.   One would come back to something like the Boulogne basis, i.e. the annuity for the earlier
years to be fixed at x million gold marks, paid partly
in cash (guaranteed by customs revenues), partly in kind—
coal, etc.   The annuities for the later years to be left for
future decision.   Germany might be granted certain minor
concessions—regarding costs of the Armies of Occupation, etc.

PARIS, *December* 29, 1920.—General Weygand called upon
me this morning.

I HAVE a great admiration for him since he is good
enough to say I afforded valuable co-operation which
assisted in obtaining the Victory of Warsaw.   Without
my rather violent pressure he would never have obtained
adequate power to act from the Polish Staff.

WE discussed the disarmament of the Einwohnerwehr
in Bavaria.   He took the line that the Germans were
endeavouring to elude the treaty and that a firm control from Paris was wanted, but he was doubtful if the
firm control would be forthcoming.

I TOOK the opposite line and said that the whole incident
had been greatly aggravated by injudicious handling, that
there was no military danger from Germany now, and since
there was no military danger there was no need for panic
measures or violent action.   The proper policy was to give

the German Government specific dates for reduction and specified numbers to reduce to. One should not forget that the Soviet might attack Poland again and might capture Warsaw this time. In that case all the elements of order in Germany would be needed to keep the country quiet.

CHAP.
III
——
December
1920

WEYGAND agreed about the Soviet danger, saying that if they attacked again they would not expose themselves as rashly as they did last August.

HE also agreed as to the absence of military danger, for the moment, in Germany, and assented to my further proposition that the real danger would come later, since the Treaty of Versailles was very vague as to guarantees against rearming by Germany after the Disarmament Commission had ceased work.

PARIS, *January* 8, 1921.—The French have rather receded from the reasonable attitude adopted at Brussels. The resumption of the Conference there seems improbable.

AT a meeting this afternoon, Seydoux,[1] the Director of Commercial Affairs at the Quai d'Orsay, said that he had seen several political men, and that they were above all anxious not to have any capital sum fixed for German indebtedness as they feared that the sum would be too far removed from French expectation. He thought, therefore, that Germany should be pressed to engage to pay an annuity of 3 milliard gold marks for five years, the fixation of subsequent annuities and total indebtedness to be left for a later period.

I HEAR confidentially that a meeting took place which was

---

[1] SEYDOUX, Charles Louis Auguste Jacques.—Charles Seydoux was born in 1870, and was educated as a lawyer, being *stagiaire* at the Hague and in London. He was later appointed as Secretary to the Embassy at Athens and Berlin, and then recalled to the Embassy at Paris.

IN 1924 he was appointed Minister Plenipotentiary. Has exercised a decisive influence on French commercial policy. Played an important part in the reparations negotiations.

attended by Loucheur, Viviani,[1] and Dubois, the last-named being dragged out of bed for the purpose.   At this meeting Loucheur is reported to have said that France could only agree to a reduction of the full sum of indebtedness provided she obtained ample guarantees for the payment of future annuities ; provided, secondly, that France got a priority for the restoration of the devastated regions ; and, thirdly, that some portion of the annuity should form the basis of a loan to France from the United States.

THE impression made was that Loucheur is anxious to have the credit of settling the reparations question.

THE above story may or may not be true.   What is certain is that something has occurred which has frightened the French Government.   There appeared to be no wisdom in pressing the French delegates to come to Brussels if when they got there they would prove recalcitrant.

IT was therefore decided to replace the official meeting at Brussels by unofficial discussions here.   Bergmann is to come back from Berlin as soon as possible, having obtained the maximum powers from the German Government. It is hoped that he may be in a position to make a declaration respecting the 3 milliard gold marks per annum. This annuity will have to include the cost of the Armies

---

[1] VIVIANI, René Raphael.—Viviani, Premier of France at the outbreak of war, was on his way back from Russia when he heard of Austria's declaration. At once he controlled the situation, and, to prove France's pacifist intentions, the troops were withdrawn 10 kilometres behind the line.   A few days later he uttered the speech which for brilliance of eloquence and appeal is probably unequalled in France.

HE was born in 1863, and established an early reputation as a lawyer and an orator.   The speech in 1906 in which he professed himself an atheist brought him his greatest fame ; his wealth of metaphor and imagery secured him always an immediate attention in the Chamber.

CLEMENCEAU and Briand in 1906 and 1909 appointed Viviani as Minister of Labour ; but the Government's attitude towards the railway strike of 1910 caused Viviani to tender his resignation, and the Briand Cabinet was broken up, though re-formed.

VIVIANI became Premier and Foreign Secretary in June 1914.   His eloquence remains unchallenged, but his greatest claim to fame rests on the control he exhibited during the early days of the war.

of Occupation, and will consist, in a considerable part, of payments in kind, calculated at probably a high figure.

It is hoped that by these means we shall be able to present the Supreme Council with a full report on most of the subjects soon.

The opponents of the present French Ministry are confident that they will turn the Government out in the course of the next few days.

> On January 12, 1921, the Leygues Cabinet resigned ;
> and on January 15 M. Briand formed a new Ministry.
> In the Chamber on January 20 M. Briand declared
> that the basis of his foreign policy would be the
> closest possible co-operation with England.

Paris, *January* 14, 1921.—The causes of the fall of the Leygues Ministry are still much discussed. It appears to have been mainly due to the insufficient authority and ability of Leygues, to the failure of Marsal [1] as Finance Minister, and to general disgust at the bad financial and commercial situation. All the shops in Paris say they are selling nothing. To a minor degree it was due to a dislike of the reasonable policy adopted by Leygues towards Germany at the Brussels Conference and to the idea that he did not stand up enough to England.

The position is somewhat this—the unreasonable elements of public opinion here resent the counsels of moderation which have been received from London. They are alarmed at America withdrawing from the Council of Ambassadors

---

[1] Marsal, François.—Marsal first entered politics in 1920, when he was appointed Minister of Finance in the Millerand Cabinet. Four years later he became himself leader of one of the transitory Governments which were faced with the reconstruction of French finance. Marsal's Government lasted five days.

Marsal is a firm supporter of the League of Nations ; he has prominently upheld Poincaré's policy, especially with regard to the Ruhr occupation. His great interest lies in a study of the political problems of the French colonies.

and reducing her Army on the Rhine, but instead of becoming more reasonable and desiring closer co-operation
with England, they are inclined to shout that they have
been abandoned, and proceed to act so that their remaining
friends will be forced to abandon them.

THE more sensible elements of opinion, voiced by Bourgeois [1] in the Senate, realise that the financial position of
France is extremely critical, and that there is no hope of
any large immediate payments from Germany.

THE real difficulty is Poincaré. If he is in the Government, he will insist upon his old unrelenting views.

IN one way it may be thought that it is better to have the
extremists in the Government than out of it.

PARIS, *January* 17, 1921.—We have had very constant
conferences with the other financial delegates and have
advanced a long way towards preparing our report to the
Supreme Council.

THE main point of discussion has been whether or not it
was necessary to come to some immediate understanding
regarding the total figure of damage and of German

---

[1] BOURGEOIS, Léon.—M. Bourgeois, an ardent and idealistic pacifist, was the
chief spokesman for France on the League of Nations Commission ; the great
interest he had shown since 1907 in international arbitration and the preservation of peace made him an indispensable member of the Council and
Assembly. His devotion to the interests and ideals of the League secured
for him an international reputation, and in 1920 he was awarded the Nobel
Peace Prize.

PUBLIC interest was first attracted to Bourgeois in 1892, when he was
Minister of Justice in the Ribot Cabinet. At that time the Panama
prosecution was causing a great stir, and Bourgeois pressed the attack with
such zeal that he was accused of having exerted wrongful pressure in order
to obtain evidence.

IN 1895 he formed his own Cabinet ; its views were decidedly Radical, and
the Senate refused to vote supplies. Bourgeois hoped that public opinion
would weigh with him, but the people remained indifferent, the Cabinet
was dismissed, and Bourgeois's reputation as a statesman was somewhat
damaged. His great claim to distinction was in his genuine efforts to promote
international friendship, and it was largely due to his zeal that the conception of a League of Nations became an actual achievement.

indebtedness. It is clear that agreement between the
German and French Governments on this point will be
difficult, and it is more than likely that if the Governments
come to terms, public opinion in the two countries will
disagree and the respective Governments will fall.

IT is also becoming increasingly apparent that the Repar-
tion Commission has let things drag on so long that it is
now practically impossible to present the German Government with the figure of damage and debt by May 1. The
expedient suggested that the Supreme Council should
authorise the Reparation Commission to put forward a
compromised figure will not hold water for a moment.
It is totally opposed to the treaty, which provides for a
judicial statement of claim under ten specific heads, after
giving the Germans an opportunity to be heard on them.
This point really governs the whole discussion, and nobody
appears sufficiently to have realised how difficult—if not
impossible—it is for the Allies now to bring themselves
into conformity with the text of the treaty.

PARIS, *January* 17, 1921.—Bergmann returned yesterday
from Berlin, but brought back no definite offer. His
main points appear to be the difficulty of cash reparation
and unwillingness to agree to five annuities of 3 milliard
gold marks each, as a temporary solution, unless the total
indebtedness of Germany is first fixed.

THE more the German budget is examined, the more inadequate does the system of indirect taxation appear to be.
Alcohol, in particular, is foolishly under-taxed compared
with England.

PARIS, *January* 18, 1921.—Saw Bergmann this morning.
He has quite changed his tone since Sunday. Instead of
saying that the German Government would not agree to a
temporary arrangement for five annuities unless the total
indebtedness were first fixed, he now says that he is in

favour, and that Simons is also in favour, of not waiting for the fixation of the capital debt. If both parties would agree to fix the total soon, but without precise date, the date of May 1 might disappear.

MEMORANDUM (OF CONVERSATION WITH BERGMANN)

PARIS, *January* 18, 1921.—The following conditions might form the basis of discussion with the German Delegation at Brussels :

1. A TEMPORARY arrangement to be made regarding annuities for the first five years.

2. THE fixation of capital debt to be arrived at as soon as possible, but the temporary arrangement not to be postponed for it.

3. THE basis of the temporary arrangement to be 3 milliard gold marks per year, but during the first two years the annuity not to be more than 2 milliards. The annuity for the three following years to be dependent on an index scheme, but to be 3 milliards, provided that the index scheme gives a result compared with the present conditions.

4. BEFORE the end of the five years the capital debt to be fixed and new annuities settled for subsequent years.

5. IN the first two years $1\frac{1}{2}$ milliards to be paid in kind and $\frac{1}{2}$ milliard in cash.

6. PRICES and quantities to be fixed according to present conditions.

7. THE cost of the Armies of Occupation to be cut down to 240,000,000 gold marks. The question whether this sum should be included or not included in the annuity to be left over for subsequent discussion.

PARIS, *January* 20, 1921.—My anxiety about the French Government and the reparations scheme is lest Loucheur, who is very nimble and inventive, should want to start

some new plan of his own. I had intended to go to
London yesterday to report, but, on second thoughts, de-
cided it was wiser to stay here and keep in touch with the
French Government. Loucheur is too prolific in ideas.
So far, I hear he is pretty satisfied with the Brussels plan.
His view is that the reparations question will almost
certainly cause the death of three French Ministries before
it is settled, and will, if the aggregate of reparation is
insisted upon inopportunely, kill more Ministries than
Landru has killed women.

BRIAND apparently troubles little about the financial
question and leaves matters pretty much to Seydoux,
subject to Loucheur's irruptions. So far, the Government have managed the French press with considerable
success, but Pertinax is again giving trouble, being well
informed, acute, and unreasonable.

PARIS, *January* 24, 1921.—A long conversation with
Loucheur and Doumer. The latter stated emphatically
that France was on the verge of bankruptcy, and that unless
the total of damages was fixed at something like 200 or
210 milliards of gold marks (£10,000,000,000) and an
annuity of 12 milliards of gold marks (£600,000,000)
was imposed on Germany, France would be unable to meet
her obligations.

LOUCHEUR confirmed the dangerous condition of French
finance, but did not appear to me to be very much in favour
of Doumer's plan. He, however, did not formulate a
plan of his own.

I AT once pointed out to Doumer that the figures he now
gave were practically double those agreed upon at Boulogne.
He said that Boulogne was not an agreement, only a project,
and that all reserves had been made as to the figures. I
rejoined that, however that might be, London regarded the
discussion at Boulogne as serious, and I did not think they
would accept or debate on any figure like 200 or 210

milliards. Apart from this argument, it was, in my judgment, out of the question to expect any payment like 12 milliards of gold marks a year from Germany, which, at the present exchange, made a total of 150 milliards of paper marks, or more than three times her total revenue to-day. We were just as anxious as they could be to obtain payments from Germany on as large a scale as was compatible with security and reason. But the plan he had sketched appeared to me to lead to nothing but the bankruptcy of Germany and no reparation at all.

DOUMER had indicated that if the Germans did not pay, the Allies would impose a debt administration similar to that in Turkey. I said the two cases appeared to me very different, and every effort must be made to avoid being driven into a crisis of force.

IN my judgment, the Doumer solution is altogether inacceptable, and it is necessary to say so quite plainly.

EXPERTS' CONFERENCE, BRUSSELS

THE main recommendations of the Allies are set out below.

THESE recommendations were made after impartial examination of the actual position. Full consideration was accorded to the representations of the German delegates, who were given an opportunity to state their case. It may fairly be claimed that the Experts' suggestions are those best calculated to lead to an improvement of German finance on technical and scientific lines. The Report carefully avoids the tone of the blind and reckless creditor who cares only for the rapid encashment of his debt, without reference to the position or the solvency of the debtor.

Recommendations

(1) GERMANY to pay 3 milliard gold marks per annum for the next five years, future payments to be fixed at a later date.

(2) THE capital sum of reparation to be fixed as early as possible, i.e. as soon as Germany's capacity can be stated with certainty.

(3) Limitation of costs of Armies of Occupation to 240 million gold marks per annum.

(4) No cancellation of plebiscite in Upper Silesia, but inter-Allied control of coal distribution after plebiscite.

(5) No interference in German public finance or with customs, provided obligations are carried out.

(6) Economic clauses of treaty not to be used to hinder German trade.

PARIS, *January* 24, 1921.—An interesting dinner to-night, after the arrival of the British Delegation.

LLOYD GEORGE was in wonderful spirits—had much chaff with Sir Henry Wilson about being Prime Minister of England (temporary), like a General with special rank. There was a good deal of talk about the benefit of a politician's training as compared with that of a soldier. A politician was always fighting and had daily practice in warfare. The soldier only fought on rare occasions. This difference made a politician much more wary and a better fighting instrument.

WE had a tremendous discussion about German capacity to pay and about the quantitative theory of currency. Lloyd George does not believe in the quantitative theory and holds the popular heresies respecting balance of trade determining exchange values, etc. But he was extremely quick in taking in other arguments, and is evidently considering whether the debasement of a currency which freed a country from much of the burden of its debt is not an advantage. All these other countries will pay off their debt on a debased currency at a half, or a quarter, or a tenth of its original value. We shall feel the burden of ours at a higher level. Shall we therefore not be at a disadvantage ?

8

WINSTON says that £150,000,000 a year is much more than Germany can pay. L. G. thinks it high, but does not object to the idea. The strong point he makes is that Germany must be told her maximum debt, otherwise she cannot recover.

MY view is that it is impossible to obtain agreement between the French and the Germans respecting total indebtedness. We must, therefore, be content with something like a temporary solution. Once this is in working force, the whole atmosphere will calm down. It will be easier to fix the total debt a year or two hence than now.

PARIS, *January 26, 1921.*—This morning I continued the conversation with Loucheur and Doumer.

I TOLD them I had seen the Prime Minister, who held fast to the Boulogne Agreement and would not discuss on any other basis. He was also unwilling to give the priority to France for the devastated regions, which was part of Loucheur's scheme. Loucheur said : " Well, there is nothing to do but to drop my scheme."

HAVING realised that it was useless to talk except on the Boulogne basis, he rather appealed for support on sentimental lines, and promised to send me figures regarding the French budget, etc.

THE conversation at breakfast with the P.M. and the Belgian delegates, Jaspar and Theunis, was mainly on the lines of the unreasonableness of the Doumer attitude, and the necessity of getting the total German debt fixed not above the Boulogne basis, and the great desirability of a permanent instead of a temporary arrangement. They all take it as axiomatic that unless the total of the German debt is fixed, German recovery is rendered impossible. This I believe to be a profound misconception.

THE Paris terms might be divided into the following heads :

(1) ANNUITIES payable during the first five years.

(2) FIXED annuities for the subsequent years—sixth to forty-second.

(3) THE 12 per cent. export tax.

OF these heads, it may be said that German assent could be won to the first and third. This only left a divergence of view under head (2), and the extent of this divergence was probably this—whether the 3 milliards per year should be increased to 4, 5, or 6 milliards or not. It was not conceivable that the Germans who accepted 3 milliards for the first five years would not agree to 3 milliards as a minimum for the subsequent years. Whether they would agree to accept an increase of 3 milliards to 4, 5, or 6 was, therefore, the limit of the divergence—not a very unbridgeable one.

CHAPTER IV

EFFECT OF THE SPA DECISIONS

German resentment at Paris decisions—An argument with Dr. Simons—
The American view—German counter-proposals for London—Lloyd
George on French policy—Attempt by Lord D'Abernon and M.
Loucheur to devise compromise with German experts.

ERLIN, *February* 3, 1921.—On return here last night
I found public opinion very excited about the Paris
decisions.   These are condemned as totally inacceptable : everything is objected to—the forty-two years, the
12 per cent., the total capital sum, which is said to exceed
the total present wealth of Germany.   Public feeling is
so strong that Germans have broken off dinner engagements and other social fixtures with members of the
Entente.   Kühlmann,[1] in particular, was to have dined with
General Malcolm last night, but wrote to say that under
present circumstances he could not come.

THE views of the French Embassy appear moderate and
sound.   They say the first cause of irritation was the
fact that the five annuities scheme, which the French
experts had practically persuaded the German Government

---

[1] VON KÜHLMANN, Richard.—For six years, from 1908 to 1914, von Kühlmann
was Councillor to the Embassy in London ; during that time, three distinct
personalities operated as Ambassadors—Wolff-Metternich, Baron Marschall
von Bieberstein, and Prince Lichnowsky.   Von Kühlmann was a capable
and clear-sighted diplomatist who realised that militarism was a very
temporary strength and aid in the establishment of national position.   In
the closing years of the war he attempted a compromise with France, but
withdrew when she refused to relinquish her claims to Alsace-Lorraine ; he
realised that, at that moment, it was psychologically impossible for Germany
to yield the two provinces.

IT was in June 1918 that von Kühlmann as Foreign Secretary brought
about his own downfall.   He had reiterated his disbelief in militarism, and
it was on the eve of the successful German offensive that he protested—
irritatingly enough to the German leaders—against achievement by force.
His speech caused the demand for his resignation.

HIS success as a diplomatist was due to his capacity for assimilation of knowledge and his energy in directing policy.

to accept, was not seriously taken up by the Supreme Council. The German Government, who thought they were negotiating on one basis, suddenly found themselves confronted with a decision on a totally different foundation.

THIS is to some extent the fault of the German Government itself in not accepting the five annuities basis more rapidly. The sudden proposal regarding the 12 per cent. export tax had not been properly understood. Nobody here had grasped that this might be considered in some way as a substitute for anti-dumping legislation.

BERLIN, *February* 3, 1921.—Dresel, the American Commissioner here, has just been to see me. He says that the position reminds him strongly of that in May 1919, when the peace terms were first published in Germany. I asked him to what extent the agitation was caused by the precise terms, and to what extent it would have occurred no matter what terms had been decided on. He replied : " I think I saw signs more than a week ago that an agitation against any Paris decision was being organised. At the same time I [Dresel] consider the position as very serious, in that it may lead to a strong concentration on the Right and the formation of a Government of a reactionary character."

I POINTED out to Dresel—rather with a view to its being passed on—that there was no such very great difference between the Paris terms as formulated and terms which the Germans had either accepted in detail or would almost surely have been willing to accept.

BERLIN, *February* 4, 1921.—A long conversation with the Minister for Foreign Affairs this morning.

DR. SIMONS opened by saying: " I understand you regard the Paris decisions as favourable to Germany. How do you arrive at this conclusion ? "

I REPLIED : " Favourable is perhaps too strong an expression, but they are certainly not unfavourable. My reasons are : With regard to the first five years, the payments demanded do not amount to those under the proposals of M. Seydoux. As I understand the German Government were prepared to agree to the latter, Germany has no reason for complaint. Regarding the fixation of the total debt, Germany has continually urged the necessity of being informed of her total indebtedness. It was Germany's friends who pressed for giving Germany this satisfaction. For myself, fixation of the total has always appeared dangerous, but Germany demanded its immediate settlement. I consider the 12 per cent. tax as favourable to Germany. It might replace anti-dumping taxation abroad, it gives the Entente an interest in German export trade, and will to a great extent allay their feelings regarding Germany's economic recovery."

DR. SIMONS then said : " Concerning the export tax, I have an open mind. In fact, in 1919 I considered a scheme somewhat similar. Regarding the first five years : after a struggle I did get the Government to agree to the plan—subject to certain conditions, Upper Silesia, etc. It was very disappointing and surprising to discover that the Paris Conference proceeded, not on that basis, but on absolutely different lines put forward by Loucheur and Doumer. Why was the original basis abandoned ? The French Ambassador had arrived at an agreement with me officially on the subject, and was supported by the British Chargé d'Affaires."

VERY few arguments were produced by Dr. Simons against my view that the Paris basis could not be considered as unfavourable to Germany, except that the total sum was excessive. He fully recognised that the financial necessities of France must be taken into consideration. Speaking politically, some means must be discovered of easing the position of France. He inclined to the view that some method should be found under which England, France, and Germany could work together economically and industrially : under this joint scheme England and France would work for themselves, the Germans would work partly for themselves and partly for reparation.

BERLIN, *February 5*, 1921.—It looks this morning as if the German Government, or some members of it, were beginning to realise that they have gone too fast and too far in their hostility to the Paris decisions.

I HEAR that Dr. Simons was principally concerned that the discussions in London should start from the five annuities basis and work towards the Paris basis, rather than the other way. This is a characteristically German attitude of mind ; so far as the practical effect is concerned, it matters more where one finishes than where one starts.

I HAVE seen Dresel, the American Commissioner. He tells me that German public opinion has not yet begun to cool down about the Paris decisions, and that even quite sensible men such as Professor Bonn, the economist, have almost lost their heads. They have also succeeded in frightening Dresel himself about the effect of the 12 per cent. export tax on American commerce. He continues to say : " Remember that our people in Washington will criticise very closely any scheme which burdens American-German trade."

BERLIN, *February 6*, 1921.—An amusing local episode is that the new Italian Ambassador (Frassati), who made a violently pro-German speech before leaving Rome, who was pro-German throughout the war, and who expected to be received here with acclamation, has been left kicking his heels for ten days before being officially received.

I PRESUME this is to show German displeasure at Italian acquiescence in the Paris decisions.

BERLIN, *February* 10, 1921.—The ways of German public opinion are very peculiar. Three days ago not only was the whole press unanimous in their determination not to discuss on the basis of the Paris proposals, but private individuals of all classes regarded these proposals as absolutely inacceptable.

Two days ago the German Foreign Office published their reply, which is described as " a conditional acceptance." The acceptance is much more visible than the limiting conditions, and to-day the papers and all the public appear to have fallen in with this new view almost without protest.

LLOYD GEORGE's Birmingham speeches, with their friendly personal allusions to Simons, had a great effect. The speeches of Loucheur and Doumer in the French Chamber, stating that France would have got much better terms at Paris but for English opposition, have convinced the more sensible people here that the German side of the case was adequately taken into account, as in truth it was.

IT will, however, take some weeks before social relations between Germans and English get back to the point where they were a month ago. The first shock was too severe.

I EXPECT the Germans will bring forward in London some abstruse calculations to prove that in order to carry out the Paris decisions German workmen will have to work some twelve to fifteen hours a day. On this " work-hours basis " one can really prove almost anything, and Rathenau, whose idea it is, and who is a clever writer and speaker, will probably get his colleagues to adopt it.

MY own view is that the best line for the Germans to take would be (*a*) to accept the first five years and the 12 per cent., concentrating their efforts to obtain modification upon the fixed payments from the sixth to the forty-second year. Or, again, they might (*b*) endeavour to get the cost of the Armies of Occupation included in the annuity ; or (*c*) endeavour to get the 12 per cent. included in the annuity ;

but I think this last-named plan—which is Laurent's—
inferior to (*a*), not only from their point of view but intrinsically.

BERLIN, *February* 17, 1921.—A French friend who has returned here from Paris is deeply impressed with the determination in France not to accept any concession whatever on the Paris decisions.   He appears to have made it his business to see men of all sections of opinion, and found that disappointment with the amounts fixed at Paris, irritation at the attitude of Germany, and the growth of impatience at repeated delays, would render Briand's task in London most difficult.   Any concession whatever on the total sum fixed would mean his certain downfall.

THE French Ambassador will see Simons directly the latter returns here—to-morrow or the day after—and will convey to him the above impression in the clearest terms. The French Government considers it a duty not to allow any ambiguity to exist.

MY friend told me that in Paris they are firmly determined to execute the prescribed sanctions by themselves if the Allies will not join with them.   When asked what sanctions, they reply : " Those foreseen in the Treaty of Versailles, and discussed at Spa."

THIS tone is the more noteworthy since the French Embassy was extremely calm and conciliatory ten days ago and appeared satisfied with the Paris basis.

BERLIN, *February* 24, 1921.—Dr. Simons called on me this evening and said that they had endeavoured to the utmost to base their proposals upon the Paris decisions and to push their counter-proposals to the extreme limit of what Germany could pay, but he could not deny that the German proposals would certainly arouse strong opposition in France.   Dr. Simons added confidentially that his language at the London Conference would be pitched in quite a different tone from some of his recent speeches. The Paris decisions had caused such a shock of surprise and anger in Germany that it would have been fatal, not only to the Government but also to the success of the negotiations, if he had not to some extent taken the popular view. It was obviously better for him to go to London as an exponent not so much of his own views as of the popular will. To have adopted any other attitude in presence of the violence of public feeling would have meant suicide. Dr. Simons said a rumour had reached him that disarmament would be discussed in London before reparations. He thought this undesirable, as he regarded disarmament as a finished question. Bavaria must disarm. It would not be wise to run the risk of spoiling the pitch for reparations.

FIRST LONDON CONFERENCE, 1921

THIS Conference, which was held in St. James's Palace, and presided over by Mr. Lloyd George, lasted from February 21 to March 14. During the first fortnight the Allies were exclusively occupied with an unsuccessful endeavour to end the hostilities between Greece and Turkey, and to induce both to accept a partial revision, in Turkey's favour, of the Sèvres Treaty. The German Delegation arrived in London on February 28, and made its first appearance in the Conference Chamber on March 1, when Dr. Simons submitted Berlin's counter-proposals to the demands made by the Paris Conference on January 29 in respect of reparation. The character of these counter-proposals, coupled with the recent repudiation by the German Foreign Minister of Germany's responsibility for the war, aroused deep resentment in the Allied camp. Accordingly, the Allied delegates proceeded to draw up an elaborate schedule showing the Reich's defaults under various heads, together with a scheme for the immediate application of territorial and economic sanctions, unless the German

Government agreed forthwith to accept the Allied demands of January 29.   On March 3 this ultimatum was presented by Mr. Lloyd George to Dr. Simons. The following days were characterised by numerous public and private sessions of the Conference, which were frequently of a stormy character.   Finally, on March 7, in the face of Dr. Simons's declared inability to accept the Allied demands, Mr. Lloyd George announced that the threatened sanctions would be put into operation forthwith.   The Rhine ports of Düsseldorf, Duisburg, and Ruhrort were occupied by Allied troops on the morrow (March 8).   Two days later (March 10) the German Government appealed in vain to the League for intervention under Article 11 of the Covenant against the Allied occupation of further German territory, an occupation for which Berlin contended that the Treaty of Versailles provided no legal justification.   On March 23 Germany addressed an equally vain appeal to Washington for mediation by the United States.

LONDON, *March* 1, 1921.—Called on the Prime Minister this morning about 10.30, an hour before the meeting of the Reparation Conference, and found him sitting in the Cabinet-room dressed up in a frock-coat and quite smart— a very rare occurrence for him.   As usual there was a roaring fire behind his back and an open window in front of him.

HE said he had talked over the matter of applying pressure on Germany, through his Customs device, with Sir Robert Horne, who seemed to think the idea practicable.   The idea is to pass a law compelling English buyers from Germany to pay half their bill to the German seller and half to the Government of their own country.   I told Lloyd George that I had spoken to Loucheur about his scheme —that Loucheur had laughed at it to begin with, but ended by thinking it might be an effective means of pressure.

L. G. SAID : " The French can never make up their mind

whether they want payment or whether they want the enjoyment of trampling on Germany, occupying the Ruhr, or taking some other military action.   It is quite clear they cannot have both, and they have to make up their minds which they desire.   As far as we are concerned, we are strongly against any military adventure.   I prefer economic pressure to military."

HE said that during the war his experience had been that nearly all financial theories proved to be incorrect. Lord Cunliffe was right when he said : " It is a fortunate thing for England that, at the time of the Great War crisis, two people were in charge of English finances who knew nothing about finance—i.e. Lloyd George and myself."

IN the Cabinet, McKenna used to come and tell them that England could only go on paying for another three months. Asquith, who was attracted by these theories, rather agreed ; Runciman also agreed ; but he (Lloyd George) and the other men who knew nothing about finance felt sure that this was wrong—and they proved it.   The problem was just whether you could dig up enough coal to make munitions and steel, and if you could either grow or import enough food to feed the people who were doing it.   There was nothing very complicated about it, and all the financial theories turned out to be moonshine.

LONDON, *March* 3, 1921.—Saw Philip Kerr this afternoon.

HIS view of reparation was that nothing permanent could be settled now ; whatever was done now would have to be revised in two years, when he expected America would come in and make a kind of general clean-up, remitting Europe's debts to her, provided that Germany was released from the greater part of reparation.

IF this is a correct surmise of the future, there seems to be no reason at all for endeavouring to fix a total sum of indebtedness in the present stage, as this has no practical value on the above hypothesis, and serves only to accentuate the difficulties between French and German public opinion.

GIVEN removal of prejudice as to the remoter future, there would be no difficulty in arranging an agreed scheme of reparation satisfactory to France, Germany, and all others concerned to cover the next few years.

ON March 8, 1921, the three Rhine ports—Duisburg, Düsseldorf, Ruhrort—were occupied by the Allies.

LONDON, *March* 8, 1921.—Dr. Simons called upon me this morning previous to his departure for Berlin. He said he would arrive in Berlin to-morrow (Wednesday) afternoon. A meeting of the Cabinet had been called that evening. He would probably see the Reichsrat on Thursday, and a meeting of the Reichstag would be held on Friday. Already they were talking about a change of Government. There would be severe attacks from the Right, and also from the Communist side. Two possible successors had been discussed for the post of Minister of Foreign Affairs—Helfferich,[1] the firebrand, and Müller,[2] the Majority Socialist leader. However, he was quite ready to fight them both. When questioned as to the probable course of subsequent events, Dr. Simons said that sanctions are ugly things ; one never knows exactly

[1] HELFFERICH.—A prominent exponent of German nationalism. He was gifted with a remarkable head for figures and had a wide knowledge of international finance, yet was no State financier. His opinions on State finance were too frequently impaired by his political bias. He delivered a violent attack on the Government in the Reichstag on the eve of Herr Rathenau's assassination, but after that brought himself less into public notice, being possibly himself in danger of assassination. Died 1924, in a railway accident.

[2] MÜLLER, Hermann.—Born 1876. A leader of the Majority Socialists. Signed the Versailles Treaty as Minister for Foreign Affairs of the newly constituted Reich. Has remained moderate and supported other Governments in their policy of fulfilment. Became Chancellor in 1918.

what will result from their application.   There may be a great movement of popular feeling in Germany.

In the course of subsequent conversation Dr. Simons agreed in the view that on many points considerable progress had been made in London towards a settlement. The reservation regarding Upper Silesia, which had been such a stumbling block, would disappear in the course of nature.   In conclusion Dr. Simons said : " I am not leaving any experts here.   Any further negotiations will have to be an entirely new chapter.   The application of sanctions makes a definite break with the past phase." His general tone was calm and sensible, free from acrimony no less than from contrition and regret.

London, *March* 10, 1921.—I may be accused of excessive optimism regarding the reparation negotiations, but it seems to me that the London Conference was nearer success than people generally imagined.   It may be that if I could get others to take my view, negotiations might be resumed with a good chance of settlement.   If the different demands put forward by the Allies as a result of the Paris Conference are examined in detail, it will be found that the German Delegation in London agreed to almost all the important conditions.

They agreed to the Paris plan for the first five years.

They agreed to the 12 per cent. on exports taken as an index of an additional variable annuity.

At the end of the five years they agreed to the principle of a variable annuity dependent on German prosperity, this plan being taken as an alternative to a certain portion of the fixed annuities established in Paris.

Outside the points mentioned in Paris, both sides agreed in principle to reduce the forty-two years to thirty years.

Both sides agreed to the mode of payment proposed by Mr. Lloyd George, under which importers from Germany should pay 50 per cent. of the purchase price to their national Treasury.

FURTHER, both sides agreed to the proposal that different creditor countries should receive payments in different forms—e.g. France, per coal ; England, per 50 per cent. on imported goods.

As to the reservations made by the German Delegation, which are probably the main cause of the break-down of the Conference, the most important of these reserves was that regarding Upper Silesia ; but the fate of Upper Silesia will be determined in the course of a few weeks, and the reserve will, therefore, evaporate.

THE other three reserves, namely :

(a) THAT regarding the right to borrow ;

(b) THE demand for favourable treatment for German commerce ; and

(c) LIBERTY for the German Government to control their own customs tariff,

are, in my opinion, of very minor importance.   They could all be adjusted with a certain amount of negotiation.

WHAT then are the points outside the reserves which caused the break-down ?   The main difficulty was to obtain agreement regarding the immediate fixing of the total sum of indebtedness, together with the demand for minimum payments after the first five years without any reserve as regards the economic prosperity of Germany.

ON these points it would seem that further discussion should soon lead to agreement, more particularly if the difficulty of fixing the total sum of reparation is turned by increasing the amount of the variable annuity from the sixth to the thirtieth year and diminishing the amount of the fixed annuity.

THE Prime Minister's proposal to this effect was accepted in principle by the German Delegation.

IT would thus seem, on a general review of the discussion, that considerable progress was made towards agreement, and the parties are not now separated by any divergences of view which would not be amenable to reasonable dis-cussion.

THE Conference in London was hampered from the start by two facts—that Dr. Simons had not public opinion in Germany behind him in his endeavour to reach a reasonable compromise, while the French Delegation practically had no powers of discussion or negotiation, and were cramped by an imperative and narrowly restricted mandate. If the delegates who represented France and Germany had enjoyed the normal latitude usually conferred on men of far inferior rank and status, there can be little doubt that a settlement would have been arrived at.

LONDON, *March* 14, 1921.—On Friday afternoon, March 4, Loucheur and I were instructed by the Prime Minister to endeavour to find a bridge between the French and German positions.

I CALLED upon Loucheur [1] at the Hyde Park Hotel late in the evening, and after some discussion we arrived at an agreement, under which France would accept as a temporary solution the five annuities on the Paris basis, provided that we agreed to assess the total sum due for

---

[1] LOUCHEUR, Louis.—The war gave Loucheur an opportunity to demonstrate his genius for construction. Born in 1872, his early training prepared the way for his highly successful career as an engineer and a contractor. In 1910 Briand realised the value of non-politicals who yet possessed great technical ability, and appointed Loucheur as Under-Secretary. The new Under-Secretary soon became familiar with the political atmosphere, and politics and business became interdependent.

IN 1921 Loucheur was appointed Minister for Liberated Regions in the Briand Cabinet, and was prominent in his negotiations with Rathenau over the reparations question.

PARLIAMENT dealt Loucheur a bitter blow in 1925, when, as Minister of Finance in the Briand Government, he presented some ambitious schemes for the reconstruction of the national finance. Twice the Finance Commission rejected his measures, and Loucheur was forced to resign, having held his portfolio for seventeen days.

LOUCHEUR owes his success to his tremendous energy and to the abundance of his ideas. He has numerous interests, is a proprietor of *Le Petit Journal*, and shows a marked preference for advanced ideas.

damages at 180 milliards.   Subsequent discussion showed
that Loucheur regarded total damages as the same thing
as total indebtedness, which I did not.

THIS agreement was reported at a meeting between the
Prime Minister and Briand on the next morning.   The
meeting was followed by a secret conference at 1 Carlton
House Terrace, between them and Dr. Simons.   (The
fact that this Conference had been held leaked out, and
was published, without comment or disclosure of what
occurred, in the *Weekly Dispatch* of the next day, Sunday.)

IT was decided by the Prime Minister and Briand that
financial experts should draw up a proposal on the lines
agreed to, but when the Allied financial experts met in
the afternoon, again at 1 Carlton House Terrace, Loucheur
had entirely changed his attitude and said that no temporary
arrangement would be acceptable to French public opinion
or to M. Briand.

ACCORDINGLY, when the German financial experts joined
us at 3.30 (the Allied experts having met at 3.0), discussion
was difficult and ended in no practical conclusion.

ON the Sunday morning I had a further conference with
Dr. Schroeder,[1] who made further proposals and certain
concessions.   I had luncheon with Briand and Loucheur
at their hotel.   They both maintained the attitude that if
Germany persisted in subordinating any offer to a satisfactory result in Upper Silesia, no successful negotiations
were possible.   They remained hostile to a temporary
solution, and the French subordinates—notably Laurent

---

[1] SCHROEDER, Dr. Franz.—Dr. Schroeder has been one of Germany's most
consistent financial advisers and directors.   For six years after the conclusion
of war he was Secretary to the Treasury and devised important schemes for
the reconstruction and stabilisation of Germany.

HE had been utilised by the Imperial Government in 1916, when he became
Director of the Imperial Treasury Office.   Earlier in his career, in 1902, he
was for three years Prussian Minister of Finance.

BORN in Danzig in 1874, Dr. Schroeder's experience of finance has been
technical rather than political.   He is a believer in democracy, and his
views are liberal yet nationalist.

9

and Seydoux—who had previously been friendly to a temporary arrangement, now declared that, since the total sum of reparation had been settled in Paris, any recession to a temporary arrangement was quite unthinkable.

AFTER luncheon on Sunday I motored down to Chequers and saw the Prime Minister. Loucheur and Theunis followed soon after.

THE result of our conference at Chequers was that the Prime Minister, Lord Reading, and I motored up together and devised a scheme under which the fixed annuities for the subsequent annual periods should be replaced by a large percentage of exports, the underlying idea being that it was essential to provide some guarantee for the later years, while it was also essential to avoid a fixed sum, since French and German opinion were too far apart.   This proposal was accepted very unwillingly by the French and Belgian delegates at the conference in the evening, but was dropped on Monday morning when it was found the Germans subordinated everything to Upper Silesia.

LOUCHEUR and I had a midnight Conference on Sunday/ Monday at the Savoy Hotel with the German delegates, at which I endeavoured, without success, to bring the Germans to formulate their proposal in a more acceptable form. They, however, adhered obstinately to their four reserves —notably to their reservation about Upper Silesia—and it was fairly apparent that Loucheur rather desired them to formulate their conditions in an unacceptable form ; in this he succeeded.   But even had he taken the other line and assisted me, I do not think the result would have been different, for the German delegates had definite instructions to make the most positive reservations regarding Upper Silesia.

AT the Conference meeting on Monday morning (which Loucheur and I attended after a further meeting with the German delegates at 10 a.m.), the Conference, largely on French and Belgian advice, declined to discuss the German proposal in detail so long as the German reserves were maintained. The question was raised whether the full meeting of the Conference called for 12 o'clock should be postponed until 5 o'clock in order to allow Lloyd George to have a private interview with Simons. He was in favour of this course, so was Bonar Law, but it was rejected by the French, Belgians, Italians, and Japanese, largely on French and Belgian initiative.

THROUGHOUT the Conference the Belgian delegates appeared to be largely under French inspiration, and to take an ultra-French view. In this attitude they showed some considerable modification of their line in Paris.

SUMMARY OF VARIOUS PROPOSALS FOR A SETTLEMENT OF THE REPARATIONS QUESTIONS, MADE AT BOULOGNE, BRUSSELS, PARIS, AND LONDON, JUNE 1920—FEBRUARY 1921

A. Reparations Clauses of Treaty of Versailles

1. GERMAN liability to consist of payment for all damage done Allies' civilian populations and their property (Art. 232).
2. BY May 1, 1921, the Reparation Commission—
   (a) to notify Germany of the total amount of this liability ;
      (b) to present Germany with a schedule of payments for discharging this liability within thirty years (Art. 233).
3. THE Reparation Commission to have power to modify this schedule, but not to cancel any of the liability (Art. 234).
4. GERMANY to pay (in gold and commodities) before May 1, 1921, the equivalent of 20 milliards of gold marks (Art. 235).

B. The Boulogne Agreement, June 21, 1920

GERMAN debt to be fixed as follows :
1. COST of Armies of Occupation.
2. FORTY-TWO annuities of 3 milliard gold marks,

running from May 1, 1921 ; five annuities of 3 milliard gold marks, running from May 1, 1925 ; thirty-two annuities of 4 milliard gold marks, running from May 1, 1931.

Equals 269 milliard gold marks.

3. ANNUITIES paid before falling due to be capitalised at following rates of interest :

> 8 per cent. to May 1, 1922.
> 7.50 per cent. in 1922–3.
> 7 per cent. in 1923–4.
> 6·50 per cent. in 1924–5.
> 6 per cent. in 1925–6.
> 5·50 per cent. in 1926–7.
> 5 per cent. in 1927–8 and following years.

C. Herr Bergmann's Suggestion to Lord D'Abernon, January 1921

FOLLOWING conditions to form Basis of Discussion :

1. COST of Armies of Occupation not to exceed 240 million gold marks per annum.
2. (a) TEMPORARY arrangements for five years, based on annuities of 3 milliard gold marks ; first two annuities to be 2 milliards only and remainder a minimum of 3 milliards.

    (b) Fixation of capital debt to be arrived at as soon as possible.
3. WHOLE offer subject to result of Silesian plebiscite.

D. Allied Experts' Recommendations, Brussels, January 1921

1. LIMITATION of costs of Armies of Occupation to 240 million gold marks per annum.
2. FIVE annuities on scale of magnitude of 3 milliard gold marks.
3. FIXATION of capital debt at as early a date as possible.
4. No cancellation of plebiscite in Upper Silesia, but inter-Allied control of coal distribution after plebiscite.

5. No interference in German public finance under Article 248 or with customs, provided obligations are carried out.

6. No concessions as regards sequestered and liquidated property other than in very minor and personal instances.

7. ASSURANCES to Germany that economic clauses of treaty will not be used to hinder German trade.

E. *Paris Proposals, January* 29, 1921

1. FORTY-TWO annuities, running from May 1, 1921, of—

    (*a*) 2 milliard gold marks for 2 years
    (*b*) 3   ,,   ,,   ,,   ,, 3 ,,
    (*c*) 4   ,,   ,,   ,,   ,, 3 ,,
    (*d*) 5   ,,   ,,   ,,   ,, 3 ,,
    (*e*) 6   ,,   ,,   ,,   ,, 31 ,,

equals 226 milliard gold marks, plus 12 per cent. on German exports.

2. ANNUITIES to be discounted at—

    8 per cent. until May 1, 1923,
    6 ,,   ,,   from May 1, 1923, to May 1, 1925,
    5 ,,   ,,   from May 1, 1925.

3. No State credit operation outside German territory without consent of Reparation Commission.

4. REPARATION Commission to hold watching brief over German customs, with power to administer if Germany defaults in her reparation obligations.

F. *Dr. Simons's Offer, March* 1921

1. PRESENT value of Paris annuities (discounted at 8 per cent.) is calculated at 50 milliard gold marks.

2. THIS capital sum (less deliveries under Article 235, valued at 20 milliard gold marks), 30 milliard gold marks.

3. GERMANY will pay this by—

    (*a*) Issuing a loan of 8 milliard gold marks (said to be equal to 10 milliards deferred payment), to be raised in the world markets. This loan to be free from taxation and to be at lowest possible rate of interest.

(*b*) Five annuities of 1 milliard gold marks, running from May 1, 1921. These annuities to be credited at the rate of interest—5 per cent.— of the amount of reparation debt not immediately covered by the loan or annuities. Interest thus uncovered shall be added to capital amount on May 1, 1926 (about 22 milliards of gold marks).

4. THIS offer conditional upon—

(*a*) Upper Silesia remaining German.

(*b*) Removal of restrictions upon commercial relations.

(*c*) Relief from further payments or deliveries under treaty.

(*d*) Renunciation of Allied right of liquidation of private German property.

G. Mr. Lloyd George's Reply, March 3, 1921

GERMANS must accept Paris proposals or submit counter-proposals which will in other equally satisfactory ways discharge their obligations under the treaty (subject to Paris concessions).

H. Dr. Simons's Offer, March 7, 1921

WILL accept Paris amounts for first five years and will give full equivalent for 12 per cent. export tax, though at least 8 milliards will be paid by raising a loan (with priority over claims in Art. 248). Has authority to make no definite offer for fixing capital amount of debt (and, when questioned privately, will not say whether he can make an offer for remaining 25 years such as to equal Paris proposal). Offer for first 25 years conditional upon reservations regarding—

(*a*) Upper Silesia.

(*b*) No economic restrictions on German commerce.

(*c*) No restriction on German borrowing powers, as contemplated in Paris agreement.

(*d*) No interference with customs, as contemplated in Paris agreement.

I. Mr. Lloyd George's Reply to Dr. Simons, March 7, 1921

DR. SIMONS's offer unacceptable, as—

1. SUBJECT to Upper Silesia plebiscite.
2. CONTAINS no definite offer after first five years.

LONDON, *March* 22, 1921.—Before leaving for Berlin I called at Downing Street about 5 p.m. and had a long talk with the Prime Minister. As usual, the big fire behind and the open window in front.

HE said that he was anxious for me to go back as soon as possible, as he was not now getting any clear impression as to what was going on in Germany or as to what people were thinking.

REGARDING Upper Silesia, he said : " It is entirely due to England that Germany has a chance of getting the whole or part of Upper Silesia. President Wilson was anxious to give the whole country to Poland, so were the French ; the English were alone in resisting. I brought the whole Cabinet over to Paris, and they sat—with brief intervals for sleep—from 6 p.m. Saturday till 10 p.m. Sunday. The discussion was a very fair one ; there was no rancour against Germany—no bitterness. The whole of the evidence was reviewed and the decision come to that, in fairness to the country, it could not be given to Poland. We should have been favourable to giving it to Germany, but we compromised on a plebiscite. My inclination is that the country should be kept together, and I will not agree to partition unless I am obliged to. We are all interested in German prosperity. After all, if we wish Germany to pay we have to leave them something to earn money with,"

REGARDING reparations, he said : " You ought to tell Simons to put forward his scheme for the restoration of the devastated areas by German co-operation. I do not say necessarily by German workmen, but a large amount of the material required could be prepared in Germany and delivered to the devastated regions and set up there with little additional labour. If the 50 per cent. import payment on goods coming to England works smoothly, it may show us the way to a satisfactory solution."

I GATHERED that the Prime Minister was very hostile to any further military advance into Germany. He appears to think that his refusal to associate himself with the sanctions established at the London Conference (occupation of Duisburg, Düsseldorf, and Ruhrort) would have raised all sorts of clamour, but he is fully alive to the undesirability of sanctions in general.

SIR EYRE CROWE is said to be doubtful as to the efficacy of the sanctions and as to their desirability. Lord Curzon is strongly of the same view, and considers that the London Conference ought not to have been broken up. I presume he would have given the Germans seven days for fresh proposals.

THE truth is that the second and third delegates and the subordinate Ministers generally have extraordinarily little influence in deciding the line to be adopted in foreign policy, where Western Europe is concerned. The P.M. makes up his own mind and acts upon it, without excessive regard to the opinion of his colleagues.

THE P.M. said that probably Horne would be Chancellor of the Exchequer. He prefers Horne because he regards him as the least orthodox of all the possibles and the most indifferent to financial and economic theory. When I told him I was, in principle, an orthodox partisan of sound currency, he blanched with horror, and one felt that one had lost half his confidence and all his friendship.

CHAPTER V

BACK TO BERLIN

Berlin's principal reaction to London sanctions—An interview with Prince
Lichnowsky—France's precipitate publication—A German Royal Prince
on Lloyd George and reparations—German laments.

BERLIN, *March 25, 1921.*—Returned last night and have CHAP.
seen a good many people in the course of the day. V
THERE is no doubt that the Germans are at heart dis- March
appointed regarding the voting in Upper Silesia,[1] saying 1921
that if the industrial districts are separated the country

[1] ON March 20, 1921, there was held in Upper Silesia, under the authority
of the Inter-Allied Commission, presided over by General Le Rond, the
plebiscite provided for by the Treaty of Versailles. The provisional results
published on the morrow showed a substantial majority for the German
population. This was confirmed by the final figures issued on April 23,
which disclosed that 707,605 electors had voted for Germany, as against
479,359 for Poland. In the light of these figures, German opinion contended
—and in a measure expected—that the whole of Upper Silesia would be left
within the boundaries of the Reich, a thesis which found widespread support
in England, but was resolutely opposed by France and Poland. Owing to
the repeated delays of the Allied Governments in reaching an agreement
among themselves as to the final allocation, on the basis of the plebiscite,
of the various Upper Silesian districts, the summer witnessed the armed
invasion of Upper Silesia by an army of Polish partisans led by M. Korfanty.
A large German " irregular " locally raised body, the Selbstschutz (" Self-
protection "), commanded by General Hoefer, offered active resistance to
Korfanty's supporters. A truce was finally arranged, largely owing to the
intervention and mediation of the British Government, and of the British
Commissioner, Sir Harold Stuart. The Allied Commissioners, however,
were unable, even by July, to record an unanimous vote on the partition of
the province, and informed the Ambassadors' Conference in Paris to this
effect. The question of a decision was thereupon remitted to the Supreme
Council, which met in Paris on August 8, 1921. But no more than an
earlier Conference of Allied Experts on the subject could Mr. Lloyd George
and M. Briand agree on the new frontier. On August 12, therefore, on the
proposal of the Italian delegates, Signor Bonomi and the Marchese della
Torretta, the Supreme Council decided to invite the League Council to
record its own opinion on the partition. The League Council, in its turn,
referred the problem to a Sub-Committee consisting of its four non-permanent

cannot live.   They all praise the attitude of the English and Italian troops in the plebiscite area, but are extremely bitter about the French, whom they accuse of having assisted the Polish roving bands.

REGARDING reparations, there is remarkable apathy as to military occupation.   Whether a few more towns are occupied or not does not seem to touch them.   They are more sensitive about the customs frontier on the Rhine and about the 50 per cent. levy on German exports.

GERMAN expert financial opinion considers that Simons's last offer in London went beyond German capacity, and they are, I believe, sincerely glad that his offer was rejected by the Allies.

[IT transpired in later years that the failure of the London Conference was probably due to Dr. Simons not going to the full limit allowed by his instructions.   He was informed, so the story runs, by Germans who professed to be judges of British opinion, that the Government would never agree to sanctions.

IT may be well, while the facts are still in my memory, to note the inner meaning of the Paris Conference, which lasted from January 23 to 28, and the London Conference, March 1 to 9.

THE Paris Conference had been preceded by Brussels, where friendly and impartial financial discussion between the Entente and Germany had nearly led to agreement. It was recognised there that discussion of the total sum

members—Belgium, Spain, Brazil, and China, assisted by a Swiss and a Czecho-Slovak expert.   The Council, after considering its Sub-Committee's report, decided on October 14 upon a wholesale partition of Upper Silesia between Germany and Poland.   This decision was confirmed on October 17 by the Allied Governments and communicated to Berlin.   Indignation in Germany was universal and acute, and brought about a ministerial crisis. Chancellor Wirth was forced to resign, but, at the request of President Ebert, formed a provisional business Cabinet, which accepted the unpopular decision of the Allies, under strong protest.

would necessarily lead to a breakdown of negotiations
and that it was indispensable to confine the debate to a
temporary solution if success was to be attained.

LLOYD GEORGE came to Paris determined to arrive at a
practical solution and not to exact from Germany excessive
terms, but he unfortunately took the view that a temporary
solution would not enable Europe to settle down. At
intervals during both the Paris and London Conferences
he agreed, as a kind of compromise, to a temporary
arrangement, but this was always done against his own
judgment, and it never happened to coincide with the rare
moments when the French and Germans were also agreeable
to a temporary settlement—so nothing came of it. I have
always regarded this as a great misfortune, believing that
German and French public opinions are too far apart for
lasting settlement to be reached now. The best preparation for a permanent agreement would be the smooth
working, for two or three years, of a temporary scheme.

THROUGH all the early part of the Paris Conference L. G.
was fighting the French to induce them to reduce their
terms. He only agreed to the Paris decisions after a
struggle with Briand and after prolonged discussion with
different experts.

THE sanctions agreed to in Paris were not a subject of
prolonged discussion and were more or less slipped in by
the French without adequate consideration. The French
were certainly unjustified in publishing them at the same
time as the Paris terms, since it was clearly agreed that,
as a matter of courtesy to Germany, the sanctions should
not be communicated simultaneously with the conditions.
As a matter of fact, although not communicated to
Germany, they were published in all the French papers
simultaneously with the decisions, and this made the
Paris decisions appear much more anti-German than they
otherwise would have been. In fact the whole tone of
Paris seemed to be more hostile to Germany than it was

in reality, and it proved later impossible to persuade the German Government that Paris terms constituted a compromise, to which we had great difficulty in bringing the French.

WHEN it came to London, Lloyd George again began with the strong desire to arrive at agreement and to make the terms possible of acceptance by Germany. But Simons's opening statement was so unsatisfactory that it was almost impossible to assist him or to build negotiation on so unacceptable a basis. Notwithstanding this, however, every advance made by the Germans in private discussion towards a possible basis of agreement was taken up by the English experts with a real endeavour to agree. Several confidential meetings took place, one at Lord Curzon's house in Carlton House Terrace. Other confidential conversations took place at the Savoy Hotel between myself, or Loucheur and myself, for the Entente and the German technical delegates for Germany. At all these meetings we displayed a desire to negotiate and come to an understanding, provided the German terms were defensible. Unfortunately they were indefensible. Financial offers were hedged round with all sorts of reservations about Upper Silesia, etc., which gave opponents of agreement a chance.

ALTHOUGH Lloyd George made severe speeches regarding German responsibility, he was only brought to do this by the impossible attitude adopted by Simons. I do not think that Simons was deliberately against an agreement, but (a) he was afraid of public opinion in Germany, which he had partly himself created by his speeches, (b) and being rather precise and juridical in mind, he is not disposed to leave any ambiguity, whereas in so difficult a negotiation ambiguity is not only useful but indispensable.

THE French delegates were, I think, themselves quite reasonable and sensible, but they received by every post letters from Paris telling them their ministerial life was not worth a minute's purchase if they made any

concession. In the middle of the Conference Doumer
came from Paris with a message from Millerand to the
same effect. They were almost compelled to be intransigent,
and feared the failure of the Conference much less than
their own failure to gain public support.

LOOKING back over the whole of the negotiations, my
opinion is that the best course would have been to allow the
Brussels discussions to continue and to have been satisfied
with a temporary solution. Failing this, I do not think
that any advantage would have resulted from even stronger
British pressure at the Paris Conference for a further
reduction of the French claims. The French delegates
could not have accepted. If they had accepted, the French
Chamber would have refused. This would have led to a
very unpleasant situation between London and Paris. It
may, and probably will, come to this before the end of
this reparation discussion, but I do not believe that at
that time it would have been wise deliberately to diverge
from France and from Briand, thus bringing about his fall
in favour of some less broad-minded minister.

LLOYD GEORGE has always said that it would have been
better to have had Poincaré as French Premier, instead of
Briand. The French would soon have found that the
Poincaré policy led to no satisfactory result. However,
once Briand was in, Lloyd George felt bound to support
him and to facilitate his task.]

BERLIN, *March* 28, 1921.—The situation here is not at
all satisfactory. There is a decided reversion to Junkerism,
and I hear that in many of the officers' clubs quasi-penal
lists are drawn up of those officers who associate with
ex-enemies.

THE application of the military sanctions has not produced
a normal or healthy reaction—it has turned the Germans
sour. Feeling against France is intensely bitter. Compared with the French, the English are almost popular,

but I do not know how far our influence would go if it was applied to make them agree to some measure acceptable to France.

THE military advance has not caused nearly the same sensation as the economic measures. It is too soon yet to say how the 50 per cent. tax will work, but the Government still stoutly declare that they will contribute nothing to assist exporters. The Italians appear hostile to levying the 50 per cent. on German exports to Italy, but the Belgians seem determined to apply all and every means of compulsion, though they are nervous of its effect upon the trade of Antwerp.

IT is difficult to make out what has occurred to the Belgian Government. Their attitude altered between the Paris Conference and London. In Paris they were reasonable; in London they appeared anxious only to bring about a break. Explain this who can.

BERLIN, *March* 28, 1921.—I hear that a very detailed report on German capacity to pay was drawn up by the Belgian statistician on the Reparation Commission, M. Fürst, and was signed by all the Reparation Intelligence Bureau in Berlin. As this report concluded against the ability of Germany to pay anything like the Paris terms, it caused an outburst from Jaspar and Theunis, who hurriedly telegraphed from London—in conjunction with Loucheur—to have the document withdrawn or suppressed. A copy which was sent me never reached its destination and must have been intercepted somehow.

THEY had previously lauded their statistician to the skies ; now he will barely escape with his life.

BERLIN, *April* 3, 1921.—Lunched to-day with Prince Lichnowsky,[1] a former Ambassador to London. He has

[1] LICHNOWSKY, Prince Karl Max.—In 1912, after eight years of retirement in Silesia, Prince Lichnowsky was unexpectedly appointed as Ambassador in London in succession to Baron Marschall von Bieberstein. The German

withdrawn from politics and lives a retired life, but has
still a certain amount of influence in Democratic and Majority-Socialist circles. The Right, of course, detest him.

HIS most intelligent and talented wife has become a
very popular author of quite incomprehensible poetry.
I have tried to read her books, but have failed completely
to make any sense of them. However, others have been
more successful.

LICHNOWSKY says that with few exceptions people in Germany still think that England is united with France in
wishing for Germany's economic destruction. The English
Government always ends by giving way to France and by
agreeing to the imposition of impossible terms on Germany.
He quoted the Conferences of Versailles, Paris, and London
in support of this view.

I REPLIED : " I don't know what happened at Versailles.
As far as regards Paris, the terms agreed to there represented an enormous reduction on the original French
demand. They were not more than half what Doumer
put forward. Instead of being grateful to us for having
obtained this great concession, German opinion only

Embassy during his tenure of office lost its reputation for " withdrawal "
which it had acquired under Count Wolff-Metternich. Any friendly feeling
which was established between Germany and England in the time prior to
the war was largely due to Prince Lichnowsky's genuine desire for peaceful
relations and his success as a political host.

EARLY in his diplomatic career Prince Lichnowsky had twice been attached
to the German Embassy in London, and had acquired an admiration and
regard for England ; he aimed at development on British lines.

A CONSERVATIVE by tradition and position, Prince Lichnowsky was not
without an understanding of democracy. In 1910, during the conflict
which arose out of the Prussian Franchise Reform, he urged that concessions
to democracy were imperative and unavoidable.

PRINCE LICHNOWSKY made desperate efforts to avoid war, for which he was
unprepared. But his personal influence in Berlin—he had not the brilliance
and initiative so necessary in German political circles—was almost negligible.
The recognition of his honesty and untiring efforts to secure peace was shown
by the provision of a guard of honour on his departure from London.

GERMANY criticised his policy and his attitude. His unpopularity was so
great that he retired to Switzerland.

screamed out that the terms were impossible. To prove
to you how bad French public opinion considered the
Paris terms you have only to read the debates in the French
Chamber, and to take into account the fact that the first
thing the French did after the break in London was to say
that they were no longer bound by Paris. Does not
this suggest to Germany that it was somewhat unwise
to exclaim so much against the Paris conditions ? Nearly
the same thing happened in London. We urged you to
consult us unofficially before making your declarations in
London. Instead of that, you kept the terms of your
proposal absolutely secret, and finally put them forward
in a speech which could not but be considered a mockery.
This compelled a severe reply and the application of
sanctions—for which you are much more responsible than
we. With the best will in the world we could not save
the situation. Ask your delegates : they will tell you we
did what was possible to give them an opportunity to
retrieve the false move they had made, but to every proposal
which you put forward there was attached some fatal condition which took it to the bottom like a heavy stone."

BERLIN, *April* 14, 1921.—An interesting dinner at Prince
Lichnowsky's last night, meeting several of the leading
officials and the editors of the *Vorwärts* and the *Berliner
Tageblatt*. At dinner I sat next to Theodor Wolff,[1]
the proprietor of the *Tageblatt*. He is strongly in favour
of Germany making new proposals, but what proposals
would meet the case ? I told him that at the present
moment I could put forward nothing precise. That

[1] WOLFF, Theodor.—The editor of the *Berliner Tageblatt*, a Liberal organ of
great influence and wide circulation. Contrary to its rival, the *Vossische
Zeitung*, the *Berliner Tageblatt*, while by no means pro-British, does not
believe in a Franco-German and Continental rapprochement against Great
Britain. Wolff, however, although personally hostile to Poincaré, has ever
been a steady advocate of the policy of fulfilment, and a no less steady
opponent of Prussian militarism.

was their business, not mine. I had given them, as Wolff
recognised, very sound advice in the past. Now the counter-
proposals must come from the German side. I indicated
that they must be a clear proof of genuine sincerity and of
goodwill to meet their obligations. The effect of their
proposal in London had been to make even those of the
Allies who were friendly to them convinced that they
were not playing up. That was exactly the wrong line
to take.

AFTER dinner I talked mainly to Dernburg, and to the editor
of the *Vorwärts*. The former, an ex-Colonial Minister
and a very intelligent banker, with strong American proclivities and a violent American accent. He has little of
the Prussian, and appears to hold Democratic moderate
views. Simons he considers much too much of a purist
and a stickler for precise legal phrases. " What folly to
haggle about what will happen after the sixth year !
None of us knows what will happen even next year. Who
could tell what Germany's capacity would be in 1927 ?
Besides this, there is the question of America's intervention."

DERNBURG would have made some agreement for the first
three or five years and given such assurances as were necessary regarding the later period, trusting to subsequent
negotiations and to the logic of facts. If, when the
time came, Germany was unable to pay, the fact would
be patent from the condition of her trade and finances,
and even the French experts would by then have become
convinced. He does not believe in Rechberg's plan,[1]
or rather he does not believe in Rechberg's figures, saying
that the estimate of 9 milliards of marks a year for Germany's profits on industrial concerns and banks is ludi-
crously exaggerated. I replied : " That does not make the

---

[1] RECHBERG.—A well-known writer in the press on economic and diplomatic
subjects, and a sculptor of considerable talent. His political judgment is
not equal to his artistic performance or his skill in controversy.

10

plan necessarily bad ; the offer of participation in industry might be considered as proof of Germany's goodwill, and if the figures are small, as you say, this should be to some extent a measure and an indication of Germany's capacity or incapacity to pay."

THE *Vorwärts* man rather laughed at Simons, saying that Simons believed there were only two statesmen— Aristides and himself. The general tone of all was to consider Simons too nice and precise and punctilious about ability to carry out his promises—too juridical and not political enough or diplomatic. However, they think he will survive—having squared Fehrenbach in the train, and the press after his arrival here.

BERLIN, *April* 18, 1921.—My interview with Simons to-day was quite cordial, but left me with the impression that the odds are decidedly against a satisfactory solution. All the minor schemes for Allied participation in German industry, for German substitution in the American debt, for contribution in kind to the devastated regions, are well enough in their way, but they do not go very far towards the total annuity required. I strongly favour their discussion, but I realise that they do not answer the main question—nor can it be answered at all to the satisfaction of Paris, unless the Germans accept the Paris resolutions as a basis.

I HAVE never thought the vehement opposition of the Germans to the whole basis of Paris justified. Their outburst against Paris was really caused by the violent and provocative manner of publishing the Paris decisions, i.e. the publication of the sanctions at the same time as the conditions. This was done notwithstanding the fact that the Conference had clearly stipulated that they should not be communicated at the same time. As a matter of fact the way they were published was even worse than simultaneous official communication. If the Paris terms had been properly conveyed to Germany, with suitable explanations, I am inclined to believe that Germany would have accepted them. Whether we can get Germany round to this now is more doubtful. It appears to be the best thing to try for.

BERLIN, *April* 18, 1921.—Dresel, the American Commissioner, does not appear to have much information regarding the American attitude. He is anxious to facilitate some kind of an arrangement under which Germany should take over a portion of the American debt. It is all very fine to talk about America not being willing to accept a shaky debtor such as Germany, in place of rich nations like England, France, and Italy. I admit that the exchange for England would be a bad one, but I am not sure that the exchange would be unfavourable as compared with France and Italy. All three countries—France, Italy, and Germany —appear to be on the verge of bankruptcy, and France and Italy, apart from their financial difficulties, claim a kind of sacred moral right not to pay, which Germany, if she takes over the debts, would not have. Anyhow, I hope America will be brought in in some way or another, for it is clear that the restraining forces on French nervosity in regard to this subject require all the strengthening they can get from any quarter of the compass or any side of the Atlantic.

BERLIN, *April* 23, 1921.—I hear from a fairly good source that one of the most able and experienced Princes when asked recently by a visitor his opinion as to the proposals made by Germany with regard to reparations, said that he was not an expert on the subject, but was willing to stake his reputation on the honesty of Simons. " When Simons put forward the proposals in London, he believed that they contained the uttermost that Germany could possibly pay."

THE royal personage was dubious about Germany being able to put forward anything like an accurate statement of what she could pay. It was just as likely to be overstated as understated, and he was absolutely convinced that until an independent inquiry, possibly by an international commission, had been made, no satisfactory solution of the reparations problem would be found.

FRANCE, he considered, was like a bull rushing wildly at the red flag hung on a stone wall. She was well in her stride to her own ruin. Her attitude was utterly incomprehensible. Her blindness to her own interests was reacting on the other countries, including Germany, whose interests were bound up in those of France. He looked on Lloyd George as a very wonderful man, a man of genius, but could only ask : " Has anything happened to him ? Is it that he is worn out and leaving himself in the hands of advisers who have neither the intelligence nor the foresight which have been such conspicuous qualities in this extraordinary man ? "

SPEAKING of the responsibility for the war, he said that, in his opinion, after the mobilisation of Russia, it was quite impossible to prevent Germany going to war. " I can give you my oath that the Kaiser never wanted war. I cannot speak of those who surrounded him.

" APART from the question of responsibility, I believe in the reparations—the loser must pay. Settle this question of ' how much ' and ' how,' and I believe you will have settled Europe. One thing I am sure of, and that is that, whatever benefit may accrue to the Allies through the enforcing of the ' sanctions,' it will not be in the form of reparations."

BERLIN, *April* 24, 1921.—For the last two days the Cabinet has sat almost continuously, the only intervals being time for meals and for short wrangles with the party leaders. Public opinion cannot make up its mind regarding the

German-American negotiations. They are inclined to blame
Simons for having placed Germany so completely under
America's decision. " We have stripped ourselves
naked," the Right says, " and bound ourselves to agree
to anything America decides." On the other hand, more
reasonable people see the advantage to Germany of bringing
America in.

DR. SIMONS's position appeared to be hopeless on Friday,
but stronger on Saturday ; to-day he has gone back again.
His only chance of survival is the complete inability of
everybody to produce a suitable substitute.

THE Socialists are of two minds about joining the present
coalition, or even forming a Government themselves.
Here, again, the absence of capable men is the dominating
factor. The tone of their principal papers is that if they
were sure of fair treatment from the Entente on better terms
than were given to the bourgeois parties, then they would
take power, but they will not assume office if Germany is
to be treated perpetually as under-dog without a fair chance
of recovery. The accusation is made against the Entente
that promises of generous treatment towards a democratic
Government have not been kept, the attitude of France in
particular being no less harsh than if she had to deal with
a militarist or monarchical régime.

THERE is some justice in this view, and the Entente might
have made a greater differentiation between its attitude
towards democracy and its attitude towards militarism ;
but in all these questions the Germans themselves are
very much to blame, in that their pacific attitude has
not been sufficiently clear. The fact is that while the
progress of disarmament, the delivery of coal and other
things, under the treaty, have gone forward at a rate
which I consider astounding, the Germans get very little
credit for all they have done. This is due in a large
measure to their manner of doing things, and to their
inveterate quibbling.

BERLIN, *April* 24, 1921.—Viviani's visit to the United States will, I think, cost his country more than any visit since the Queen of Sheba came to Solomon. Viviani appears to have been obliged to renew direct assurances to America, not only that France would pay her debt to the last sou, but that she never had the smallest hope of not paying.

CHAPTER VI

THE LONDON SCHEDULE OF PAYMENTS

Talks with Lord Curzon and Lloyd George—Lloyd George's difficulties with the French—The London Schedule of Payments—Briand on the Ruhr—Dramatic call of the Reparation Commission—Hot arguments between financial experts—Reception in Berlin—Stresemann's four questions to Lord Curzon.

SECOND LONDON CONFERENCE, 1921

ON April 27 the Reparation Commission, in accordance with Article 233 of the Versailles Treaty, fixed Germany's total liability in respect of reparation at 132 milliard gold marks (£6,600,000,000), and notified Germany of this decision on the following day. On April 30 the Supreme Allied Council reassembled in London, where it sat, almost continuously, until May 5. Having declared all the German counter-proposals hitherto submitted to have been inadequate and unacceptable, it discussed the framing of a fresh ultimatum to Germany, and instructed the Allied experts to work out a definite and detailed plan, which would lay down the time and methods whereby Germany should discharge the totality of her reparation obligations, as fixed by the aforementioned decision of the Reparation Commission. It was agreed by the Allies that a refusal by Germany to comply with this decision should entail the occupation of the Ruhr as the chief sanction. Indeed, military preparations for this occupation were ordered on May 2, the French Government decreeing the mobilisation for this purpose of a class of French reservists. But Mr. Lloyd George secured for Germany the granting of a respite of six days in which to accept the new Allied ultimatum, which specified the fulfilment by her of certain stipulations relating to disarmament and war criminals as well as to reparation.

THE so-called "London Schedule of Payments" of May 5 had been practically completed by the experts

CHAP.
VI

April
1921

of the Supreme Council on May 4, when the Reparation Commission was urgently summoned by telephone
from Paris to London, and rather summarily invited
to endorse the work of the Council itself.

WHEN the Allied Ultimatum and the Schedule of
Payments reached Berlin on May 6, the German
Cabinet of which Dr. Simons was the Foreign Minister
had fallen, and President Ebert experienced no little
difficulty in persuading other political leaders to
form a new Cabinet in the present circumstances.
Finally, Dr. Wirth, of the Catholic Centre, was
prevailed upon to accept the Chancellorship, and on
May 11, thus twenty-four hours before the expira-
tion of the time-limit in the Allied ultimatum, the
new Government, with the approval of the Reichstag,
signified its acceptance of the terms laid down by
the Allied Governments and the Reparation Commission.

LONDON, *April* 29, 1921.—Arrived London at 5 p.m.
and saw George Curzon. He has been laid up for the
last week with one of his old attacks, and still looks weak.
Outside his illness there is some friction over his not having
been asked to attend the Lympne Conference. The
excuse was that the Belgians and Italians would not be
invited and might be annoyed if it was a full official conference. This would not occur if it was only a private
meeting between the two Premiers. At the last minute,
however, Vansittart, Lord Curzon's private secretary, was
asked. Not much balm in Gilead.

CURZON is strongly against occupation of the Ruhr, but
seems to doubt how far it may be possible to control the
menace. He did not take up my suggestion, that it was
indispensable to bring in America, with any particular
enthusiasm.

ENGLAND and America working together can restrain
France and can bring Germany up to the scratch ; alone,
I doubt England being able to do either.

A Cabinet Committee composed of Montagu, Worthing-ton-Evans, and Winston Churchill have elaborated a new plan under which Germany would have to pay 2 milliard gold marks a year fixed, plus a sum equal to 25 per cent. of her exports. Bonds both for the fixed and varying portions of this would be issued. This does not appear to me at all a bad plan. The Prime Minister will listen to nothing which does not include the maintenance of his scheme of 50 per cent. on imports into England. He says that without this England will get nothing ; France and Belgium will manage somehow to take all the German payments. Most of his colleagues think the 50 per cent. scheme sketchy, but they will not succeed in pulling him out of it. No mule is in it with L. G., once his mind is set on the unorthodox, with all the experts against him.

London, *April* 29, 1921.—It may be well to set down the position to-day. It is about as follows :

Regarding the occupation of the Ruhr, this is demanded by certain sections in France : the Poincaré group, partly for political reasons, partly as security for cash ; the Foch party, who believe that it will lead to the breaking-up of Germany and the permanent establishment of the French frontier on the Rhine.

Is it possible to prevent the occupation of the Ruhr by inducing the Germans to accept the Paris Allied decisions ? French feeling is so high that they will undoubtedly occupy the Ruhr unless Germany accepts the Allied demands without further delay.

The Germans seem as intractable and heavy-handed to-day as ever. When hours count and military enthusiasm is mounting, they make a quite incomprehensible proposal which gives the impression of subterfuge.

The utmost that England will be able to secure at the forth-coming conference is French agreement to the sending of an ultimatum to Germany requiring her to accept the

Allied proposals within so many days or submit to the occupation of the Ruhr. The Allied proposals will be based substantially on the Paris terms, possibly with certain modifications favourable to Germany. This would certainly be the case if England had her way, but any modification on Paris would probably involve the fall of Briand.

THE French want to occupy the Ruhr in the first days of next month without considering any further proposals ; the British, though just as determined as the French to secure adequate reparation, will certainly not agree to any more than the Paris terms, and wish an ultimatum to be sent to Germany giving her so many days in which to accept the Allied demands. Failing acceptance, England will co-operate in the occupation.

THERE are strong arguments against this policy, but it is no longer a question of opinions but of facts, and unless Germany accepts, the French will occupy the Ruhr. Germany must decide between accepting the Paris terms and giving France a strangle-hold on her throat.

IT is no use Germany looking to England for impossibilities. We induced France to accept the Paris proposals at the cost of a considerable straining of Anglo-French relations. England will now probably secure for Germany a chance of escaping the occupation of the Ruhr if she faces the facts and accepts without qualification the new Allied proposals. If she does decide to reject our proposals, she must do so with a full comprehension of what she is doing.

LONDON, *April* 30, 1921.—At an interview at Downing Street this morning I urged :

(*a*) THE necessity of bringing in America ;

(*b*) THAT the Ruhr occupation would be absolutely fatal. Once it was carried out, the menace would no longer subsist. I GATHER that the Prime Minister is quite doubtful whether it will be possible to prevent occupation of the Ruhr.

LONDON, *May* 2, 1921.—Between Saturday and Sunday the P.M. was hard pressed by the French. He found very considerable opposition against sanctions, in the Cabinet, the majority of the ministers being strongly against the Ruhr occupation, and particularly against any English participation in it. The leaders of this view are Winston and Montagu. Mond is rather anti-German. Winston is said to have been brilliant, taking a very broad, sensible view and putting it admirably.

REGARDING the desirability of bringing America in to the negotiations, both L. G. and Curzon appear to be pessimistic.

IN the Technical Committee which has sat so continuously, Worthington-Evans has done extremely well, muddling along with a little bit of French, but mainly in English, and riding off inconvenient proposals without giving offence. A very clear financial head.

THE new proposals are a great improvement on Paris in that they reduce the fixed annuities payable by Germany, replacing them by a levy calculated on German exports. This will probably become, in effect, a tax on German exports and has two advantages—it corrects the valuta advantage to Germany and would secure a large sum without imposition of a fixed minimum. It also has the advantage that its produce is incalculable, and therefore avoids criticism from either one side or the other.

LONDON, *May* 3, 1921.—Dined quietly with a leading French statesman at the Carlton Hotel.

I TOLD him exactly what I thought of the position in Germany, and he appeared quite disposed to agree. The main point I made was the absence of proper safeguards in the treaty regarding the control of military armaments and preparations in Germany after the Control Commission had ceased work. I said : " If you can get effective safeguards or guarantees on this point, it is worth a large sacrifice either in reparations or in immediate disarmament and disbandment of the Einwohnerwehr. There is no present military danger—the danger, if any, is in the future." The second point I made to him was the desirability of giving better terms to a democratic Government in Germany than to a Government drawn from the Right. The Allies had not really kept their word in giving easier terms to a democratic Government as opposed to a monarchical. This was a mistaken policy and ought to be corrected. HE said he thought the chances of Germany accepting the new scheme were about even money. It came a little too soon. He thought public opinion in Germany was not quite ripe. If the same proposal was put forward three months hence, Germany would certainly accept.

REGARDING the occupation of the Ruhr, he said that all his information was that there would be no difficulty with the miners. He thought it would go just as smoothly as the occupation of Duisburg, etc. I replied: " The point is not that it shall go as smoothly, but that it shall be more effective."

LONDON, *May* 4, 1921.—Since Saturday, when the meetings of the Conference commenced, we have been sitting almost continuously, either at the Supreme Council or in the Financial Sub-Committee—mainly the latter. We sat all through Sunday until 1 a.m. Monday morning, and were up again most of the following night.

THE result of all the work is a diplomatic Note to Germany threatening the occupation of the Ruhr if the financial terms are not accepted within six days. This Note encloses the financial terms—what Lloyd George calls the " pie," the diplomatic Note being the " pie-crust." The " pie " appears to me quite a good solution. If I were in the place of the Germans I should accept it ; as the fixed annuities are much reduced and as the conversion of the fixed annuities into bonds will enable Germany—either the State or German individuals—to repurchase their own obligations at a considerable discount. Thus the

nominal indebtedness of 6½ milliards sterling, which was
fixed by the Reparation Commission, is first of all reduced
by interest being only immediately payable on a section of
it, and will be reduced in the second instance by the possible
repurchase by Germany of her own bonds.

THE earlier portions of the Conference were critical, as
the French wanted an immediate advance into the Ruhr.
This L. G. very successfully resisted. Now the difficulty
is the precise legal form in which to clothe the communication to Germany. The Commission of Reparation
have been telephoned for to Paris. The telephone message
only went at 7 p.m. yesterday and they were expected to
start at midnight. They will probably come with a party
of about fifty, including statisticians and secretaries, and
will have a miserable journey.

LAST night again the Drafting Committee was up all night,
but I did not attend their meeting, being tired out.

LONDON, *May* 7, 1921.—The results of the London Conference as far as regards reparation finance appear to me
reasonable and satisfactory. I believe that Germany can
pay the fixed annuities of 100 millions sterling a year, and
there is not much danger for her in undertaking the variable
annuity equal to 25 per cent. on exports. There is every
advantage in Germany getting through the present crisis
on the chance of a revision later when America comes in.
It is now clear that no settlement of world-indebtedness is
possible without the intervention of America and concessions
by America.

THE French press is already beginning to criticise the
London terms. Happily the French Chamber will not
meet until the die has been cast and until Germany has
either accepted or refused. In both cases the criticism
of the Chamber will come too late. This is fortunate. As
it is, the ill-humour of *Le Temps* and other journals will
do a good deal to reconcile Germany to the terms.

LONDON, *May* 9, 1921.—The biggest fights of the recent Conference took place over the following points :

QUITE at the beginning Lloyd George and Briand nearly broke over the question whether the Germans should be given an ultimatum allowing them six or eight days in which to comply, and thus avoid the occupation of the Ruhr. Briand eventually gave in about this, but not willingly.

ANOTHER great fight was between Loucheur and myself about the French demand that the gold reserve of the Reichsbank should be transferred to occupied territory as a guarantee. I said this proposal was insane—it would probably cause a crisis in German exchange, and would be resented throughout Germany as an evident attempt to destroy the financial fabric. The finances of the whole of Europe were in so delicate a condition that no such experiment could be justified. While, on theoretical grounds, it may be true that the main cause of value in all paper currencies is the limitation of supply rather than gold backing, I felt that no opportunity could be less favourable than the present to test this theory. Financial nerves were too over-strung.

ANOTHER fight took place in the Finance Sub-Committee over the question whether German indebtedness not represented by issued bonds should carry interest or not. Loucheur maintained that French public opinion would never stand the annulment of interest on so large a portion of the debt. After considerable discussion I gave in, basing myself on the ground that it would only make a difference to Germany at the end of a very long period and that before then some new arrangement would be entered into.

LLOYD GEORGE took up the point in the Supreme Council and urged, with considerable force, that Germany would never agree to a clause under which she had to pay interest. Finally, the point was submitted to a new sub-committee, which I did not attend. They discussed vehemently for

a couple of hours and brought back a draft, which was
incorporated.

THE next day it was discovered that this draft did not clearly
establish the principle that Germany was not responsible
for interest. Indeed, it said just the opposite, so at the
last minute fresh words were added clearly establishing
that, except from some adventitious sources, no interest
was payable by Germany on this balance. It was fortunate
that this error was detected, as it meant a liability on
Germany for an annual sum of 16 millions sterling during
about fifteen years.

THE fact is, in these conferences, so much work has to be
cramped into so short a space that enormous issues are
decided in a few minutes, and drafts are agreed to without
adequate consideration. In this Conference the Financial
Sub-Committee were given, at midnight, two drafts by
the Reparation Commission, each of about four typewritten
pages of foolscap, to review and revise before the next
morning, when the final signature had to be appended by
the plenipotentiaries. We discussed one of these drafts
for three hours. This was the financial ultimatum ; but
the other document, which was a modification of the
powers of the Reparations Commission, we had to take
as drafted by Sir John Bradbury. There was no possibility
of revising it.

SIR MAURICE HANKEY, the Secretary to the Cabinet, who
came in to the Treasury Conference Room at about 1 a.m.,
when everybody was arguing vehemently on the financial
draft without much order or method but with deafening
noise, said he had formed the impression that we must
all be mad. Montagu, who attended many of the meetings
of the Financial Sub-Committee but who does not know
French—in which the discussion was mostly conducted
—said it made him sigh for the peace of the parrot-house
at the Zoo. In reality the discussion was not other than
sensible, and the outcome was a document of moderation

and wisdom ; but to an onlooker who does not understand the language, any vehement discussion appears a wrangle of maniacs, just as a Stock Exchange appears Bedlam to the uninitiated.

BERLIN, *May* 9, 1921.—I returned to Berlin this morning and found that Kilmarnock had just sent a most important telegram to London.   This telegram read as follows :

" DR. STRESEMANN has just been to see me.   Although he did not expressly say so, he is evidently contemplating assuming office as Chancellor.   He told me that party leaders of parties forming Government were practically united in thinking that Germany should accept terms of Allies, and hoped to be able to persuade their party committees to approve this policy, but their final decision must depend on clearing up of following points, about which there was considerable obscurity :

" 1. AUTHENTIC information was required as to interpretation of protocol delivered to Germany by Reparations Commission as regards passage dealing with alteration of paragraph 19, annex 2, of Part VIII of Treaty of Versailles.   Phrase at end of first sentence of communication of Reparations Commission runs, ' or to enable any Allied Power to proceed with restoration or development of industry or life.'   Question is whether this applies only to restoration of damage caused by war or whether it means that any Allied Power could at any time require Germany to deliver any goods necessary for development of its industry or economic life.   Latter interpretation would mean that any Allied Power, e.g. Italian or Serbian, could four years hence demand delivery by Germany of twenty ships or 1,000 agricultural implements.   Such a position would paralyse German industry to such an extent that its acceptance would be impossible.

" 2. WITH regard to section 9 of conditions notified to Germany by Reparations Commission, explanations are asked for as to whether it is intended that ' GermanReparation (Recovery) Act, 1921,' shall remain in force indefinitely or whether condition notified in this section is merely intended to cover period of transition until Act in question can be repealed.   It is understood that German Ambas-

sador in London has received some communication from Mr. Lloyd
George on this question, but exact purport is not known.   Anxiety
exists as to whether, in the case of England, German industry would
be burdened to a greater extent than the 26 per cent. now imposed.

" 3. WOULD sanctions imposed on March 8, especially those involving occupation of Düsseldorf, Duisburg, Ruhrort, etc., and
Rhine customs be cancelled in event of Germany accepting terms of
ultimatum ?   Stresemann pointed out that such acceptance involved
very heavy responsibility, and would meet with strong opposition,
and unless Government which assumed responsibility were able to
point to some definite alleviation which had been gained they would
not be able to obtain majority in Reichstag.

" 4. STRESEMANN said that morning papers reported British and
Italian representatives on Upper Silesian Plebiscite Commission
had reported in favour of Pless and Rybnik and a part of Kattowitz
district being given to Poland and the remainder of plebiscite area
being allotted to Germany.   French representative, on the other
hand, was reported to wish allotment of whole of industrial area to
Poland.   He recognised, however, regretfully that, in view of large
Polish majorities in districts said to be allotted to Poland in British
and Italian reports, those areas must be regarded as lost to Germany,
but if she retained greater part of industrial districts, he thought that
by a great effort (group undecipherable) might succeed in fulfilling
economic conditions imposed by Allied ultimatum.   If, therefore,
he were assured that British and Italian Governments would stand
by proposals of their representatives (as reported in the press), he would
be ready to assume responsibility for the carrying out of economic
conditions.   Without industrial area, however, German industry
would be so handicapped that it would not be capable of assuming
those obligations.   Furthermore, any Government which accepted
Allied terms and then was faced with loss of region in question could
not last a fortnight.   Before deciding advisability as to whether it
would be possible for him to form a Government capable of carrying
through acceptance of Allied terms, he would greatly appreciate
some form of private assurance to the effect that His Majesty's
Government would not allow any solution of the question other than
that founded on report already made by British representative on
Plebiscite Commission.

" STRESEMANN spoke with great earnestness and moderation in a

I I

thoroughly businesslike spirit, and I am convinced that if he could be reassured on above points, he is persuaded that he can secure acceptance of our terms.

" IT is of the utmost importance that I should receive an answer at the earliest possible moment, as the question of forming a Government can scarcely be delayed beyond to-morrow."

I AT once telegraphed a further message, giving my views on the four questions raised by Stresemann, the object being to facilitate the formation of a Government decided to accept the Allied terms and capable of carrying through their execution.

WHILE I ventured to advocate a reply facilitating this solution, I confess I was not hopeful of anything speedy or of anything definite which would enable Stresemann to undertake the formation of the Government on an adequately solid basis.   My telegram read as follows :

" REFERRING to Lord Kilmarnock's telegram (No. 202), of the four questions raised by Dr. Stresemann, three appear easy to answer :

" As regards point 1, it is clear that clause mentioned can only apply to damage done during the war, otherwise stipulation would constitute a perpetual option and would be intolerable.

" As regards point 2, I believe it was discussed in conversation between Prime Minister and Dr. Sthamer, to which Dr. Stresemann might be referred.   As I understand the question, the 50 per cent. levy will remain in force until new scheme is working smoothly and until it is shown that collection in Germany is as satisfactory to us as collection in England.

" REGARDING point 3 it would seem that, as sanctions were applied for non-fulfilment of treaty obligations, they lapse naturally when these obligations are fulfilled.

" REAL point of difficulty is No. 4.   Germans state that no German Government which accepted ultimatum and did not succeed in retaining greater portion of industrial area of Upper Silesia would last a fortnight ; on the other hand, it appears singularly impossible to pledge ourselves in advance to any given solution.   Perhaps, failing a more positive statement, point might be met by a declaration that we shall adhere to strict and impartial execution of Treaty of Versailles in respect of destination of industrial area.

" I should be glad if your Lordship would inform me whether the above views meet with approval of His Majesty's Government.

" Dr. Stresemann and Schiffer are coming to see me to-morrow morning, and I shall have to see other party leaders in course of next two days.

" My general impression of situation is that chances are in favour of acceptance by German Government, the main obstacle to acceptance being recent events in Upper Silesia and uncertainty felt here respecting eventual fate of industrial area. A reassuring declaration from His Majesty's Government regarding Upper Silesia would probably settle the issue."

Berlin, *May* 10, 1921.—In reply to the telegram I sent yesterday, I received this morning a reply as follows :

" Your telegrams Nos. 202 and 204 of May 9.

" The questions raised by Dr. Stresemann affect, in the majority of cases, the Allies as well as ourselves. While, therefore, we are quite willing to state our own opinion and are communicating it to the Allied Governments with the expression of a hope that they will concur and will instruct their representatives at Berlin accordingly, we cannot at this stage commit them to full acceptance of our views.

" Subject to this reservation you may return the following answers :

" 1. The intention of paragraph quoted from communication of Reparations Commission was to enable the Allied Powers to receive payments in kind for other purposes than reparation of actual war damage ; no right is claimed of demanding particular articles which have already been manufactured, but only of placing orders on commercial lines in Germany for such articles to be manufactured and delivered and the value to be credited to German reparation account. This proposal was inserted at our suggestion, and was in no sense intended to injure German industries, but rather to make payment easier to the debtor by introducing a more flexible method. Moreover, it was contemplated that recourse to this method should be kept within narrow and reasonable limits, and that, if necessary, definite assurances on this subject would be sought by us from the other

Allied Powers, while any such orders must of course receive the prior approval of the Reparations Commission.

" 2. THE second question is one on which we can speak definitely for ourselves.   It was our intention to retain ' The German Reparation (Recovery) Act, 1921,' in operation in order to enable us to exercise the option of collecting sums due for reparation in the United Kingdom instead of in Germany, should we so desire ; but no increase in the total burden on Germany would thereby be involved, since it was not our intention to collect more than the 26 per cent. contemplated in the protocol.   The above explanation relates only to the policy of His Majesty's Government towards reparations from Germany, and does not, of course, affect our freedom as regards the general fiscal policy which we may find it necessary to adopt towards all nations irrespective of reparation.

" 3. THIS question was not specifically raised at the recent Conference, but in our opinion the sanctions imposed on March 8, especially those involving the occupation of Düsseldorf, Duisburg, and Ruhrort and the Rhine customs, ought to be cancelled in the event of Germany accepting the ultimatum, and we are communicating this opinion to the French Government.

" 4. SILESIA.—It is impossible, without prior consultation with our Allies, to give assurance asked for in concluding paragraph of this sub-section.   But in our discussions with our Allies German Government may rely upon our desire to pay due regard to the important German interests involved and to press for equitable settlement on basis of strict and impartial execution of Treaty of Versailles.

" WHILE Cabinet was sitting to-day, the German Ambassador called and was received by the Prime Minister, who answered the same questions, when put by him, in the above sense.

" BY far the most important consideration is that a German Government should be found able and willing to accept the terms laid down in London, and thus escape the calamitous consequences that will otherwise ensue.

" PRIME MINISTER further advised German Ambassador that if his Government decide to accept they should not attach any conditions to their acceptance.   This might provoke the very consequences which it is desired to avoid."

BERLIN, *May* 12, 1921.—Stresemann called upon me this

morning and I communicated to him the substance of Lord Curzon's telegram giving the British Government's replies to his four questions. Never did the communication of a diplomatic document cause greater emotion. As I read out one answer after another, it was evident that the communication from London was of profound importance to German politics. It appeared to me that what was going through S.'s mind was the reflection that, had the answer—so unexpectedly favourable in its tenor —been received forty-eight hours sooner, there would not have been a Wirth Cabinet, but a Stresemann Cabinet.

I said that I was glad the substance of the answers was so gratifying. No time had been lost, since His Majesty's Government had replied fully and specifically to his questions within a few hours of their reception. Such instances of almost electrical promptitude were rare even in the most efficient communities.

My impression is that the Volkspartei have an ardent desire to join the Government and will probably succeed in doing so. They constantly point out how essential it is that a party which is supported by 90 per cent. of the industrial world should not be absent from the Ministerial bench. How far it may be really desirable to have them there appears doubtful. There are strong arguments both for and against. On the one hand, they represent the most energetic and capable section of the capitalistic community ; on the other hand, they are at heart monarchical. Briefly, they are a danger both within and without, and I would sooner see Dr. Wirth Chancellor than anyone except Stresemann.

Berlin, *May* 12, 1921.—Tuesday was a hectic and agitated day—constant interviews with the party leaders, with the press, and with various intermediaries. Up to the last moment the issue of the vote in the Reichstag was doubtful. Not that the majority had any doubt as to the desirability of accepting the ultimatum, but that for party reasons no section wanted to bell the cat.   In the result, both the Social Democrats and the Centre, who constitute the majority, and who form the basis of the new Government, explained to the public that they only accepted office at a heavy personal sacrifice.   The new Government is not very strong either in ability or in Reichstag support, but it is frankly democratic and entirely free, or as free as any German can be, from the old Nationalistic views.   Wirth himself is an ex-schoolmaster, but has retained a freshness of outlook and a boyishness of appearance which would become his former pupils.   He is said to be largely under Erzberger's [1] influence and to owe his position largely to his secret support.

BERLIN, *May* 12, 1921.—The Reichstag last night adopted a resolution accepting without reservation the terms of the Allies, as determined at the recent Conference in London. THE final official figures for the voting show that 220 voted for acceptance, and 172 for rejection.

[1] ERZBERGER, Mathias.—In 1903 Mathias Erzberger, one of the youngest members of the Reichstag, emerged from obscurity by his attitude towards colonists in German South-west Africa.   His insistence on colonial affairs brought his whole party, the Centre, into disfavour in 1906, but Erzberger had achieved his object and was marked—he was only thirty-one—as a rising politician.   During the war he was sent on various missions to Stockholm, Switzerland, and Holland, his sensitiveness to the changes of political atmosphere making him particularly valuable.   In 1918 he was Foreign Secretary, and in the chaos which the Peace Treaty occasioned his prevision and firmness alone gave stability to Germany.
HE was assassinated on August 21, 1921, by Schulz and Tillessen, two members of a secret association.   The Coalition Government of 1919 had Erzberger as Chancellor of the Exchequer; it was his task to readjust Germany's financial affairs, to devise a system of taxation which would meet the enormous demands made on her.   Erzberger's brilliance could not avert oppressive taxation, and his schemes occasioned discontent, notwithstanding his true spirit of democracy and care for the people.   In the anti-royalist revolution of 1921 his position was not forgotten; he was a marked figure.

CHAPTER VII

WIRTH, RATHENAU, AND ROSEN—EASTERN AFFAIRS—
UPPER SILESIA

German experts on Turkey—Germany's new Foreign Minister—" A
benevolent tiger "—Krassin's visit to Berlin—Rathenau enters Cabinet
—Rabindranath Tagore's success in Berlin—Wirth's plea for Allied
forbearance—Bad reports from Upper Silesia—Maltzan on German-
Russian relations—Lloyd George on French security—Keynes on the
mark—England, Germany, and Asiatic policy—Talks with German
financiers on the mark—Rosen on the late war.

Berlin, *May* 14, 1921.—Had the opportunity to-day CHAP.
of a long talk with one of the most knowledgeable VII
men in Germany, a specialist on Eastern and Turkish May
affairs. 1921

His general view of the Near East is that the Turk is
naturally so conservative that the most advanced radicals
there are more the slaves of tradition and inherited ideas
than a Tory squire. Even the Young Turks were conservative. One of the strongest Turkish traditions was
respect for England, and my friend declares that both
throughout the war and even now the large majority of
the Turkish population are incurably Anglophile. They
detest the French, the Italians they call " Macaroni,"
while the Germans they never really liked on account of
their precision, although they respected their military
efficiency and their ability and readiness to supply bak-
sheesh.

During the war the Turk proved an expensive Ally.
A large portion of the German gold reserve had been poured
out in Turkey, a long daily train of food had to be sent to
Turkey, and assistance of all kinds had to be given them.
If these refreshers had ceased, Turkish military assistance
would have ceased at the same moment.

In 1916, at a luncheon with the Kaiser, the latter had been
warned that Turkish affairs were going very badly for
Germany, but the representative of the General Staff,

Colonel Bauer, had violently interrupted, and had persuaded the Kaiser that it was otherwise.

My friend regards Turkey as having been one of the essential causes of Germany's downfall. " It was the grave of Germany." When asked what he meant by this, he replied : " I will explain how it all came about. In 1911 Kiderlen-Waechter,[1] who was a great friend of mine, had prepared a treaty between Germany and Russia, which treaty was based upon the sacrifice of Turkey. Kiderlen-Waechter did not dare put this treaty through without consulting Marschall, who was then Ambassador at Constantinople. Marschall refused it, both from considerations of policy and because he was a genuine Turkophile. So the idea of the treaty was abandoned and Russia was lost to Germany. That was one of the ultimate causes of our disaster.

" Again, in 1914 it was, in last analysis, a great mis-fortune for Germany that the *Goeben* and *Breslau* got into the Dardanelles. If they had happily been stopped, Turkey would not have come into the war. The war would then have lasted a few months. Germany would have been beaten, but defeat would not have been the catastrophe

---

[1] von Kiderlen-Waechter, Alfred.—Kiderlen-Waechter's hostility to militarism made him personally disliked by the Emperor ; he was essentially a diplomatist, though not Chesterfieldian.

In 1852 Kiderlen-Waechter was born in Würtemberg, the home of South-German spirit of independence and democracy. His strong personality and unconventional style made him prominent, if not always popular, in German political circles. His capable handling of the " Kaiser crisis " in 1908 when he was acting Foreign Secretary proved his ability, and in 1910 he became actual head of the Foreign Office.

The East claimed much of his interest, and he hoped at one time to succeed Baron Marschall von Bieberstein as Ambassador at Constantinople ; dis-appointed, he turned his attentions to Anglo-German relations, and it was his attempts to break up the " Entente Cordiale " which led to the famous Agadir incident. A lesser statesman would have been sent into retirement by the unfavourable results of that act of aggression, but Kiderlen-Waechter was too indispensable and his determination too assured. His death, more than a year before the outbreak of war, deprived Germany of a strong intelligence.

that it is to-day, a catastrophe which it will take a hundred years to repair."

FROM another reliable source I hear that, even with the *Goeben* at Constantinople, the Turks were only manœuvred into the war against their will, by Enver Pasha, by Talaat Pasha, and by Germany's diplomacy.   At last, after immense difficulty, on October 27, 1914, the German Embassy secured from the Sublime Porte an order for the German Admiral on the *Goeben* to sail north and attack the Russian coast.   The order came to the German Embassy sealed in an envelope addressed to the Admiral. An official, against the will of his colleagues and of the Ambassador, broke open the letter in order to be sure what it contained.   When he had read it, he determined not to send on the original to the Admiral, but sent a copy, together with a verbal message through a naval officer.   This was enough for the commander of the *Goeben*, who set forth and attacked Odessa.   Two days later —October 29—there was a report all over Constantinople that the *Goeben* had been defeated or sunk.   The Russian Ambassador had been to the Grand Vizier to protest against the attack.   The Grand Vizier, thinking the *Goeben* had been sunk and that the Turkish written order had sunk with her, had the face to deny that any order to attack Russia had been given.

As soon as the German Embassy heard of this, an envoy went to Yeni-Keui, saw the Grand Vizier, and said to him : " The order of which you deny the existence, because you think it was sunk with the *Goeben*, is in a safe place.   It is at the German Embassy at Therapia.   Pray cease to deny that the Turkish Government has given the order to attack Russia." The Grand Vizier turned deadly pale, but did not thereafter dare to deny the existence of the order.   The Russian Ambassador left Constantinople.   Turkey was at war with the Entente.

THE Grand Vizier was genuinely against the war, and was

Anglophile. Of the eleven Ministers, six voted against declaring war, but Enver, Talaat, and German diplomacy were too clever for the majority and forced their hand.

My informant says that the English are the only people who can do anything in Turkey. The others will never inspire confidence nor gain authority. " With all your mistakes, you have not really lost the position."

GRAF WOLFF-METTERNICH [1] had been recalled from the Constantinople Embassy at the instigation of the Turkish Government because he could not be cured of the pernicious habit of protesting against Armenian massacres. He had caught it in England. The Grand Vizier had said to him : " I should like to know who you imagine you represent—Germany or Armenia. We cannot tolerate your perpetual reproaches."

BERLIN, *May* 18, 1921.—All sorts of stories reach me from Upper Silesia concerning the outrages committed by Korfanty's [2] Poles.

---

[1] WOLFF-METTERNICH, Count Paul.—Wolff-Metternich's policy of moderation during his years in London proved unwelcome in Berlin, and the Ambassador was sent into retirement on the succession of Marschall von Bieberstein. For eleven years Metternich had sincerely done his best to overcome difficulties, but the question of Germany's naval power taxed all his abilities as a diplomatist. Count Metternich urged that the continual increase in the German Navy was the real impediment to better relations between England and Germany.

METTERNICH tried to make compatible his own patriotism and his desire for England's friendship ; his own views, which were dependable because always expressed with extreme caution, earned for him appreciation in England in spite of his reserve, which gave rise to certain " hermit-like " traditions.

AFTER the Agadir incident, the Imperial advisers urged increase in the size of the Navy, and Metternich's counsels of moderation became particularly unwelcome. With these influences at work, Wolff-Metternich soon gave way to Marschall von Bieberstein, and retired in some disfavour, though he was later dispatched to Turkey to nurse Germany's policy there.

[2] KORFANTY, Wojciech.—Korfanty's interests were centred in democracy and the freedom of the people. In 1902 he contravened the laws of the press and was imprisoned for four months, and three years later he took a violent part in the religious controversy as a Catholic.

IN 1921, when the League of Nations ordered a plebiscite in Upper Silesia,

GENERAL NOLLET, who certainly cannot be accused of being pro-German, but who is an honest old fellow and a good soldier, is reported to be none too pleased with what has occurred.

BERLIN, *May* 19, 1921.—The German Government appears so far to be determined to carry out their obligations under the ultimatum with vigour and without reserve. I doubt if they can keep up the pace for long, but, for the moment, the initial momentum of the Reichstag vote is carrying them along.

BERLIN, *May* 26, 1921.—Events here have moved very fast and, in regard to reparations, most satisfactorily. Since the vote in the Reichstag on May 10 and the installation of Wirth as Chancellor, the German Government have shown not only good faith but almost alacrity in carrying out their obligations in respect of disarmament and reparation. More progress has been made in a fortnight under Wirth than in a year under Fehrenbach and Simons. So far this action does not appear to have aroused any particular hostility. Everyone is glad that the menace of the Ruhr has been removed.

IT is too soon to say much about Rosen, the new Foreign Minister. Two days before he was appointed, Wirth said to me : " Rosen may not be the kind of man I want." He was eventually appointed as something like a " Hobson's choice," also largely on Socialist support, particularly

Korfanty came to the fore—he was then High Commissioner for Poland—against the threatened domination by Germany. With an organised force, Korfanty occupied the whole of the south-eastern part of Upper Silesia. For a time the rural districts were indisputably in his possession, and the Allied forces sent by the League of Nations were forced to retire to the towns which were reduced to idleness. Prompt reinforcements and Korfanty's difficulty in paying and controlling his followers ended inevitably in the failure of the insurrection. The economic results showed a great loss in output, but Korfanty had succeeded to some extent in demonstrating the Polish hatred of German domination in many of the districts.

that of Breitscheid, Independent Socialist, who is the guiding star of Socialism in foreign politics.

ROSEN's appearance is that of a somewhat sleepy and benevolent tiger, with a secondary suggestion of slyness. Talking to him is rather like playing chess with an automaton. As you speak you get no indication whatever from his facial expression or from his eyes what impression your words are making. Finally, when you stop speaking, he replies with " Queen to queen's eighth—checkmate," or some other pat with his paw, and relapses again into feline self-concentration. He is an authority on Persian literature and art, as well as an exponent of Oriental calm.

JUST at the moment the Germans appreciate English advice —we are for the time being popular and influential.

BERLIN, *June* 1, 1921.—Krassin [1] has been here during the last week and has had meetings and luncheons and dinners with various German industrials. He appears to have won their ear to some considerable tune, but what precisely he offered or settled is not clear—nothing very definite, probably. The present policy in Moscow appears to be to

---

[1] KRASSIN, Leonid.—Krassin was born in 1870 at Kurgan, Siberia, where his father was a civil servant. As a student in the Technicological Institute in St. Petersburg, the young Russian actively engaged in revolutionary movement, and was for this reason expelled from the Institute in 1891. He then returned to Siberia, where he became associated with Lenin. In 1897 he went to Berlin to complete his technical education at the Charlottenburg Politechnicum. From Berlin he took an active part in organising revolutionary societies in Russia. After the Bolshevik *coup* in 1917, Krassin was appointed by Lenin Commissar for Foreign Trade, and in this capacity he was responsible for the creation of the Soviet State monopoly of all foreign trade. In May 1921 Krassin was sent by the Soviet Government to establish relations with the Government in London, and was there successful in negotiating a trade agreement by which for the first time the sovereign status of the new Government in Moscow received international recognition. Krassin was appointed Ambassador in Berlin in 1922, and Ambassador in Paris in 1924. He was transferred from Paris to London in the course of the following year, and died in London in 1926.

create capitalistic islets in a communistic sea, and Krassin
promised to see that capitalists who exploited these islets
should be afforded the necessary labour.   Labour would
be paid according to the standard communistic rates, but
special inducements in the way of food or boots or caps
would be allowed to remunerate extra work.   The impression Krassin left here was that Moscow was going to
abandon the communistic basis as rapidly as possible, but
in proposing this policy Lenin had met with violent opposition from certain quarters.   I hear from another source
that the appearance of Moscow has already somewhat
changed and that signs of commercial activity are apparent.
Krassin praised Lloyd George very warmly to his German
audiences.

THE result of these interviews does not appear to have
been to arouse any hopes in the German breast of a regenera-
tion of Russia through German industrial support.   The
leaders of industry here recognise fairly well that they would
be too weak if alone and would lack the necessary political
backing.   They regard it as essential to have England
and America with them in their Russian enterprises.

BERLIN, *June* 1, 1921.—Rathenau has been appointed
Minister for Reconstruction.

WIRTH considers this a great stroke, since he regards
Rathenau as the best speaker in Germany and as a genius
on industrial organisation.   Others say that Rathenau
brings no political support and is so theoretical and fanciful
that his presence in the Government is certain to lead, at
no distant date, to violent conflicts and not much practical
result.   I myself rather incline to this view, although I
like Rathenau personally.

IN appearance he is a compound of Lenin and Trotsky,
and I am not sure that his face has not moulded his opinions.
He had the misfortune to be born to wealth and to be at
the head of a large industrial undertaking, but he could be

on occasion as ruthless as Snowden looks, while he has not the same intellectual balance.

BERLIN, *June* 1, 1921.—Spent most of the day with Sir Harold Stuart, who is on his way through to Warsaw and Oppeln. He seems clear-headed and sensible and goes to Upper Silesia with an open mind. The principal point appears to be to obtain very definite instructions from the French and Italian Governments to their military commanders that force must be used against the insurgents. It is ridiculous to have troops in Upper Silesia in a situation like the present, paralysed by instructions that in no case are they to use their arms. It is worse than the militia in Pitt's time, who were enlisted under the condition that they should only be sent abroad in case of actual invasion. I AM rather pleased with the new team we have in Upper Silesia. Both General Henniker and Colonel Wauchope are cool, sensible men. The former team in Upper Silesia, though they have done their work gallantly, appear to me stale and over-strained. They have had a most trying and difficult job. A cat may look at a king, but a French major-general may not be argued with by any colonel. And our representatives were colonels.

BERLIN, *June* 2, 1921.—Rosen asked me to come and see him this morning. I FOUND him in a condition of great nervousness regarding the parliamentary fate of the Wirth Government. He said : " We have done marvellous things towards carrying out the ultimatum, but we have got very little in exchange. Can the English Government not say something regarding the cancellation of the sanctions of March 8 (occupation of Düsseldorf, etc.), or regarding the fate of Upper Silesia ? "
IT is not quite true that the Allies have done nothing to recognise the loyalty of the measures carried through by

Wirth. The saving of the Ruhr, the dispatch of a large English force to Upper Silesia, are definite material results.

THE internal trouble here comes from the fundamental antipathy between the Volkspartei and the Socialists. The assistance of both is wanted to make the Coalition strong enough to carry through the reparation programme, but the simultaneous support of both is almost unattainable through their mutual distrust and animosity. Stresemann himself would be amenable. But his followers are less directly interested and are afraid of losing votes to the Nationalists. Wirth, who inclines personally pretty much to the Left, would be glad to do without the Volkspartei, but he finds his democratic supporters shy of appearing in Socialist company without the respectable backing of the industrials behind the Volkspartei.

BERLIN, *June* 3, 1921.—Rabindranath Tagore, the Indian poet, was here to-day.

A BEAUTIFUL specimen of the apostle, with flowing hair and beard. More impressive in appearance than most of the conceptions of Christ. A slow, smooth, quiet voice, which rather charmed me. He has had a tremendous reception in Scandinavia and Germany. Helen went to one of his readings yesterday, but not only could not get into the room but could hardly get into the street, so great was the crowd.

TAGORE says he has talked with most of the intellectuals here and finds the German mind looking about for some new philosophy to replace militarism. He appeared surprised when I told him that the universities—both professors and students—were considered very monarchistic and bellicose. His experience with the philosophers had been rather that of weariness with the old pre-war conceptions. He had been greatly impressed by the depth of hatred against the French and by the relative popularity of the English.

With some exceptions, all the Germans he had discussed the matter with had expressed confidence in our generosity and sense of fair play. Even Stinnes had said to him : " They are a great people, and at heart generous when they are not misled." Tagore had been surprised how little abuse of England he had heard, considering his own nationality and reputation. He gave it as his opinion that the result of the war had been a great coarsening of feeling throughout Europe, a greater indifference to disorder and to human suffering. To him all Europe is alike ; one European is like another European ; our culture and our characteristics are similar : no European realises how much identity there is, nor how small are the divergencies between countries whose main stock-in-trade consists of nationalistic antipathies.

BERLIN, *June 5*, 1921.—The naturalness of some of the newer European States has a certain attraction. The representative here of one of these States is married to a lady, who startles the official mind by saying : " We have been married two years, but we were together four years before."
QUITE a child of nature.

BERLIN, *June 5*, 1921.—Wirth is showing great courage and determination. He is loathed by the Nationalists and there is considerable jealousy against him on the part of the Volkspartei. They cannot get over not being in the Government ; at the same time they cannot muster up courage to join it.
THE Government complain that they have not obtained from the Entente sufficient recognition of their good behaviour regarding the ultimatum and reparation, but this is unjustifiable. The tone of Briand's speeches has completely changed, and Barthou has declared that the 1919 class will be liberated at once. I am almost surprised at

the rapidity of the response from France. All this constitutes progress compared with a month ago. I doubt if
this is sufficiently realised here.

THE war increased the German's respect for, and his dislike
of, the English, but has done nothing to diminish his
belief in his own superior sturdiness compared with the
French. This will continue subconsciously and sub-
cutaneously whatever happens—even though France
possesses an overpowering army and the Germans have no
organised means of resistance. I was struck by this basic
feeling when I was here in 1900. It is just as strong now.

WHAT does it proceed from ? The inherent distrust and
contempt of the slow man for the quick—of the sturdy,
solid, masculine sense for the nimble and graceful intellect.
The world has always believed that slow is sure—and no
one is more convinced of this than the slow themselves.

BERLIN, *June* 6, 1921.—Had a long talk with the Chancellor
last night.

HIS chief theme was that it was a great mistake on the part
of the Allies to speak of their policy " towards Germany."
There was not one Germany, but two Germanys. The
right policy depended upon whether the Allies were faced
with a democratic Germany which sincerely desired peace
and work and reconciliation, or by a country led by reactionaries or Communists—both of the latter appeared
to prefer catastrophe to commerce. In the past, sufficient
distinction had not been drawn between the two conceptions.
He hoped, now democratic Germany was in the saddle,
and had declared her resolute will to a wise policy, that
the good intentions of his country and her proofs of performance would be recognised by friendly assistance of
a palpable and demonstrable character. There was no
need to fear extreme measures from the Majority Socialists.
They were really of the small bourgeoisie type—not
Socialists in the ordinary sense. Put something in the

12

stomach of the working classes of Germany ; let the German public see that the German democratic policy had brought about an easier fate for the Fatherland, and all would be well.

THE Chancellor continues to make on me the impression of a very sincere man of great courage, faced by an almost impossible task in which he both requires and deserves assistance.

BERLIN, *June* 9, 1921.—The German Government persevere in making great efforts to carry out their obligations under the ultimatum, and their policy has been supported in the Reichstag by a large majority. In the realm of financial fact they have paid over approximately 50 millions sterling to the Reparation Commission in Paris—partly in gold, partly in Treasury bills. They have continued the process of disarmament with commendable rapidity, and they have obtained from Bavaria a satisfactory undertaking respecting the disbandment of the Einwohnerwehr. This is a big result for a month.

WITH regard to Upper Silesia, which, as I have stated, forms an exception to the above favourable picture, although nothing definite in the way of pacification can be announced, yet the firm attitude of His Majesty's Government and the careful direction of British policy in Upper Silesia give ground for the hope that the period of hesitation and prevarication is past. The general opinion of our best officers in Upper Silesia is that it only requires resolute action in conjunction with the Italian and French forces to clear out the insurgents.

BERLIN, *June* 9, 1921.—Had a conversation to-day with a member of the German Foreign Office, who is considered the best authority here on all that concerns Moscow or emanates from it. He said :

" THE Soviet Government is still spending a large amount

of money on propaganda in Germany. There is no good in attempting to stop this. If it is stopped in one direction, it will be spent in another. I don't think, however, they are making much headway or many converts. But they are none the less continuing to spend money and to appoint agents. I see no reduction in their propaganda expenditure nor any sign that they are getting near the end of their available resources for evangelistic purposes. Jewels and other valuables are still going to Holland and America. They would sell them here, but our people cannot afford to pay the price. The danger from Communism in Germany is certainly less than it was, but it must not be neglected. Compared with last August there is improvement—great improvement. Last year the whole of Germany would have become Bolshevik if Warsaw had fallen. That is quite certain—I can prove it by documents, chapter and verse. At that time the Bolsheviks had succeeded in capturing or hoodwinking the Nationalist organisers here, telling them that Russia and Germany must work together to throw off the Western yoke. All our extremists on the Right took the bait. At the same time, Moscow told their Communist friends in Germany, ' We will only employ the Nationals until we have won the position ; then we will cut their throats and enjoy ourselves in a Communistic paradise.'

" The German Government has a list of the proposed Communistic committees which were to rule Germany. Radek was to be the head. In Danzig the organisation was complete and the Communists were already marching out to meet their brothers from Russia.

" Curiously enough, a letter has just come into my hands from another source giving an account of a recent interview between General Ludendorff and an envoy from Moscow—an ex-officer of the Russian army—which goes to show that the same combination is being engineered again.

" As to the present condition of the Russian army, the German view is that they have no capacity for fighting outside Russia, and, generally speaking, are war-weary and unwilling to engage in foreign adventures. Otherwise they could not have resisted the temptation of falling on the Poles during the trouble in Upper Silesia, since hatred and under-valuation for the Poles is ingrained in all Russians, whether they are Communists or Imperialists.

" As regards the attribution or partition of Upper Silesia, Moscow favours the Polish solution, mainly because it is the worst available. The Poles, they believe, are certain to mismanage the industry—its collapse would be another capitalist failure ; this would redound to the advantage of Communism."

BERLIN, *June* 11, 1921.—A conversation with Dr. Rosen, the Minister of Foreign Affairs, yesterday.

HE told me that he assumed office with a great desire to improve relations between England and Germany. If this proved impossible, he would immediately resign. He advocated this policy, not out of affection for England— which he disclaimed—but because he regarded it as the wisest and safest course for Germany.   This did not exclude a desire for improved relations with France, which might follow as a corollary on improved relations with England. He had done his utmost to treat France as well as England and to allow no grounds for the suspicion that she was the least favoured nation. But this attitude required some reciprocity.

LONDON, *June* 21, 1921.—Luncheon with L. G. to-day, the only other person present being his private secretary.

I URGED the great desirability of doing something to assist the German Government in the Reichstag—some declaration regarding the removal of sanctions, or assistance for Upper Silesia.

L. G. replied : " As regards sanctions, I think there

will be a conference in Paris in July, at which we shall certainly urge the view that they should be removed ; but I expect, as Briand has only just succeeded in getting reparations through the Chamber, he is afraid to do much until the Chamber goes away for its holidays.

" RESPECTING Upper Silesia, I am anxious to save for Germany as much of the industrial area as possible, but I expect the French are heavily pledged to the Poles."

REGARDING control of German armaments after the disappearance of the Control Commission, I suggested international supervision as preferable to national. He appeared inclined to agree with the view that England should guarantee to protect France in the event of unprovoked attack by the Germans. He said, however, if we guarantee their security we must make it quite clear to them that there is to be no military hegemony of Europe and no operation of military adventure. We should have to put it very clearly that, if we guarantee them from attack, they must not provoke attack by aggressive attitude, and that they must restrain the Poles. It was a choice, in a way, between an English policy and a Polish policy.

HIS idea is that once Russia gets on her legs again, Germany will join with her to resist French military domination, just as France joined with Russia to resist German military domination.

TALKING over the reparation question, I said that its partial settlement appeared a great achievement. The Prime Minister said we only arrived at it by successive stages and numerous conferences. We brought the French gradually down and round to our terms : a large section of French opinion was much incensed at this. " They accused me of hostility and they accused you of having brought the Germans round to acceptance by making promises re Upper Silesia. These suspicions are quite groundless, but probably you and I are the two most unpopular men in France to-day."

BERLIN, *June* 29, 1921.—Before leaving London I met Keynes and had some discussion with him regarding reparations. He claimed some credit for having urged the Germans to accept the ultimatum, and said that he had taken particular pains to have his article advising acceptance telegraphed in full to the German press. He went on to say that while he had recommended acceptance he did not believe that Germany could pay the amounts stipulated. He anticipated that at the beginning of next year Germany would find it impossible to make the necessary remittances. In his opinion, German exchange would continue to fall, his anticipation being that it would drop, on an average, one point per day for the next two or three years, until it arrived at 1,000 marks to the £ sterling.[1] The mark had only been maintained at its present level owing to the large speculative purchases of marks abroad, particularly in America. These speculative purchases would now almost certainly cease, and there was nothing to stop exchange falling rapidly.

I VENTURED to point out to Keynes that his anticipation of the future was based upon very uncertain psychological factors. How was it possible for him to say that people who previously bought marks because they vaguely thought that Germany was a great country, would now cease to do so ? I should prefer to base anticipation upon something more physical, such as the amount of notes issued from the German printing press. The amount of these would be determined by the attainment or non-attainment of equilibrium in the German budget, so that exchange really depended in the main on German State finance. Speaking generally, I was more hopeful than he appeared to be, since payments on account of reparation were fairly well settled for the present year. The subsequent burden might be met in

[1] As a matter of fact, exchange soon fell much more rapidly. Later, the mark fell catastrophically, reaching in October–November 1923 the level of Mks. 18,000,000,000,000 to the £ sterling.

part by some credit transaction, if no other means were
available. But reparation in kind would go a longish
way if coal were counted at its world-price and not at an
unduly depressed internal German price.

TURNING to the general subject of exchange and world-
prices, Keynes said that he was now in favour of some
inflation. He had formerly been in favour of deflation,
but the correction had gone too far, and he saw no in-
consistency in now urging that deflation should certainly
be stopped even if the engine was not reversed. It seemed
to him necessary to adopt this policy to get the commerce
of the world again in movement.

I FOUND that, speaking broadly, Keynes takes a similar
view to Professor Cassel. These are the two best authorities.[1]

BERLIN, *July* 1, 1921.—The Italian Ambassador came in
to-day and told me that he had written very strongly to
Sforza regarding Upper Silesia, insisting upon the fact
that a bad solution for Germany in Upper Silesia meant
the fall of the Wirth Government, while the fall of the
Wirth Government meant chaos and the loss of all the
ground gained for general pacification during the last
two months. Like everyone else who talks about the
" Sforza line," Frassati has not the faintest idea what the
line is. I am beginning to doubt whether it exists. Three
days ago I asked the German Foreign Office to send me a
map showing the " Sforza line " and the original Anglo-
Italian line. I shall be surprised if they have any idea
what is meant by the words they use.

BERLIN, *July* 3, 1921.—All information that comes here
from Moscow points to the increasing strength of Lenin

[1] FIFTEEN months later, Professors Keynes and Cassel were brought to Berlin
to advise the German Government on finance, largely on Lord D'Abernon's
advice. They presented (November 7, 1922) an admirable report, which
was ignored both by the German Government and the Allies.

and his relatively moderate party.   The Bolsheviks continue to spend a good deal of money in Germany on propaganda.   Most of their literature comes here through the messengers of the Ukraine Mission.   Their communications with France are said to be done through the French official Government couriers.   In England, Moscow continues to subscribe to the *Daily Herald*, and is in negotiation for two weekly papers, which will start with more or less moderate views and gradually become Bolshevik.

THERE are constant reports of Bolshevik and Turkish activity in Central Asia and Afghanistan.   A meeting is to be held in Munich next week on this subject, with the assistance of a Sinn Fein delegate and with the possible assistance of a Deutsch National.   It is difficult to say how much importance should be attached to these meetings, but the agents of disturbance in India appear very active and well supplied with funds.   Certain reports speak of purchases of aeroplanes, to be shipped from Italy.

ALL the Young Turks in Berlin—and they are pretty numerous—are thoroughly disgruntled and frightened by the acquittal of the assassin of Talaat Pasha,[1] and by the evidence given at the trial by German officers who served with the Turks during the war.   General Liman von Sanders and others gave evidence to the effect that Talaat connived at—if he was not the real cause of—the Armenian

---

[1] TALAAT PASHA.—Talaat Pasha was born of mixed Turkish and gipsy blood near Kirjali in 1870.   Educated at a secondary school in Adrianople, his first official post was a minor clerkship in the Ministry of Posts and Telegraphs. At Salonika he became acquainted with the leaders of the Young Turk movement, and after the revolution of 1908 he was elected Deputy for Adrianople.   In 1911 Talaat was prominent as one of the strongest supporters of the " Ottomanisation " of the subject races of the Turkish Empire.   He took a leading part in the *coup d'état* of January 23, 1913, and as Minister of the Interior conducted the subsequent peace negotiations with the Bulgars. Talaat was largely responsible for the Armenian massacres which followed the entry of Turkey into the Great War.   As Grand Vizier, Talaat was one of the Turkish plenipotentiaries at Brest-Litovsk.   After the collapse of Turkey, he found a refuge in Berlin, and there he was assassinated by a young Armenian on March 15, 1921.

massacres. The tendency of the evidence of German
officers was that his assassination was justified, and this
evidence settled the verdict.

BERLIN, *July* 4, 1921.—Rosen spoke to me to-day on the
subject of Talaat's assassination, saying that the Turkish
students here had all threatened to leave Germany as
a protest against the acquittal. The Minister of Justice
proposed to issue a statement giving his view of the
acquittal.

I TOLD Rosen that the matter was one for the German
Government to settle, but he would do well to remember
that public opinion in England was sensitive about Asiatic
intrigues, and there appeared to me a good deal going on
in Central Europe between the Turks and Russians and
Indians which was not of a desirable character.

BERLIN, *July* 6, 1921.—The prospect of a settlement in
Upper Silesia appears to have improved during the last
few days, in the sense that both Germans and Poles have
moderated their pretensions.

ON the German side, they recognise they must lose Pless
and Rybnik, together with a stretch of agricultural territory
along the northern border of the frontier. They still
hope to obtain the whole of the industrial area, and there
will be violent dissatisfaction if any considerable portion
of this is taken away.

ON the Polish side, I hear from a friend who has just come
from Warsaw that the more sensible people there consider
the Sforza line as the maximum they can hope for.

TALKING the matter over privately with a French business
man this morning, he fully recognised the economic folly
of giving any valuable industrial property to the Poles,
but he said : " In France we are inclined to regard the
Poles as heroes. They have a romantic and sentimental
attraction for us. When I was at school I remember

that the master who taught us German badly—and who happened to be a Pole—was regarded as a demi-god. On the other hand, I fully recognise that they are quite incompetent in business affairs, and if any industrial territory is taken, the fullest guarantees must be exacted that it shall be worked not by them but by others." I should not be surprised if the French have taken adequate precautions of their own for replacing Polish industrial incompetence.

BERLIN, *July* 6, 1921.—Another talk with the German expert on Turkish affairs.

REFERRING to the war period, my friend says that in May 1915 the Russians very nearly came out of the war. They had demanded as a condition of treating with Germany, that the Turks should agree to certain concessions to Russia, about the Straits, about the coal-mines of Heraclea, and two or three other questions. The Germans obtained these from the Turks, and the deal was to be that Russia would make peace provided Germany obtained for her these conditions from Turkey. But the negotiation broke down because Italy declared war, and the German confidential agent could not go from Constantinople to Rome to negotiate with de Giers,[1] who was charged with the whole operation.

REGARDING the pre-war period, my informant says that already in the spring of 1914 he knew war was coming, because he discovered that Russia had succeeded in obtaining a dominant influence over Rumania. The Czar had seen Talaat at Livadia in May 1914 and had said : " I want to make a new Balkan Federation in which Turkey shall be included. If the Turkish Government agree to this, you need not negotiate with St. Petersburg ;

---

[1] DE GIERS, NICHOLAS.—A distinguished member of the former Czarist diplomatic service. Russian Ambassador at Constantinople and Rome ; Minister for Foreign Affairs.

you can negotiate direct with Bucharest." The day after the Czar had said this to Talaat, Sazonoff endeavoured to minimise it, but that only made the Czar's slip more significant, and showed more clearly that Russia dominated at Bucharest.

GOING further back in the history of German diplomacy, my friend said that Kiderlen-Waechter in 1912 had determined to make an agreement between Germany and Russia, naturally on the back and behind the back of the Turks. This agreement, which was more detailed and better thought out than the Bismarck re-insurance Treaty of 1887, was already initialled, but Kiderlen-Waechter fell into disgrace with the Empress and the Empress's clique—first because he did not pay enough attention to them, and secondly because he lived with a very low-class woman. They said : " Let us have a man who pays more attention to us."

THE opposition of the Court finally killed Kiderlen a good deal before his time. Another thing that helped to kill him was the Emperor selecting Wangenheim for the Embassy at Constantinople. Kiderlen had intended to send Prince Ratibor. The moment Wangenheim arrived at Constantinople he arranged the Military Mission to Turkey under General Liman von Sanders ; that was the event that really settled the fate of Germany in the World War. The Czar had telegraphed to de Giers saying that as long as this German Military Mission was in Constantinople, cordial relations between Germany and Russia were impossible. It is interesting to compare this with the action of the Russian Government towards England in 1908–9, when they positively vetoed the idea of English officers reorganising the Turkish Army. It would appear that they adopted the same attitude towards Germany as—at another time—towards England.

MY friend told me that the fatal mistake of England in 1914 was seizing the Turkish battleships. If instead of seizing them they had sent them out to Constantinople with English crews, the feeling for England would have been so strong that the Germans would have had no chance whatever of getting Turkey on their side. Even as it was, most of the Turkish ministers were against coming in. With one exception they were all against the *Goeben* entering the Dardanelles, and it was only the popular anger with England on account of the seized battleships which encouraged the Germans to risk bringing the *Goeben* through the Dardanelles.

THE recent friendship of Italy towards Angora he attributes more to Italian hatred of the Greeks than to the pursuit of any direct advantage. He also attributes the co-opera-tion of Italy and France in Upper Silesia and other questions to the fact that the French attitude is more anti-Greek than that of the English, and, therefore, more in harmony with Italian prejudices. He says quite frankly that he wants England and Angora to come to terms, so that there may be no question of our giving way to France in Europe against concessions made by France in Asia Minor.

BERLIN, *July* 13, 1921.—Information from Turkish quarters suggests that the death of Talaat will remove a considerable obstacle to the union between Angora and Moscow. Talaat apparently fought for the view that Russians and Turks were necessarily enemies. No reconciliation between the two was possible. Enver [1] has no such persuasion, and

---

[1] ENVER PASHA.—Enver was born of humble parentage at Abana, near the Black Sea, in 1886, and received his military education at the Staff College at Constantinople, whence he went to Salonika, where he came into contact with the Young Turk movement. In 1908 Enver and Niazi Bey raised the standard of revolt with the object of restoring the constitution of 1876. Abdul Hamid yielded, and Enver entered Constantinople in triumph. From Berlin, where he was a military attaché, Enver returned in 1909 to Salonika to conduct a campaign against the reactionaries. He entered Constantinople and deposed Abdul Hamid. He commanded at Benghasi in the Italo-Turkish War, and in the war with the Balkan States that followed he com-manded, though with little success, the X Army Corps. During the course of the peace negotiations Enver removed the Grand Vizier Kiamil and

has always favoured close combination. About Kemal I know less, but the last notes from Angora have a strong flavour of Moscow inspiration, if not of actual Moscow drafting. Kemal and Enver are personally hostile to one another, but Kemal is practically obliged to fall back on Moscow both for ammunition and money.

BERLIN, *July* 14, 1921.—Dined last night with Rathenau to meet the Chancellor, the only other guests being Cuno,[1] of the Hamburg-American line, and Melchior,[2] the banker, both from Hamburg. I think the scheme was to make me realise how serious the position of the German Government would become if a rapid and favourable solution of the Upper Silesian question did not intervene, but this scheme—if it existed—was shattered by the fact that the

subsequently filled all offices with nominees of the Young Turk Committee. In 1914 Enver made himself Minister of War, and demanded and received in marriage the Princess Nadzie, the Sultan's niece. In the Great War Enver took credit for the successful defence of the Dardanelles, and gradually established himself as the absolute ruler of Turkey.

AFTER the Turkish collapse, Enver fled first to Germany, and then to Russia, where for a time he assisted Denikin to defend the independence of the Caucasus.

IN 1920-1 he was in Moscow, where he was appointed Director of the Asiatic Department by the Soviet Government. In 1922 he went to Central Asia after a quarrel with Moscow and assisted the revolt of the Turconians and Bokharans against Soviet tyranny, but was killed a year later in battle.

[1] CUNO, Wilhelm.—Cuno was a business man of high standing, the Chairman of the Hamburg-American Line, who, on the failure of the Wirth Ministry, was given the task of forming a " non-political " Cabinet of national reconstruction. It was unfortunate for Cuno that his office coincided with the French invasion of the Ruhr ; he was left to decide whether Germany would give way to French demands or attempt passive resistance. He decided in favour of this latter course. However, passive resistance had to be fed with paper money, and results on the mark were catastrophic. Moreover, Cuno was unable to induce German opinion to accept even the reparation compromise proposed by Great Britain. So, finally, he had to make way for a Stresemann Cabinet.

[2] MELCHIOR, Dr. Carl.—Dr. Melchior is one of Germany's greatest financial experts. In 1919 he was appointed a member of the German Peace Delegation, and became also a member of the Financial Committee of the League of Nations. He is a director of several German banks.

Chancellor was so tired that he could not take much part, while Cuno and Melchior, representing very important Hamburg interests, were both rather optimistic and took the line that the country was behind the Government in its determination to carry out the ultimatum.   Rathenau was more pessimistic, and said that negotiations for some modification of the ultimatum ought not to be delayed.

MELCHIOR rather surprised me by saying : " We can get through the first two or three years, with the aid of foreign loans, or possibly of further bank note issues. By the end of that time, foreign nations will have realised that these large international payments can only be made by huge German exports, and these German exports will ruin trade in England and America, so that the creditors themselves will come to us to request a modification."

RATHENAU said that his negotiations with Loucheur were going on satisfactorily.   He is to meet Loucheur again at Wiesbaden, but is evidently alarmed that England might take umbrage if Germany negotiated too much with France.   He said he was anxious to come to London at an early date.

RATHENAU inclines towards the issue of a German loan, the proceeds of which would cover Germany's indebtedness for the first few years, and would serve also to provide France with immediate cash.   In my opinion, this is all very well as an objective, but where could a German loan be floated ?   However that may be, negotiations on this basis, and the lure of immediate cash, would give France a reason for making concessions.   Briand, laden with gold, would have a good reception in the Chamber for concessions regarding the sanctions, and Upper Silesia.

RATHENAU's house in the Grünewald is a fantastic production.   He built it on his own plan, without an architect, but the result is hardly an encouragement for this excursion into freedom and independence.   The walls are decorated with most extraordinary frescoes, and one is met in the

entrance-hall by a gigantic picture of Adam and Eve,
the work of an advanced artist, apparently designed to prove
that if advanced art had flourished in the Garden of Eden
there would have been no question of a state of primeval
innocence.

BERLIN, *July* 20, 1921.—Rathenau appears to have gained
great influence in the Cabinet lately and to have become
something like Vice-Chancellor with special responsibility
for the reparation question, and to some extent for foreign
affairs.   So far I find him satisfactory, but he is subject
to constant fits of depression and imagines twice a week
that all is lost.

IN their present mood the German Government are more
or less ready to take advice from England.   I am by
no means confident that this tendency will last and am
wondering in what way the favourable wind which blows
to-day can be utilised for something permanent.   For the
moment I do not see anything specific which it would be
wise to attempt, but the subject merits consideration and
one should not let the opportunity slip.

BERLIN, *July* 20, 1921.—Information from Moscow, which
has come through Turkish sources here, goes to show that
Tchitcherin [1] regards co-operation between Turkey and

---

[1] TCHITCHERIN, George Valentinovitch.—By tradition and upbringing an
aristocrat, Tchitcherin became imbued with Socialist ideals in 1905, when
he was on diplomatic service in Berlin.   He at once gave up his appointment
and became associated with the Central Socialist Bureau in Berlin.

FOR a year he was an active organiser of combined German and Russian
Socialist activities, but these led eventually to his arrest and imprisonment
at Charlottenburg.   Tchitcherin's doctrines were unpopular in Imperial
Germany, and he was banished from the country, leaving for Paris and, later,
London.

FOR some years he lived in England and, at the outbreak of the Russian
Revolution in 1917, worked to secure the repatriation of Russian refugees.
When Bolshevik Russia was considered an enemy of England, Tchitcherin
was again imprisoned, eventually released and banished to his own country.
In Russia his diplomatic experience proved useful : he was appointed People's
Commissar and put in charge of the Soviet Foreign Affairs.   In 1922 he
headed the Soviet Delegation at Genoa and Lausanne.

Russia as likely to be short-lived in view of the inherent antipathy. This was certainly Talaat's view ; he was always writing to Angora warning them against Moscow. Enver, of course, takes the other line, and will do anything to consolidate an alliance between Moscow and Angora, particularly if it consolidates his private fortune.

THE Germans appear to have washed their hands, for the time being, of their Turkish friends, and the Turks, on their side, have become very anti-German.

WITH the Wirth Government in power I do not think any German intrigue against England at all likely, certainly not with the approbation of the higher direction. Some of the smaller emissaries may continue from acquired momentum, but what they do will not amount to much.

BERLIN, *July* 21, 1921.—German military experts say that gas would be overpowering against Orientals. If we had used it against the Turks we could have done what we liked. Similarly in India—a very small army with gas would hold the country. I do not know that they are particularly good authorities on these questions, but I am struck with the unanimity with which this view is held.

THEY consider that one of the many ways that Germany lost the war was in letting the gas secret out too soon. If they had kept it in reserve until gas installations existed in sufficient quantities, they could have broken through any line, but their own military commanders were more than sceptical about the success of the gas experiment.

BERLIN, *July* 25, 1921.—At luncheon to-day I met General Lecquis, who is talked of as a firebrand, and who is supposed to have been elected Commander of the Selbstschutz in Silesia in the place of General Hoeffer. In appearance, he is a peaceable old gentleman of agree-

able manners, and at first rather somnolent. But after
a glass or two of wine he wakes up, fights all his battles
over again, and talks very willingly on the exploits both
of himself and his Silesian division. It appears that he
commanded a Silesian division throughout the war. He
speaks very highly of their fighting quality, provided
you know how to handle them. His own system apparently
was to hold Mass before any big attack and to go through
the whole ceremony with his troops. He then addressed
them—not as Germans, or as Poles, but as Silesians :
that is what they like to be called. He became quite
excited in telling the story of Caporetto, in which battle,
he said, his division pierced the Italian line to a depth of
80 kilometres. He exulted in the fact that most of his
men captured two or three chickens, while every platoon
annexed two or three pigs, the possession of which he
appeared to regard as the height of human felicity. On
the general subjects of the war he talked sensibly, estimating
German losses compared with the English and French
opposed to them as two to three—a figure which exactly
corresponds with other returns in my possession. Against
the Russians the German losses were one to ten.

REGARDING the possibility of a rising of Germans in
Upper Silesia, or of a German *putsch*, General Lecquis
said there was no danger at all. If the Germans rose,
they would have no guns or heavy appliances, and the
Government could not give them any. The Poles, on the
other hand, would have all they wanted from Warsaw or
some other source. No military commander of experience
would dream of putting himself at the head of such a
foolish outbreak.

As regards the past, General Lecquis said that he had been
in Berlin for the last seven weeks, and not near Upper
Silesia. He had been utilised by Wirth to send certain
letters there, but these were of a quieting description. The
people trusted him, and he could make them understand

13

how foolish a rising would be. Though many of his division were of Polish stock, he still received letters from them on his birthday saying : " Vile German as thou art, we love thee still."

BERLIN, *July* 26, 1921.—Had a long talk yesterday with Rosen about the causes of the late war.

LIKE everybody else here he has a personal theory on the subject, and dates the unavoidability of the war from some special day or some special deed. His opinions are all the more worth having, as during the war he was in diplomatic posts with not much to do and, as he has, according to his own statement, neither virtues nor vices, he had plenty of time for reading. The explanation he gave was that it all dated from 1908, when Austria occupied Bosnia-Herzegovina. Iswolsky considered this a terrible defeat, and vowed from that date forward to get together a combination which would crush Germany and Austria. Rosen said that he could show me the documents which prove that this was the dominant cause throughout 1908–14 ; he can trace it from year to year. He said that he had opportunity to judge the Kaiser, but had no opinion of his mental ability or his capacity for any fixed policy.

ROSEN is a queer being, more like the cat in *Alice in Wonderland* than anything else. But I have agreeable relations with him. Unlike the cat—and also unlike the Oriental which he is—his temperament is monogamous and he pursues only one hare at a time. This is now England. But, by training in the old school, he has become an unconscious and instinctive blackmailer. He cannot ask you to dinner without saying : " If you don't come I shall ask your enemy and we shall concoct something disagreeable for you." This is a pure idiom, and means nothing more than an Englishman's saying : " Do come, old man."

CHAPTER VIII

THE PARIS CONFERENCE

Paris Conference refers Upper Silesian question to League of Nations—
Rosen on Anglo-German friendship—Rathenau and Wiesbaden agree-
ment—Rathenau's London visit—General review of German position
—Disturbing news from Upper Silesia.

CONFERENCE OF PARIS, AUGUST 8–13, 1921

THIS was another conference convened by
M. Briand to discuss the Turco-Greek War in
Anatolia, the famine in Soviet Russia, the
threatened financial and economic collapse of Austria,
and various questions relating to Germany's non-
fulfilment of the Versailles Treaty, e.g. in regard to
Disarmament and War Criminals. It was agreed
to continue the occupation of the three Rhine ports,
but to end the economic sanctions decreed in March
on September 15, should Germany have discharged
her obligations by that date.

BUT the outstanding problem of the agenda was
that of Upper Silesia. A plebiscite had been held
on March 20, under Art. 88 of the Versailles
Treaty, 707,000 electors voting for Germany, and
479,000 for Poland. On the other hand, more
communes had voted for Poland than for Germany,
and the Treaty of Versailles appeared to regard
the voting of communes as the deciding factor.
On the further plea that the industrial area,
or " triangle," as it is called, must remain indivisible, Mr. Lloyd George wished to assign it
to Germany, and M. Briand to Poland. There ensued a grave deadlock, which even the personal appeal
of the French President to all the delegates, who
visited him at his château at Rambouillet, failed to
remove. On August 13 a way out was suggested
by the Italian delegates, Signor Bonomi [1] and the

---

[1] BONOMI.—Played as a sergeant in the Alpini a valorous part in the war.
He was then a Socialist deputy. Shortly after the war, he broke with the
more Radical Socialists and became leader of the Revisionists or National

Marchese della Torretta,[1] and adopted by the Conference.   This was to refer the question of the dividing line between Germany and Poland in Upper Silesia to the Council of the League, under Art. 13 of the Covenant.   The League Council accepted the mission remitted to it by the Paris Conference, and entrusted the task of working out a boundary line to a sub-committee consisting of its Chinese, Belgian, Czecho-Slovak, Brazilian, and Spanish members.   This sub-committee drew a dividing line in Upper Silesia, which was in the nature of a distinct compromise between the British and French views, and cut across the famous industrial triangle, hitherto regarded as indivisible.   It stipulated, however, that for the next

Socialists.   Formed a Coalition Cabinet after the resignation of Signor Giolitti in the autumn of 1921.   Was present at the Cannes Conference, where he presented Mr. Lloyd George with a Memorandum asking for a defensive pact between Great Britain and Italy after the model of Mr. Lloyd George's offer to France and Belgium.   His request, however, was declined by the British Premier.   Signor Bonomi participated, together with his Foreign Minister, the Marchese della Torretta, in the chief international conferences of 1921.

[1] DELLA TORRETTA, Marchese.—A member of a distinguished Sicilian noble family which has given cardinals to the Church as well as diplomats and generals in Italian history.   Was Italian Ambassador in Petrograd, at the time of the Soviet revolution.   Thereafter was sent on various special missions, notably as Envoy to Vienna shortly after the war.   Became Foreign Minister in the Bonomi Cabinet in 1921.   Presided over the Venice Conference, which gave most of the " Burgenland " to Hungary instead of Austria.   Inclined to support French as against British policy in regard to Germany, reparations, and war debts at the Peace Conferences of January and August 1921.   Claims to have been the author of the proposal referring the Upper Silesian problem to the League of Nations.   Sought an agreement with Great Britain on the Albanian question, but quarrelled with Signor de Martino over the latter's pro-British tendencies.

Was appointed Italian Ambassador in London by Signor Mussolini at the close of 1922, and remained there until 1928.   Although he still took a pro-French line at the Paris Conference of 1923, he became gradually and genuinely an admirer of British policy, and showed great tact in avoiding serious differences between Great Britain and Italy over the conference and other incidents.   The end of his career in London was crowned with success in the shape of the agreements about the Jubaland, the Egyptian-Italian frontier, the Dodecanese, the Albanian, and other questions.   He, in fact, with Sir Austen Chamberlain, laid the basis of the present good understanding between London and Rome.

fifteen years the new political frontier should not constitute an economic or customs frontier for the national
products of the plebiscite area. These recommendations by its sub-committee were approved by the
League Council and by the Ambassadors' Conference.
This award pleased none of the parties concerned.

BERLIN, *August* 15, 1921.—There is a large colony of
Russian refugees at Baden-Baden, where I spent a few days
last week. They live there in poverty and discontent,
and appear to have little cohesion. Countess Kleinmichel,
who was one of the leaders in St. Petersburg society before
the war, and a very intelligent woman, says she sees no
signs of any ability or of any coherent policy among the
Imperialist refugees from Russia. In Baden they do
nothing ; in Paris they do little but quarrel with one
another. It is noteworthy that among these Russians
the hatred of Kerensky is far greater than the hatred of
Lenin or Trotsky. The latter they regard simply as
robbers ; the former they regard as the man who over-
turned all the foundations of order in Russia, and who
made the subsequent Soviet terror inevitable. Kerensky
had Trotsky in his hands and let him go. While Russians
of pure Slav origin idle or wrangle, the Russians of German
or Baltic origin all agree in the opinion that no reconstruction
of Russia from within is by any means possible. The
Slavs have little persistency and no organising ability.
Before the war, not only was every Ministry in St. Petersburg run by German brains, but in every estate throughout
the country there was some German factor or agent who
kept the more showy Slavs up to the mark and who supplied
the needful stability.

LESLIE URQUHART, who was here to-day on his way to
Moscow, takes the same view about Kerensky, whom he
considers as a charlatan of the worst description. He
puts him below the Soviets, and almost on a level with the
Armenians, whom he loathes.

BERLIN, *August* 15, 1921.—The decision of the Supreme Council to refer the question of Upper Silesia to the League of Nations has been fairly well understood by the German press, but their first impulse was to bemoan the postponement of a settlement and to make Germany out as a great sufferer, whereas it is quite obvious that Germany ought to be extremely satisfied with the event. There is an invincible tendency in the German character to complain, and their first impulse on hearing any news is to bemoan its effect upon their own fate. However, Rosen to-day was quite sensible and said that throughout Germany they were extremely grateful to England for the attitude she had taken. If the German press was not more vocal, it was that they thought silence would be more agreeable to London and more expedient in the diplomatic sense.

THE Italian Ambassador has returned from Rome full of his success in having brought Torretta round to a sound view on Upper Silesia. He says that he and Marinis had to work very hard, but, finally, Torretta was quite convinced of the necessity of adhering to the English policy out and out. Bonomi was also quite sensible. Nobody could explain Sforza's policy about Upper Silesia.

How much of the attitude of Torretta was really due to Frassati's action one cannot say, but there can be no doubt as to Frassati and Marinis having exercised their fullest influence.

FROM another source I hear that Barrère threatened Bonomi as he was starting for Paris that France would not renew 49 million francs of Treasury bonds which fall due soon, unless Italy stood by France in the Upper Silesian question. Bonomi was rather alarmed by this menace and was only kept up to the scratch by Torretta.

BERLIN, *August* 19, 1921.—Rathenau came to luncheon to-day and we had a conversation afterwards.

HE said : " We have succeeded in getting together the

necessary funds for the payment of the milliard on
August 31, but we have put exchange down from 260
to 310 in doing it. Next November or next spring,
whenever a large payment comes, exchange will again fall
to a still lower level. This cannot go on. I am most
anxious not to arrive next spring at the position of saying,
'Germany cannot pay.' Therefore, I advocate Germany
discussing with each of her individual creditors what
are the best means of meeting the situation—whether
by payments in kind, by postponement, by loan, or
by any other means. I should like to get in touch with
some English financial authorities or with the English
member of the Reparation Commission. Loucheur will
not let me see the Reparation Commission in Paris until
my negotiations with him are complete. I resent this
restriction, but cannot afford to neglect it. Germany
could borrow now in neutral markets, and particularly
from Germans who have illicitly sent capital abroad and
who would be given an indemnity if they subscribed. If
we wait until the mark falls again to a new low level,
then we shall not be able to borrow. I say, therefore,
that we must deal with the situation rapidly, and not
suddenly find ourselves close to a due date for payment
without means of meeting it."

BERLIN, *August* 24, 1921.—The German Government is
constantly reverting to the alleged fact that there could
not possibly be in Germany a Ministry more friendly to
England than the present one.
THE effects of England's attitude in the Upper Silesian
question, of the Prime Minister's speeches, and of our
conduct of the negotiations in Paris, have not only made a
great impression on public opinion, but have even brought
the Right round to the extent that there is now in their
papers hardly any criticism of England. This attitude
will certainly last as long as the Upper Silesian question

is under discussion. Apart from cupboard-love, I think that most of the Right—with the exception of extremists like Helfferich and Westarp—recognise that England has adopted a fair, and even a magnanimous, attitude towards Germany.

IN addition to considerations drawn from the politics of the day, a good deal of weight attaches to recent revelations regarding Bismarck's attitude from 1887 to the end of his ministerial career. His inclination—one might almost say his determination—to conclude an arrangement or a treaty with England is clearly shown in Eckhardstein's three volumes, and even greater importance is attached in literary circles to the story of negotiations between Beaconsfield and Bismarck contained in the last volume of Beaconsfield's Life. The Right are, therefore, able to rely on Bismarckian authority for a change in their anti-English attitude. There appears little doubt that the mainspring of opposition to an arrangement with England between 1895 and 1905 was the Emperor William, and was due in no small part to his dislike and jealousy of King Edward VII and his personal hostility to Lord Salisbury, whom he suspected of irreverence towards the dynastic and imperial prerogatives in Germany.

BERLIN, *August* 25, 1921.—Peace Treaty signed between the United States and Germany. It contains no mention of the League of Nations or of the question of responsibility for the war. The latter omission will assure it of great popularity here.

BERLIN, *August* 26, 1921.—Erzberger assassinated.

BERLIN, *August* 29, 1921.—I have been a good deal in the minor intellectual world here lately, and have had interesting talk about Nietzsche, Wagner, and others.

WAGNER is said to have been a great drinker ; the man with

whom he lived in his early years of poverty—Wille—used
to boast that he and Richard (Wagner) often finished off
two bottles of cognac together. Wagner spoke with a
very common Saxon accent and was inclined to coarseness
both in language and in choice of subjects. In fact,
Nietzsche, who was sensitive on these matters, ultimately
broke off his friendship largely on this account. He also
ended by thinking Wagner too much of an actor and something of a mountebank. Wagner was quite indifferent to
money considerations ; his affairs were managed for him
by his wife, Cosima, a daughter of Liszt, a woman both of
extraordinary charm and great financial and theatrical-
management ability. There is some ground for the view
that another reason for the quarrel was that Wagner was
jealous of Nietzsche's friendship with Cosima.

NIETZSCHE ended by becoming a confirmed slave to drugs.
He started life strong and athletic, but had an accident
riding, and was very weak and ailing from 1880 to the
time of his death, 1890. There is no ground for the view
that he was in and out of lunatic asylums through all the
last period. Up to 1889 he was quite sane ; once he went
into an asylum he wrote no more and never came out. Like
Schopenhauer, he was a pronounced misogynist ; but there
is a lady still living, of literary proclivities, who claims to
have been his mistress in the later eighties. After many
adventures during a long career, she now goes through an
annual course of recuperation by living for a month in a
state of nature in the Göttingen Forest.

REGARDING Schopenhauer, the story is that in his case
misogyny became accentuated after his journey to Italy,
whence he returned ill. German love of research is particularly active in regard to scandal and has traced out the
prescriptions which he used, in various chemists' records
at Munich.

ANOTHER reason for the estrangement between Wagner
and Nietzsche was Wagner's anti-Semitism, which became

acute towards the end of his life. The Jews here claim that he was himself of Jewish origin, his real father being a certain Semitic actor called Geyer. Wagner did not accept this view, nor does his appearance support it. But he had many Jewish tastes, notably a mania for violent colours, both in his clothes and in the decoration of his house. He seldom composed except when decked out in some fantastic garb, with a feather in his hat, while working in a room of startling crudity in colour.

IT would seem that there is no philosopher of real note in Germany at the present day. Nothing but men of the second rank. The Germans think very little of Bergson, whom they call a philosopher for the drawing-room or the boudoir.

BERLIN, *August* 31, 1921.—A few days ago I said that Erzberger's assassination might prove a blessing in disguise for the Wirth Government. This turns out to have been more true than I thought when I wrote it. I have good evidence that Erzberger was engaged with Scheidemann,[1] the leader of the Majority Socialists, and Breitscheid,[2] one of the leaders of the Independent Socialists, in a manœuvre to turn Wirth out and make Scheidemann Chancellor and Breitscheid Foreign Minister. Breitscheid is admittedly in very close touch with the French Embassy, and has recently been in Paris for a considerable time, in contact with Berthelot. The essential object of the French was

---

[1] SCHEIDEMANN.—Born 1865. A leader of the Majority Socialists. Perhaps the best debater in the whole Reichstag, although by no means its most popular orator. Formerly an extreme Socialist, he showed considerable moderation during his tenure of office as Chancellor.

[2] BREITSCHEID.—Born 1874. Leader of the Independent Socialists in Germany. Owing to his association with French Socialists and to the evident favours bestowed on him by the French Government and other French authorities, it has been suggested that he has pro-French tendencies. He enjoys, however, great personal esteem in the Reichstag, of which he is one of the most eloquent speakers. He is agreeable and intelligent and ambitious, but at the same time rather theoretical and academic.

to get Breitscheid appointed Foreign Minister. All these

schemes are brought to naught by the assassination, and if the next fortnight passes quietly, Wirth will come out of the episode a good deal stronger than before.

BERLIN, *August* 31, 1921.—Had a long conversation with Rosen yesterday, when he again reverted to the great importance of establishing better relations between England and Germany.

WHATEVER Germany might have done during the war—regarding Ireland, Turkey, and the East—the dominant objective of German policy all over the world must be to establish relations of confidence with England. No other consideration could be allowed to interfere with this essential object ; the encouragement of anti-English aims would not be tolerated. Stringent instructions had been given to German representatives abroad to avoid all connection with the agents of countries hostile to England. He wished to lay emphasis on Germany's sincerity and determination to carry out this policy. He had reason to believe that certain English Members of Parliament were of the opinion that Sinn Fein was receiving encouragement from Germany. This was entirely false.

To strengthen England was to strengthen the forces which restrained Continental militaristic ambitions. A powerful England could bring nothing but benefit to Germany.

BERLIN, *September* 24, 1921.—A long talk yesterday with Rathenau, who is still anxious to proceed to London at an early opportunity in order to discuss with English representatives an arrangement analogous to that which he has made with Loucheur. Rathenau fully recognises that deliveries of manufactured goods to England will be unacceptable, and that German deliveries on the competitive world-market would give rise to trade hostility.

His idea is, therefore, to deliver goods to Russia and other countries to the south-east of Germany which are largely inaccessible to English producers. Payment for these goods would be made by Russia and the other countries, not to Germany, but to England, and this would constitute reparation.

RATHENAU finds Loucheur easy to deal with and amenable to argument. Loucheur has seduced Rathenau by telling him he is a light in the naughty German world.

BERLIN, *September* 26, 1921.—General Allen, commanding the United States troops at Coblenz, has been here during the last two days, returning from a cruise in the Baltic. He says that the first time Washington have taken any interest in any question at Coblenz is over the new Control Commission, and that he is surprised at their energetic attitude. Allen is strongly in favour of America taking a more active part in the European settlement, believing that this will result in the certain triumph of Anglo-Saxon common-sense views. He says that in nineteen cases out of twenty—without previous collusion—the English and American delegates at Coblenz take identical views. The same rule would obtain in other cases.

BERLIN, *September* 29, 1921.—I gather that Stresemann does not propose to take office, but to put two or three of his party into ministerial posts. The reasons given are that his wild untameable nature is unsuited to the trammels of official life, and, secondly, that he has nobody who could succeed him as party leader. The real reason is that he would not take anything less than the Chancellorship. Unquestionably a big man, and he knows it.

BERLIN, *September* 29, 1921.—I hear from a very good source that the Poles are pressing Czecho-Slovakia to make an alliance. However, the first article of the treaty the

Poles had drafted was a guarantee of Polish territory as CHAP.
laid down by the Riga Treaty. This was naturally rejected VIII
in Prague, for, as my informant admits, every party and September
every class in Czecho-Slovakia is at heart pan-Slav and 1921
pro-Muscovite. It is asserted that nothing Czecho-Slovakia
signs or promises or says will ever make them reliable
against Russian influences. Those who know them say
that they might fight the Poles or the Germans or the
Hungarians or the Austrians—never the Russians.

BERLIN, *September* 30, 1921.—The present appears a convenient moment to review the general position in Germany,
and no better criterion can be taken than to compare the
state of things to-day with that of a year ago.

THE position as regards nourishment and clothing has
improved to a very marked extent. The supply of food
is much better and one no longer hears complaints of the
difficulty in obtaining adequate nourishment. The appearance of children has improved in a notable degree. It
is, however, true that the consumption of articles of luxury
and semi-luxury has fallen off compared with pre-war, but
from this it does not follow that public health will be en-
dangered or that the working capacity of the people will
be diminished.

FALLING-OFF IN CONSUMPTION IN GERMANY

(Figures per head of population)

	1913.	1920.	Decrease per cent.
Sugar (kilograms) . . .	18	14	22
Coffee and tea (kilograms) .	2·4	0·8	66
Tobacco (kilograms) . .	1·0	0·8	20
Beer (litres)	100	42	58
Wine (litres)	43	33	23
Spirits (litres) . . .	10	2	80

THE ability of the German population to submit cheerfully
to a large reduction of their pre-war standard of living is
probably due to the fact that during the war they were

reduced to a much lower level than that of to-day. The severe privations of the war period, regarded as preliminary training, must indeed have given the German population a distinct advantage as competitors with the populations of countries where nourishment and the consumption of luxuries were maintained among the working classes throughout the war at approximately a pre-war standard. In England the population probably expects to-day at least as much nourishment and as much enjoyment as fell to their lot before the war. They will be seriously disturbed if these are not forthcoming. The German worker, on the other hand, will be amply satisfied if he obtains 75 per cent. of his pre-war allowance of semi-luxuries. Assuming that this does not diminish efficiency, it is clear that on this count alone competition with Germany in the neutral market has become even more difficult than before. But other causes are in operation and further contribute to render competition with German production abnormally difficult. The various subventions granted by the Government, the effect of which is to cheapen production, may be cited among the reasons which enable Germany to underbid all competitors. Coal is made available to industry below cost price in England ; bread has been sold considerably below its open market price ; railway transport is offered below working costs. The German budget suffers in order to enable German commerce and industry to prevail.

As to external politics, the result of the last year has been a considerable aggravation of the hostility felt against France, and an even greater reduction of the hostility felt towards England.

THE essential reason for this change of opinion in Germany is the conviction that England has adopted a broad and reasonable attitude regarding reparation and also the whole problem of Germany's recovery. Our action in reference to Upper Silesia has been noted with particular

gratitude, and it is generally admitted that if the Ruhr
is not to-day occupied by French troops, it is to English
influence that this result should be attributed. In a speech
the other day, Dr. Simons, late Minister for Foreign Affairs,
is reported to have said : " Germany has no longer a fleet
or any colonies ; therefore all causes of rivalry with England
have disappeared. On the other hand, the militaristic
menace from France must remain a danger. Apart from
this, the English have shown that they are disposed to
view without alarm, and indeed with friendliness, the
restoration of Germany's commercial and economic position.
The French have shown themselves jealous and critical.
The best chance for Germany appears to be to act in
co-operation with the great Anglo-Saxon communities—
England and America—and to endeavour to regain her
prosperity by regenerating Russia in conjunction with these
countries."

LEAVING aside relations with the great Western Powers,
the views held in Germany regarding the smaller European
States are of less importance. Italy she regards without
resentment but without respect. Her immediate neighbours on the east and south she considers as of small
account. The Germans have always had a great contempt
for the Poles, and their feelings for Jugo-Slavs and Czecho-
Slovaks, though less pronounced than those held regarding
Poland, are not essentially dissimilar.

REGARDING Russia, they nourish vast hopes, anticipating
that Germany's economic recovery is more likely to come
from this quarter than from any other. They recognise,
however, that they cannot hope to be successful in Russia
without English support and English political prestige.

As regards Central Asia and Asia Minor, Germany
appears to have abandoned—at any rate for the present—
her ambition to play an important part in these countries.
She feels that activity there might lead to jealousy and
suspicion in England, and the task of gaining England's

confidence is now the dominant pre-occupation in Government circles.

WITH reference to their Allies during the war, it cannot be said that the Germans like them better or respect them more than their former enemies. Their disposition to worship force leads them to admire a victorious enemy rather than a companion in defeat.

THEIR bitterness against France is the result of post-Armistice bullying and blundering more than of defeat in the war. At the time of the Armistice there was little bitterness against France, but a deep resentment against England, mainly due to the hardships caused by the Blockade. To-day the positions are reversed.

GERMAN feelings towards America are distinctly cordial. They are inspired to some extent by a certain similarity of outlook regarding finance, and by the fact that America has taken little part in measures of compulsion under the Treaty of Versailles.

MILITARY DANGER

IT is many months since the possibility of a military campaign by Germany in the near future constituted a real menace to European peace. The operations of the Control Commissions, whose duty it was to destroy German armaments, have been carried through with such success that, in my judgment, Germany is incapable of entering upon a campaign against the Entente or even against an isolated France with the smallest chance of success. Unless some entirely new method of aerial or chemical attack is discovered, it would seem impossible for any country not possessing heavy artillery and an elaborate aerial equipment to sustain a campaign against a modern army. Germany does not possess these. It would also appear impossible, without long years of preparation, for Germany to create the necessary military equipment. She could not even begin to create it without the fact being

discovered by foreign observers. It must be remembered
that some two millions of factory and railway hands are
members of the Socialist party. The manufacture and
transport of war material for military preparations on
any serious scale could not escape their vigilance. Alarm,
therefore, regarding the immediate present is groundless,
and apprehensions which were justified when Germany
possessed a large military equipment are now completely
out of date.

THIS does not mean that Germany will never re-arm or
that the military danger is at an end for all time. It may
indeed be worthy of immediate discussion whether some
international organisation, probably under the auspices of
the League of Nations, is not necessary after the Control
Commissions have disappeared.

A GENERAL survey of the main events of the past year
goes to show that in most directions progress towards
restoration of normal conditions has been achieved.

THE Government is stronger and has less to fear from
extremists. It has declared deliberately for a policy of
fulfilment of its treaty obligations and is supported by
public opinion. Trade and industry have improved to a
marked degree ; the condition of the people as regards
food and clothing has become more normal, if still below
pre-war level.

REGARDING foreign policy, the attitude of the Government
and of the people towards England has definitely improved
and may be considered entirely satisfactory. Our advice
is frequently sought and generally followed. Against
France the feeling of bitterness has increased, but this
might be modified by a few months of wise policy on the
part of the French.

THE United States and Russia are the two other countries
which, after England and France, mainly interest public
opinion here. Much is hoped from both : from Russia,
extended commercial relations and the eventual opening of

14

a rich field where German order will be essential to correct disorder and the inherent apathy and incapacity of the Slav ; from the United States, not only financial and industrial help, but more common-sense and business method in international questions.   The contribution on the part of America will, it is hoped, confirm and reinforce the reasonable and, in many respects, magnanimous attitude which Germany has now learnt to expect from England.

BERLIN, *October* 7, 1921.—The more I consider the Wiesbaden Agreement, the more I am inclined to think that it may be fairly characterised as a swindle based upon a fallacy.   The swindle is provided by one side, the fallacy by the other.   But even so, it may pacify Europe, and we had better use our blind eye.

THE most curious fact about this agreement is that each signatory unconsciously cuts himself off from his favourite argument.   The Germans can no longer say that the ultimatum figure is excessive, since they assume the burden of a higher delivery.   The French cannot press the extreme urgency of repair to their injured limb, since they refuse to accept material for repair unless invoiced to them 50 per cent. below cost price.

BERLIN, *October* 7, 1921.—The Wilhelmstrasse is in a great state of mind about the news which they continue to get from Geneva and from Paris that the decision regarding Upper Silesia will be unfavourable.   They are convinced that the allotment of any portion of the industrial area to Poland will bring down the German Government, and that with the fall of the present Government will perish all English influence in Germany.   Perhaps too tragic a view.   While it is of the highest importance to keep the industrial area intact under German direction, this world will not come to an end, nor will English influence in Germany cease, if a small portion of the district is lopped off against compensation.

BERLIN, *October* 7, 1921.—Accounts from the occupied area state that French officers and French troops have modified their attitude and now appear almost to desire to gain favour with the population. This is probably due to the fact that we were becoming too popular in the area and the French too unpopular. The French have, therefore, taken a leaf from England's book, and orders from Paris have apparently enjoined a change of attitude. But this change is quite likely not to last. What Briand does, Pertinax will undo.

CHAPTER IX

FINANCIAL COLLAPSE IN GERMANY—CHAOS IN UPPER SILESIA

Upper Silesian intrigues at Geneva—Polish-Czecho-Slovak Treaty—German Jutland film—German bitterness against England on Upper Silesian decision—Lord Curzon's comments—Why the Kaiser fled—Reparation Commission in Berlin—Belgian delegate's attitude.

CHAP.
IX
—
October
1921

BERLIN, *October* 13, 1921.—What the orthodox treatment for suicidal mania may be I do not know, but I have exhausted nearly every drug of the pharmacopœia—licit and illicit—in preventing suicide by the German Government during the last few days. Such a severe fit of nerves that they have been on the point of resigning at almost every hour. To-day they have recovered their courage and self-possession to some extent, and are more inclined to stand and fight, largely because they have discovered that the enemy—in the shape of the Volkspartei—do not propose to shoot. Stresemann has behaved well and has not taken advantage of the Government's nervousness.

BERLIN, *October* 13, 1921.—The following from Geneva :
THE German witnesses were badly selected, and their evidence did not make a good impression. The German Government say that they did not select these witnesses, but that they were chosen by Geneva among elements notoriously in alliance with French interests. I have not been able to check the truth of this statement, and I dare say it is erroneous.
BERGSON, the philosopher, is said to have been brought to Geneva for A. J. B.'s delectation, in place of the traditional cocotte of French spy plays, and of Orpen's art.
THE general impression here is that England was outwitted at Geneva, and that the French used means of pressure which

we neglect.   That is as it may be, but the result is that
we have lost face.   Our out-and-out friends say that we
were fooled ; those less biassed in our favour class us with
Judas Iscariot.   But this is temper as well as injustice.
I CONTEND that, compared with the Le Rond line, Germany
obtains a very favourable solution.   Compared again with
the Versailles proposal to give the whole of Upper Silesia
to Poland, the gain to Germany through the P.M.'s intervention is enormous.   These comparisons must not be
forgotten.   But the only effective means to stop whining
here will be a louder whine from Warsaw or from Paris.

BERLIN, *October* 15, 1921.—Importance appears to attach
to the conclusion of the treaty between Poland and Czecho-
Slovakia, under which Czecho-Slovakia recognises the
French treaty with Poland and becomes virtually a party
to it.   The network of French influence is thus considerably strengthened and extended.   Only a year ago the
Czechs were violently hostile to Poland, and had only
one hope, namely, that the Soviet would blot them out.
The close agreement between Rumania and the two countries above mentioned is also a remarkable achievement
of French diplomatic activity.
WHAT precise line England should take under the circumstances is not clear, but the whole position requires careful
thought and discussion.
THE endeavour of the French to regain German sympathies
—so far as this result is compatible with the supreme duty
of getting paid—is also noticeable to an increasing extent.
They have succeeded so far here that many French plays
are now running in Berlin and a French boxer occasionally
knocks out, or is knocked out by, a German champion.
Such an event would have been impossible a year ago.
THERE can be no doubt that the Geneva decision on
Upper Silesia was a great blow to our popularity and
prestige.   The change of feeling is noticeable in Berlin,

and I hear the same account from Upper Silesia and still more strongly from Cologne.

BERLIN, *October* 16, 1921.—Saw the film of the Battle of Jutland last night. A very crowded house, but not much enthusiasm and a total absence of national anthems and so forth. The German public has no use for " honourable defeat "—it prefers victory at all costs. On the whole, the film appeared to me fair and to give a clear picture of the various stages of the fight. Great importance was given to the superior strength of the English fleet and their heavier loss, but otherwise the presentment was impartial. Beatty's signal towards the close of the fight : " Follow me, and we can cut off the whole enemy fleet," was made a feature ; stress was laid on the bad visibility and the terrible smoke which made it impossible, towards dusk, to distinguish friend from foe. The Germans assert that during the night their fleet, steering south-east, crossed the track of the English fleet, steering south, probably about 2 a.m., and passed unnoticed between the main body and the rear guard. At dawn on June 1 the fleets are represented as having been 65 kms. apart, the Germans to the east near Horn Reef, the English fleet due south from the scene of the battle. The final picture gave the German claim as to the result of the battle, namely, that Russia went out of the war and that the German coast was never attacked again by the English fleet. Neither result perhaps very direct.

NEXT week the same theatre gives a film called *Nelson and Lady Hamilton*. An amusing juxtaposition, but no irony is meant.

BERLIN, *October* 25, 1921.—The peculiar mentality of the German public is well illustrated by the present phase. To-day the vast majority of German politicians, including those friendly to England, believe that the recent course of events regarding Upper Silesia has been as follows :

ENGLAND had defended the German cause at Paris.   Lloyd
George had made eloquent speeches, and had asserted
the indivisibility of the industrial area—therefore Germany
was sure to get, if not the whole of Upper Silesia, at least
the whole of the industrial area.

BUT about three weeks ago something must have happened which caused England to change her mind, and to
abandon Germany :

EITHER London was displeased with the Wiesbaden
Agreement, or England required concessions from France
in Asia Minor, or England required French support at the
Washington Conference ; whatever the cause, this much
is clear :

ENGLAND sold the German birthright.

THE English delegate at Geneva no longer defended what
was defended at Paris ; the neutral representatives at
Geneva, misled by Beneš and shepherded by Hymans,
ratified decisions which had previously been arranged
in Paris to the detriment of Germany.

As for the economic concessions which the English newspapers claim to have obtained as a set-off to the bad frontier
decision, they are worth very little, and they were communicated to Germany in a form so dictatorial that it would
have rendered any concession indistinguishable from insult.

THE above is absurd, but it represents what high and low,
rich and poor, conservative and radical alike think, and
they think it with such unanimity that it is almost impossible to make headway against their illusions.   To
some extent I have brought Rosen round to realise what
nonsense this is, but he declares that he cannot make
anybody else take the correct view, and he himself hardly
dares state it.

BERLIN, *October* 26, 1921.—Cabinet formed by Wirth.[1]

---

[1] THIS was the second Cabinet formed by this statesman, who already, in
May 1921, had taken office as Chancellor, with a coalition of the Catholic

BERLIN, *October* 28, 1921.—The genius of the German language does not lend itself to compliments.

My caddie said to me the other day : " We boys were all talking about you."

" WHY ? "

CADDIE : " You are so old, and yet you drive nearly as far as Herr Zamek."

AND the champion Zamek said : " I am so happy when I with you play—it makes me rejoice that I so many years before me have in which I may yet golf play."

BERLIN, *October* 28, 1921.—Speaking generally, the lay public here are not as depressed or pessimistic as the politicians are.   The shops are selling enormous quantities of goods, partly to foreigners, and partly also to Germans. The banks are so full of stock-exchange orders that in one of them they are three days behind in opening their letters in the Stock Department.   Even the Upper Silesians are somewhat consoled for political disappointment by the rise which has taken place in their shares.   Of course the rise is unhealthy and feverish.   We cannot be very far from a panic.   As soon as inflation ceases to increase and deflation sets in, there will be the devil to pay.

BEHRENSTRASSE here, which corresponds to Lombard Street, reminds me of San Francisco after the earthquake.   Almost every bank is being increased or rebuilt, and one can hardly get along the roadway.

SOMETHING like the South Sea Bubble.

BERLIN, *October* 28, 1921.—There is no doubt that the Geneva decision regarding the partition of Upper Silesia caused surprise and not a little resentment in

Democrat and Majority Socialist parties, for the purpose of carrying out the Allied ultimatum of May 5.   On this occasion, owing to the failure of the political parties to reach an agreement, Dr. Wirth was entrusted by the President of the Reich with the coalition of a Ministry of Affairs, which would accept, under protest, the Allied Note on the subject of Upper Silesia.

certain circles in England. In the belief that the whole question would be referred to an independent tribunal, which would hear all sides and deliver an impartial judgment, England insisted on reference to the League of Nations. Without such faith as to impartial procedure England would almost certainly not have agreed to submit the matter to Geneva. Much rested on the decision—enormous issues were involved—and it seems incredible that the subject was referred to members of the Council who had not previously dealt with the question.

BERLIN, *October* 29, 1921.—I gather that Lord Curzon's view of German complaints as to Upper Silesia is as follows : SINCE the Armistice, England's greatest aim has been to do all possible to assist the recovery of Europe, including Germany, and anything likely to retard such recovery, such as the French extremist attitude and policy of revenge, has no sympathy from us. For some time we have pursued a course of friendly impartiality towards Germany, at times seriously imperilling our relations with France.

ON the question of Upper Silesia, England fought Germany's battle : we failed to come to terms with France, so we consented to submit the case to Geneva. Perhaps A. J. B. was too ready to accept a diplomatic compromise. But he declares the solution was the best one possible, and will eventually prove to Germany's advantage. Nevertheless, England had hoped for something different.

BUT the German attitude is preposterous—they turn round and abuse us, say that they have been deserted, that Britain is the enemy, and that as France has proved herself the stronger Power they had better side with her in the future. If this is the return we are to receive for a consideration which no victor has ever before shown to the vanquished, and which has earned us suspicion at home and abroad, there will be no encouragement to pursue it.

BERLIN, *November* 1, 1921.—To give the Crown Prince his
due, one has to admit that practically all those who have
been in any way associated with him, speak well of him.
They by no means wish to infer that he was a Solomon or
a saint, but rather that his outlook on affairs in general was,
and is, sensible and moderate. The Kaiser, on the other
hand, is let down less easily by his entourage, the general
opinion being that he was utterly unpractical, hysterically
enthusiastic about any idea which was his own—or rather
which he conceived to be his own—especially if there was
anything spectacular about it. At present the Kaiser is
fully convinced that within a comparatively short time he
will be reinstated in Germany.

WHY THE KAISER LEFT GERMANY

THE best defence I had heard of the action of the Kaiser
in leaving Germany reached me the other day from a
reliable source. So much has been written in condemna-
tion of his action that it is only fair to give the other side.

> IN Germany, as in other countries, one comes up
> continually against the regrettable fact that scarcely
> anyone understands the reason why the Kaiser went
> to Holland. Some military critics say : " It was a
> terrible mistake that the Kaiser left the army." The
> answer is : " That is a negative sort of charge ;
> please say what you think he ought to have done."
> To this it is replied : " He ought to have led his army
> back, and put his country in order." Good ! and that
> is exactly what he wished to do. But Field-Marshal
> von Hindenburg and General Groener informed
> him that he would get no troops to march with
> him ! This decisive factor still seems to be unknown
> to the people in general. Then again, others say :
> " The Kaiser should have met a glorious end on the
> front." This was a technical impossibility. The
> Armistice was to commence next day, and the Kaiser
> could not have reached the front in time. Also, the

whole lines of communication were Bolshevik, and
the Kaiser had to face one of two contingencies :
either to be murdered or to be taken prisoner by his
own troops.

LASTLY, it is said that the Kaiser should have taken
his own life.   Such action the Kaiser could never have
reconciled with his religious belief, and, had he taken
his own life, what would have been said about him ?
" Ah ! the coward ! So long as things went well
he had courage to live, but now he shirks the
ordeal, which is tantamount to an acknowledgment
of guilt."

LOOKING logically at the whole question, one comes
to the following conclusions :

(1) HAD the Kaiser remained at Spa, the probability
was that the Entente would not have concluded the
Armistice on the following day, for their main object
was the overthrow of the Monarchy, principally
the German Kaiser. Would the Kaiser have been
justified in taking that responsibility simply because
he wished to remain ?

(2) HAD we been able to find troops to march back
to Germany with the Kaiser, the supply trains would
never have been allowed over the Rhine. The
troops would have been starved, and civil war could
not have been avoided. Was blood to be shed thus
as well as at the front, just because the Kaiser wished
to remain ?

(3) IF the Kaiser had attempted to return as a private
individual, he could only have remained in Germany
at the mercy of the revolutionaries and under the
surveillance of scum in red ties. Further, the
surrender for trial of the Kaiser to the Entente would,
under these circumstances, have been a much more
simple question. Holland could protect him ; the
Germany of that time could not, and the greatest of
all humiliations, the surrender of their Kaiser, would
not have been spared the people.

No one should criticise the steps taken without
being in possession of the facts.   It should not be

forgotten that Hindenburg (then the responsible adviser of the Kaiser) besought him on November 9, 1918, to go to Holland—Hindenburg, the man whom everybody believed in, and of whom everyone then said : " What Hindenburg does can only be right."

ONE should also remember that behind Hindenburg stood the hundreds of officers who had been called to General Headquarters on account of their mental ability, and not one single one of these expressed any other opinion than that voiced by Hindenburg, which was : " There is only one thing possible : the Kaiser must go to Holland."

October 24, 1921.

BERLIN, *November* 6, 1921.—My view as to disarmament —a view I continue to put forward—is the following :

THE attitude assumed in certain circles that Germany, through survival or revival of her old military organisation and equipment, is to-day, or will be in the immediate future, a grave military danger to the peace of the world, is a Rip van Winkle conception, totally inapplicable to present circumstances. The military hegemony of the Continent is to-day with France. The size and efficiency of her present Army would alone be adequate to secure this ; but in addition to her own military organisation, she is believed to have created a chain of military alliances or understandings with Czecho-Slovakia, Poland, Jugo-Slavia, and probably Rumania, which enormously enhance her military influence and power.

THE question of disarmament and future control is affected fundamentally by the altered conditions of military force in Europe.

THE view has generally been held that, after the disappearance of the existing Control Commissions, some form of international observation, if not of control, should be established. With the exception of Art. 213, the

subject is not provided for by the Treaty of Versailles.
That article runs as follows :

" So long as the present Treaty remains in force, Germany
undertakes to give every facility for any investigation
which the Council of the League of Nations, acting if need
be by a majority vote, may consider necessary."

SINCE this clause was drafted and adopted, Germany
has been thoroughly disarmed and the balance of military
power has been further displaced by the above-mentioned
military agreements.

NEW dispositions are, therefore, necessary to meet the altered
circumstances.

As far as Germany is concerned, any future danger proceeds
less from military organisation on the old lines than from
possible discovery of some new means of attack—chemical,
aerial, or submarine. It is, therefore, of less moment to
push to the last dregs the destruction of old engines of
warfare than to obtain some organisation—international
and reciprocal—which will give timely warning of new
developments.

How this can best be secured is a question of great difficulty.
But it appears certain that an adequate system can only
be established by fresh negotiations ; it cannot be imposed
under Art. 213. Negotiations with France would probably include some measure of reciprocity.

IT is very necessary to recall the fact—so often forgotten
in current controversy—that the balance of military power
has entirely shifted since 1914.

BERLIN, *November* 11, 1921.—Rathenau said to me to-day:
" I feel convinced that there will be some kind of default
by Germany before next spring and that France will then
occupy the Ruhr. This means a total disruption of
Germany and the failure of English policy.

" I KNOW that England would object to the occupation of
the Ruhr and would protest, but we cannot expect that

England should break up the Entente or go to war with France to prevent the Ruhr being occupied. Therefore, it will be occupied."

BERLIN, *November* 11, 1921.—The arrival here of the Reparation Commission fell like a bombshell. At first, the Government was greatly alarmed and thought the Commission had come to establish a Turkish control. I told them that, in my judgment, the arrival of the Commission was favourable to Germany's view, if the situation was properly handled, which it probably will not be. The essential thing was for the Reparation Commission to be guided by a correct knowledge of the real circumstances and not by political preconceptions. The Germans were, however, pacified less by my arguments than by the rumour that Dubois, the French Reparationist, had to be brought here bound in chains, and that Paris was greatly alarmed lest the visit should lead to a moratorium or other concession.

THE Belgian Reparationist, Delacroix, seems to be ultra-practical. His main preoccupation is narrowly patriotic, i.e. to get the next two instalments paid, as they will be devoted in the main to satisfying the Belgian priority. He asked what chance there was of a loan operation. I said : " None, unless the loan operation gave solid ground for the hope that a real compromise on permanent lines had been arrived at. Nobody could be expected to put up money to stave off a crisis for six weeks. There must be something more serious than that to justify the effort and the 10 or 12 per cent. which the operation would probably cost." He agreed.

BERLIN, *November* 17, 1921.—What would happen in the (I admit unlikely) event of the ex-Kaiser making a dash and appearing on German soil ?

I HAVE discussed this question in private conversation with

people of all classes here. The Government officials scout the possibility and say that the lamentable failure of the Kapp *putsch* and the threat of a general strike if a *putsch* was initiated would certainly deter even the most extreme Monarchists from making an attempt, as matters stand now. Politicians of the Left also consider that a general strike would be declared directly any Monarchist return was threatened. Although the general atmosphere is certainly unfavourable to any attempt at violence, either from the Right or from the Left, such attempts are always possible from extremists and hot-heads. I am, however, impressed by the quiet confidence of members of all the Centre parties that nothing of the kind has any serious chance of success. It is thought that the Army would remain true to the Republic, although the officers are undoubtedly monarchist at heart. Discipline is fairly good, and could be relied on against a foreign foe, but the best judges appear to doubt whether the men would follow their officers if the latter desired to support a *coup d'état*.

BERLIN, *November* 20, 1921.—It is remarkable how nine people out of ten in political circles here rather favour a guarantee to France by England or America against aggression by Germany. They argue that Germany has neither the intention nor the power to attack France ; that France will not diminish her army unless she gets a guarantee ; that as long as she possesses the army she will dominate Europe and bully everybody. The minority who differ from these views say that France will never diminish her army below the level requisite for dominating Europe ; that, come what may, she will always wish to destroy Germany and secure at least the Rhine frontier, if not still greater territorial extension.

THE treaty between Czecho-Slovakia and Poland is thought a triumph of French militarism. So it may be, but the duration will be temporary, and effective validity is doubtful.

The Czech satellite will revert to the orbit of the Moscow planet as soon as disturbing forces cease to operate quite as powerfully as to-day.

BERLIN, *November* 20, 1921.—The Reparation Commission has come and gone. It has been in Berlin about ten days. ALTHOUGH the immediate result is negative, the visit has paved the way to a better understanding of the real position and to some probable compromise regarding a revision of dates of payment, once the matter of the January and February instalments has been settled.

THE problem is really to reconcile French public opinion with the inevitable necessity of relieving Germany during the early years. It is clear the process of adjustment must be painful and probably dangerous ; however, there is no alternative but to face it fairly promptly, otherwise the whole fabric of German finance and German exchange will collapse.

IT is remarkable in these international conferences how one is brought, compulsorily, to co-operate with the Belgians and to rely upon them. On this occasion Delacroix has really won the honours of the day, and has done more to press the French to take a sensible course than anybody else. He was stronglysupported by the American.

THE said Delacroix quite realises that blind insistence on immediate payment, which is Dubois's policy, must spell disaster. He is anxious that the refusal to pay should come, not from the German Government, but from English or American (probably also French) bankers, who would decline to make the necessary advances for the January and February payments unless the future course of German finance is made clear and secure. It is obvious that banks will have poor security, if they compete hugger-mugger with the Reparation Commission. Bradbury fully agrees with this view, but was apparently less firm in pushing it than Delacroix and Boyden.

Wirth does not seem to have made a good impression CHAP.
upon the Reparation Commission, either in respect of his IX
ability or his sincerity. He was neither very resolute November
in his expression of desire to pay nor very ingenious 1921
in devising means of payment. Instead of relying on
his own sound judgment he depends on some source
of inspiration which vanishes. It was first Erzberger,
who was assassinated ; it was then Rathenau, who was
prevented from joining the Government ; now he has
nobody, and is pretty much at a loss. The Germans
are astounded at his great reputation abroad, but I fancy
that he has civic courage—whatever that may mean.

Berlin, *November* 22, 1921.—A talk this morning, with
one of the most un-peasantlike Bulgarians I have ever met,
about Bulgaria in the war. " What was the Bulgarian
attitude in the early days of the war ? " He said :
" Bulgaria had only one idea—to be on the winning side.
Most of us thought from the beginning that the Entente
would win, but Ferdinand was out-and-out pro-German.
He completely fooled all the Russian representatives, and
particularly the Russian Minister for Foreign Affairs,
who said, ' I cannot doubt the word of a King when he
tells me he is friendly to Russia.' If the Dardanelles
expedition had been successful, Bulgaria would in all
probability have joined the Entente. Indeed, if the
Entente had sent any considerable force to Salonika, that
would have convinced Bulgaria that the Entente was to be
feared and would have brought us in on that side. We
could never get on with the Turks during the war. When
we fought together, the commanders had to put a German-
Austrian force between the Turks and the Bulgarians to
prevent their quarrelling. Bulgarians of this generation
cannot forget all the Turks made us suffer in the recent
past. We could more readily be friendly to the Greeks,
although they have behaved worse in Thrace than any

15

Turk would have done, forcing all Bulgarians to emigrate by every kind of ill-treatment and injustice.   If the Greeks abandoned Thrace or it was made into an autonomous State under foreign control, we might get on fairly with Greece.   In Macedonia our hostility is much more against Serbs than Greeks.   With Rumania we are fairly friendly."

BERLIN, *November* 24, 1921.—A long talk with Wirth.
WHAT he said did not really amount to much, but I got the impression that his Francophile inclinations had received rather a severe shock, particularly through the attitude of Dubois, who appears to have refused to discuss matters on a broad basis and, rather obviously, endeavoured to trap Wirth into a declaration that Germany could not pay the January and February instalments.   He also told me that Tirard, the French President of the Rhineland High Commission, had been to see him and had talked about developing cultural relations in the Rhineland between Germany and France.   Wirth had apparently replied that it would be time to talk about this when the Rhine ports were evacuated.
REGARDING reparations, he made me a longish " Reichstag " speech, but it contained nothing new.
I AM increasingly convinced that, however much Wirth understands figures, he regards them mainly as a peg on which to hang rhetoric.

CHAPTER X

ANOTHER LONDON CONFERENCE—TOWARDS CANNES

Foreign Office and 10 Downing Street—Rathenau's economic fallacies—
Reparation and German experts—A talk with Zionist leader—Rathenau
leaves for Cannes—Maltzan on Russian intentions—French pessimism
about reparations—Germany's Anglo-Saxon sympathies.

THIRD LONDON CONFERENCE, 1921

THIS Conference was held in London, from December 18 to 22. It was really in the nature of a meeting between Mr. Lloyd George, M. Briand, M. Loucheur, and British and French experts. It had been expressly convened for the purpose of considering the notification to the Reparation Commission made by Chancellor Wirth that Germany would be unable to meet the reparation claims upon her of the Allies under the London Schedule of Payment, which would mature on January 15 and February 15, 1922. Dr. Wirth announced that Germany could at the most provide a total of £10,000,000 in respect of these two instalments, of £25,000,000 and £12,500,000 respectively. No specific agreement was reached between the British and the French Prime Ministers in regard to reparation proper. But the French statesman urged strongly on Mr. Lloyd George in secret the desirability of curtailing Belgian priority in the changed circumstances, lest it should absorb entirely the reduced German payments to the special detriment of France. It was decided between Mr. Lloyd George and M. Briand that the Supreme Council should be summoned to meet at Cannes immediately after the New Year, and that this Conference should deal, not only with the immediate reparation issues, but with the scheme for the holding of a General European Economic Conference, which should consider the best means of restoring Europe by the co-operation of the nations. Meanwhile, through diplomatic channels, France had once more raised the question of the Anglo-French alliance designed to guarantee her security, and the peace of Europe.

LONDON, *December* 18, 1921.—The hatred of Poland by Russians and Germans—particularly by the Russians—is such that it has become ingrained and inborn. It would be as wise, or unwise, to make an alliance to defend all cats against all dogs as to engage to defend Poland against Russia and Germany.

A FAR better method of dealing with the question would be to create such an understanding with Russia and Germany as to give England, as a friendly Power to Poland, influence in directing their policy.

REVERTING to recent negotiations in London, it is difficult to ascertain precisely what Stinnes proposed or what was said to him. The impression in financial circles which he made was distinctly unfavourable, but his ideas for future co-operation in Russia may have found acceptance among certain politicians. The P.M., contrary to the general view, clings tenaciously to his original conceptions, or still more to his original prejudices, flies back to negotiations with Krassin like a fish to water, on the smallest excuse. Rathenau is, of course, in close touch with Moscow. Whether Stinnes subventions Moscow, as alleged, may be doubtful, but he has certainly a very well equipped secret service throughout Russia, and has probably made his plans for securing much that is valuable in the way of Russian concessions.

PERSONALLY, I regard immediate action in Russia as premature. For a long time to come, nothing of real value can come out of Russia, but it may be wise to prepare for the future position. Not much, however, will be lost by waiting, while a good deal of harm will result from precipitancy.

BERLIN, *December* 18, 1921.—The root fallacy of Rathenau and his school is to imagine that balance of trade is a cause

and not a result.   They say Germany has a debit balance
of trade, therefore she cannot pay this or that.   The truth
is that she has a debit balance of trade because she has not
been compelled to pay, has not been compelled to tax ;
because Germany is consuming more than she legitimately
could if she met her obligations.   What is in reality the
result of non-payment of reparations is put forward as a
proof of inability to pay.   It is not only the cart before the
horse, but the cart dragging the horse.

APART from the question of reparation and of the desirability
or the danger of obtaining for England certain quantities
of goods without payment, the most important problem
of the economic future is the equalisation of the cost of
production between Germany and, say, England.   If Germany can continue to produce goods for the English and
for neutral markets at 50 per cent. of their cost in England,
our trade in neutral countries is doomed, and our in-
dustrialists will only retain the home market when it is
protected by heavy anti-dumping legislation—a policy
which will accentuate their disabilities in neutral markets.
How to obtain equalisation of the cost of production is
admittedly a difficult problem, but it is clear that a first
step must be the removal of all indirect subventions to
German industry which enable it to under-cut foreign competition, while a second measure would be the levying of
such taxes in Germany as will bring the German tax level
to at least a parity with the tax level in England and France.
When the results of these measures and of tax reduction in
England have made themselves felt, it would be possible
to say more clearly how the industrial forces on the two
sides can be brought into fairer competition or possibly
into organised co-operation.   At present the difference
in conditions forms a handicap which is so great that no
close estimate of rival productive merit is possible.   Taxes
on one side, subventions on the other.   Even weights are
required.

BERLIN, *December* 18, 1921.—Interest during the last week in London was concentrated upon an article in the *Daily Chronicle* and on a speech by the Lord Chancellor. Both took the line that political economists and professors had estimated Germany's paying capacity too high—that nothing was to be made of the policy of the ultimatum—the only path to safety lay in a new conference to revise the whole question of reparation in conjunction with the general European economic position. To this conference Germany and Russia must both be invited.

FRENCH support would be essential. It would seem, however, that the policy itself is so contrary to French views that no agreement on the proposed basis can possibly be arrived at.

A VARIETY of schemes have been discussed during the week, but no scheme has been finally adopted. If America would come into the negotiation and would forgo her claim to be paid by Europe, an arrangement would be easy. But as she has steadily refused to adopt this attitude, and expresses annoyance at anyone who suggests it, this avenue is not hopeful.

THE idea is gaining ground in England that the demand on Germany for the payment of reparation can only be satisfied by an increased export of German goods, and that this increased export would destroy English industry. There is much which is inaccurate in this view. The true cause of the danger of German competition is not the demand for reparation, but the fact that German cost of production is infinitely below the British and American level. This is due partly to German workmen working more and getting less ; partly also to improved methods and improved economy devised during the war, but mainly to the fact that German industry is subventioned while ours is taxed. For Germany the war was a period of hard work at low cost on a bare subsistence. For us it was a period of high production at improved wages and on an improved

standard of living.   The English workers learnt to expect
more, the German workers learnt to expect less.   Add to
this high taxation which has to be paid in England, low
taxation which is not paid in Germany, and you have the
contrast.

IN so far as the payment of reparation affects the question,
the result of exacting payments must obviously be to increase
and not to diminish German cost of production, provided
the indemnity is paid by taxation and not by inflation, and
that the present practice of subventions to German industry
through insufficient railway rates, through coal, and through
food subventions is abandoned.   The idea that by abandoning the demand for reparation England would diminish
the danger of German commercial competition is ludicrous.
Exactly the opposite would occur : the danger would be
increased.

BERLIN, *December* 22, 1921.—The success of English
policy in Ireland and in Washington has altered the
atmosphere here.   The tone is as satisfactory as it was
before the Upper Silesian decision at Geneva.

DETAILS regarding the Prime Minister's proposal at the
London Conference are confused and contradictory, so
that no comments of value have been published ; but the
general impression is that the problem has been approached
on wide and liberal lines, so that the whole prospect of the
German—if not of the European—future has brightened.
Whether or not a solution is arrived at this week—and the
vastness of the scheme renders a rapid solution improbable
—so much fresh air has been admitted to the debating-
room that discussion should never again be restricted to
the prosaic and sordid details of reparation on the old lines.

BERLIN, *December* 25, 1921.—The President of the Jewish
Community at Jerusalem—Dr. Weizmann—has been to
see me two or three times.   He has been lecturing here

to get immigrants for Palestine and to supply the acutest need of the community—money. Germany can supply excellent Jewish immigrants, but gold—to the extent required, £1,000,000 a year—takes a deal of paper money.

WEIZMANN says the Jews here are mainly in intellectual professions—doctors, professors, lawyers ; in England they are all in business or politics. In Germany the Jews are not only much more a race apart than in England, but they differ from the native races more widely. In England natives have many Jewish qualities—fidelity to the given word, love of family, love of compromise, preference for surly manners and distrust of civility, rather glaring taste. Scotchmen are even more akin to the Jews. In Germany there are few characteristics in common, the Prussian conception of a negotiation being menace and blackmail.

I TOLD Weizmann the theory that the Old Testament was the essential source of " Prussianism," and that the pretension to be the " chosen people " and " salt of the earth " had been clearly stolen from Jewish tradition. He did not explode as I expected, but rather acquiesced, saying, however, that Prussians were really Slavs. " This theory," he added, " is to some extent borne out by the fact that in 1914 Jewish intellectuals in Germany were the most overbearing and aggressive Prussians of the whole crowd." He had been here then and had found them quite intolerable. To-day their tone was altered, particularly as regards England.

HE perceived an extraordinary change of public feeling regarding England during the last two years. There was an increasing desire to co-operate with us in Russia, and an increasing belief that considerable mutual benefit might result from this co-operation.

HE said that in 1914 the Kaiser's Government had a definite plan to utilise the Zionist movement for an extension of German influence in the Near East. This

he could prove by documents.   He might have added that
what they tried to do in 1914 they will conceivably attempt
again in 1934.

TOWARDS CANNES

BERLIN, *December* 29, 1921.—Rathenau came to see me
yesterday on his way to the train.   He has been sent for
to Paris, and will proceed to Cannes.   He anticipates as
a result of the Cannes Conference a rather bad partial
solution—something which will just work, but will not go
far towards final settlement.

HE considers that a whole year of conferences—financial
or economic—is required in order to educate public opinion
and to bring about a real comprehension of the position
and its necessities.   He does not believe that France will
agree to any real settlement until Poincaré has been in
office and has failed.   Briand's fall he considers inevitable,
and indeed indispensable to a solution.

As regards England, he was gratified by his reception and
was impressed by the ability of the people whom he saw.
He cordially endorses the Prime Minister's views regarding
Russia, saying that the sooner you begin negotiating, the
sooner you will arrive at some solution ; it is always so
much time gained.   This I consider very doubtful, believing rather that premature fidgeting with the question
delays any satisfactory solution.

RATHENAU views the economic position in England as
extraordinarily bad.   He sees no improvement in prospect
and anticipates increasing gloom and unemployment in
1922.

I ASKED whether the French were displeased with his
presence in London.   He said, " Not at all."   He had
four friendly conversations with Loucheur, and quite
understood that Briand did not wish to see him as it
might raise difficulties in the Chamber.   The French
knew that he (Rathenau) had pressed all the time that

England should make concessions regarding French priority, and in other ways meet the views of France. REGARDING the position in Germany, Rathenau was gloomy. He anticipates a very bad time when the " opium dream of inflation " comes to an end. There must either be an acute crisis or a prolonged period of depression.

BERLIN, *December* 30, 1921.—Maltzan called upon me this morning. He is again at the head of the Russian Department of the Foreign Office, after having been appointed Minister at Athens, rather against his will, by Rosen. Although generally considered very pro-Soviet and rather anti-English, he says that he has always co-operated with English representatives and has never taken any step regarding Russia without following the English example. The German Trade Delegation only went to Moscow six weeks after the English. He again declared to-day that his idea was to conform to our policy on all points.

MALTZAN'S view is that to form a big syndicate between the Great Powers would merely frighten the Russians, who would give it no concessions. He says: " Let us obtain concessions from the Russians individually; we can exploit them in common subsequently if that appears desirable. Individually we shall obtain much more than collectively. Only bring the Russians to a big conference if you know precisely what they will offer. Private conversations or a small conference must come first. Anything like a joint demand from the West is certain to be turned down."

MALTZAN says that the French negotiations with Russia since October have been devoted to the sole object of preventing Germany and Russia coming together. The French have spurred the Russians on to demand reparation from Germany. Germany, however, does not recognise that the Treaty of Versailles is binding upon her towards Russia. The Russians quite see the French game : to make sure that the Germans should know that negotiations were proceeding, they put the French courier in the same carriage as the German from Riga to Moscow.

BERLIN, *December* 30, 1921.—I gather that the French are expressing themselves to their intimate Allies in Central Europe in a very pessimistic sense regarding the outcome of the Cannes Conference. They say they will not be satisfied with anything except full payment, and that the prospects of payment by Germany are not bright. Whether this is their true view or not I cannot say, but it is certainly the language they hold. They no longer talk about occupying the Ruhr. Albert Thomas, the ex-Minister of Munitions, and a Socialist, at a dinner with some German Socialists the other day, told them that in his view the only way to improve relations between France and Germany was to have Poincaré as Premier. As his hearers expressed surprise at this view, he wrote it on a menu, dated and signed it, adding: " I am not drunk."

AGAINST French pessimism—real or professed—may be set German optimism. It is held that the mere fact of other larger questions being considered together with reparation is a great gain to Germany.

WHILE German opinion is inclined to be optimistic about the reparation negotiations, it is pessimistic regarding the trade outlook here for next year, and still more pessimistic regarding the outlook for trade in England. As regards Germany, leading people say : " We shall have a sad to-morrow when we wake out of our dream of inflation. Our present prosperity is fictitious and the result of drugs." Meantime, whether other branches of industry are prosperous or not, the bank note industry hums. Last week the total note issue increased another 4 milliards of marks—or £200,000,000 if calculated at the old par— roughly the total active circulation of England before the war. *Sic itur ad*—the Moscow or Vienna level.

BERLIN, *December* 30, 1921.—A long conversation to-day with one of the leading personalities here, who spoke freely on the express condition that his name should not be mentioned. He is one of the most influential men in the country.

HE said: " Rathenau is risking his whole reputation. If he comes back from Paris and Cannes without a success, he is a dead man. Stinnes has only one idea, to bring Rathenau down.

" IN my judgment, Germany can accept a great deal, and public opinion will support Wirth in accepting a great deal, provided he obtains counter-concessions. I mean, he could go pretty far in the direction of prolonged financial control, and even in the direction of prolonged military supervision, provided that in exchange for the first, time was given Germany to recuperate financially ; and provided that against the second the Rhine Provinces were evacuated, or some considerable measure of reciprocal control or disarmament was established.

" REGARDING Allied control over the Reichsbank," he said, " I do not myself attach much importance to it, nor do I think it would arouse opposition here, particularly if foreign capital is brought in to assist the Reichsbank. This would be a justification of foreign members on the Board, or foreign controllers. Allied capital to increase the strength of the Reichsbank would greatly facilitate negotiations.

" EVERY sensible person recognises that, although Wirth is no genius, he is the only possible man for the moment. But he can only be kept in power if he is able to show definite gain for Germany from his fulfilment policy. My meaning is that a good deal of give-and-take on both sides of the account is better than demanding smaller concessions from Germany and giving nothing in exchange. Give our Government orators something to talk about.

" As to currency, we cannot stop the issue of notes at

once. We are like an automobile which cannot be stopped in five yards, but I believe a limit to further issue of 50 milliards would carry us through our difficult period until the new taxes begin to come in, and that the mere fact of fixing a definite limit to the issues would do a great deal to restore stability to exchange. We all recognise that the deflation period is going to be disagreeable. We shall have men out of work, factories shut down, etc. But there has got to be a limit to printing notes—that we recognise. Do not pull us up too short ; give the car time to stop without skidding."

BERLIN, *December* 31, 1921.—Concerning the political attitude of the present Government, there can be little doubt that Dr. Rathenau's recent visit to London was productive of benefit, in that it strengthened the conviction of the Government here regarding the reasonableness and fairness of the English attitude.

EARLY in the year, England and the United States were the two countries to which the Germans looked with some degree of hope—and the same is true to-day. There have been fluctuations of opinion : England particularly has been regarded at different moments as an exponent of generous and far-seeing statesmanship and as the embodi- ment of the traditions of " perfide Albion " ; but it is roughly true to say that the hope of Germany lies in the develop- ment of friendly relations with England and America. To some extent America has belied expectation, so that the centre of expectation is more than ever London. Differences of opinion arising between England and France as to the policy to be adopted towards Germany to enforce compliance with the terms of the Treaty did not give the Germans much encouragement, as they believe, or at any rate assert, that such differences were usually settled at their expense. Nevertheless, it was appreciated that England took the broader view of the situation, and the sympathies of the people inclined more to her.

To some extent the presence of control officers in Germany militates against the resumption of normal friendly relations, but the attitude and conduct of the English officers of the Commission have been admirable. By their tact and reserve they have robbed their mission of half the offensiveness inseparable from a compulsory disarmament.

CHAPTER XI

THE CANNES CONFERENCE

Is Europe disarmed ?—The French at Washington—Russian influence on French press—A snub to Rathenau in Paris—Belgium and reparations—Theunis and Loucheur—Briand and Belgian press—Lloyd George's Memorandum on French security—The Anglo-Belgian Pact.

BERLIN, *January* 4, 1922.—Talking of French action at the Washington Conference, someone said to me to-day : " In the field of diplomacy the French are the best tacticians and the worst strategists in the world. Their big moves are often blunders, but at diplomatic details and the management of small questions they are past-masters."

BERLIN, *January* 5, 1922.—I hear from Paris that Rathenau was left entirely alone by the French for the first four days after his arrival. They did not even return his cards. Briand was furious about his being in Paris, said it was an English trick—an endeavour to force his hand.
ANOTHER Franco-German incident was that the Reparation Commission convoked Fischer, the Head of the German Delegation, to a meeting on Saturday. When they came together, they received a message from Fischer to say that his day was fully booked up and that he was not able to come. This created a terrific hubbub.

THE CANNES CONFERENCE, JANUARY 6–13, 1922

THE session of the Supreme Council was attended by MM. Briand (Chairman) and Loucheur, for France, Mr. Lloyd George and Sir Robert Horne for Great Britain, together with Lord Birkenhead and Sir Laming Worthington-Evans; Signor Bonomi and the Marchese della Torretta for Italy, MM. Theunis and Jaspar for Belgium. The Reparation Commission also sat, and a German Delegation, headed by Dr. Rathenau, was present. Lord Curzon was frequently in consultation with the Prime Minister, while other notable figures in the background were M. Henri de Jouvenel and M. Franklin-Bouillon ; also the then Premier and Foreign Minister of Greece, MM. Gonnaris and Bottazzi.

THE Conference had been preceded by conversations held in Paris between Allied experts, chiefly British and French. On arriving at Cannes on January 4, Mr. Lloyd George handed to M. Briand a striking Memorandum on Reparation, Security, and Reconstruction, in which Great Britain offered to guarantee France against an unprovoked attack by Germany on certain conditions, including French participation, and Russian, in a conference designed to ensure the economic reconstruction of Europe and an all-round pledge of non-aggression. A resolution in favour of such a conference was moved by Mr. Lloyd George on January 6, and adopted. It was also decided to invite the co-operation of the United States, which was represented at Cannes by Colonel Harvey, the American Ambassador in London, as observer. The Supreme Council then proceeded to draw up a skeleton agenda for the proposed Genoa Conference, and to appoint an Allied Committee of five to work out the more detailed agenda.

ON January 10 the Supreme Council also decided to appoint an organising Committee to lay the foundations of an International Corporation or Consortium to facilitate the economic reconstruction of Europe, and particularly of Soviet Russia.

THE negotiations on the subject of an Anglo-French Pact of Security between Mr. Lloyd George and M. Briand did not proceed altogether smoothly. French opinion resented the time-limit, the non-reciprocal character, and the absence of any military convention in the draft suggested by the British Prime Minister. French opinion also looked with suspicion upon Mr. Lloyd George's attempt to conclude with the Belgian ministers a separate Anglo-Belgian Pact based on very different stipulations.

The suspicions of Paris were quickly aroused, and motions were passed by two Parliamentary groups, in the Senate and Chamber respectively, which reflected on M. Briand's conduct of the pact negotiations as unduly prejudicial to the national interests. M. Briand was grotesquely accused of subservience to British policy because he allowed Mr. Lloyd George to give him a golfing lesson on the local links. On January 11 M. Briand was peremptorily recalled by President Millerand in order to answer his parliamentary critics. He answered them in the Chamber on the following day, but resigned without waiting for a vote of "no confidence" to be carried against him. M. Briand's fall created great perturbation among the Allied Delegation at Cannes. Still, on January 13 the Supreme Council met, with a French observer, and resolved to confirm such of its decisions as had been unanimously and definitely reached, such as those relating to the proposed Genoa Conference. Similarly the Reparation Commission, after hearing Dr. Rathenau and other German technical delegates, took upon itself to grant Germany a moratorium in respect of the cash payments due by Germany on January 15 and February 15, provided that the Reich, pending a definite readjustment, undertook to pay 31,000,000 gold marks every ten days, and submitted full proposals within a fortnight for a Reparations scheme covering the year 1922.

On January 13 President Millerand requested M. Poincaré to form a Cabinet on the morrow. Mr. Lloyd George, on his return journey, had a private conversation with M. Poincaré in the Paris railway-station ; this merely served to accentuate mutual distrust.

January 6, 1922.—Cannes Conference opened.

BERLIN, *January* 11, 1922.—The Cannes Conference was convened, on Mr. Lloyd George's initiative, with the object of bringing about the pacification of Europe and

16

its economic reconstruction. England's policy, and the large contributions she was prepared to make to further the aims in view, are perhaps best illustrated by the following extracts from Mr. Lloyd George's declaration to M. Briand at Cannes on January 4 :

" WITH regard to the safety of France against invasion, Great Britain will regard this as an interest of her own and is, therefore, prepared to undertake that, in the event of unprovoked German aggression against French soil, the British people will place their forces on her side.   There will be a double value in this guarantee, since it will not only safeguard France in the event of German attack, but will make any such attack extremely improbable.

" IF Germany is certain that the British Empire will stand by France in any future war, she will not be tempted to keep alive dreams of revenge.   It is of great importance to divert the German mind from such ambitions, as well as to provide for the defeat of those ambitions should they mature.

" THE British people understands the claim of France to be guaranteed against invasion, but is not willing to be committed to military liabilities for breaches of peace elsewhere, and participation in military enterprises in Central and Eastern Europe it would not contemplate.

" ENGLAND looks for agreement by France to an immediate summoning of an economic conference at which all the Powers of Europe, including Russia, will be represented.

" ENGLAND offers France and Italy her intimate and earnest co-operation in building up a great system of European accord which will put the maintenance of peace between the nations and the reduction of national armaments in the forefront of its aims, for only so, in their belief, will Europe secure that sense of safety amongst nations, great and small, which, through many centuries of its political life, it has never yet attained.   If the Economic Conference is agreed to, it will create an opportunity for the Great

Allied Powers—France, the British Empire, and Italy—
to inaugurate an era of peace in their own continent, whose
war-sodden fields record a history more terrible than of any
other continent in modern times."

BERLIN, *January* 12, 1922.—Lloyd George's Memorandum
to Briand, offering France a guarantee of her security
against an unprovoked aggression by Germany, is a most
interesting document.   In the original, however, it
was even more interesting, for Lloyd George laid down
a number of conditions, from the standpoint of Great
Britain's interest.   France was to renounce the submarine, she was to agree to a really international régime
for Tangier, she was to undertake to refrain from
backing the Turks against British policy.   Finally, she
was to promise her participation in the right spirit in the
Economic Conference to be held at Genoa.

THE submarine consideration, in particular, would have
removed a serious danger to our overseas communications.
THIS Memorandum was actually given out by the Prime
Minister to Lord Riddell, for distribution to the British
press.   But, just as Lord Riddell was handing copies
to the British correspondents, M. Sauerwein, of *Le
Matin*, happened to come upon the party, and was
shown a copy of the Memorandum.   He at once rushed
off with it to M. Briand, who hurried from the luncheon
table to the entrance-hall of the hotel, and pressed upon Lord
Riddell the need for delaying publication until he (Briand)
had had an opportunity of discussing the Memorandum
with Lloyd George, for otherwise, he pleaded, great mischief
might be done to Anglo-French relations.

LORD RIDDELL, after some hesitation, yielded to Briand's
entreaties and withheld the document.   When the latter
was reissued to the press the following day, Briand had
prevailed upon Lloyd George to omit the afore-mentioned
conditions.

BERLIN, *January* 16, 1922.—Belgium both desires and deserves all that she can be given, but I hear from Cannes that British and French financial experts are becoming restive over the priority which entitles Belgium to the whole of the first 100 millions payable by Germany under the head of Reparation. In view of the rapidly diminishing capacity of Germany to make payments, there has been something more than a desire to modify the above-mentioned arrangements which were made at Spa. Loucheur is supposed to have taken the initiative in proposing some modification, and rather violent scenes are reported between him and the Belgian delegates.

No better defenders of the interests of the small country can be found than Theunis and Jaspar : the first, a business man of proved capacity combining habitual bluntness with a facility for rhetoric when occasion demands it ; the latter, a very vigorous lawyer with an immense capacity for work.

BERLIN, *January* 17, 1922.—There has been a good deal of heart-burning about the text of the Anglo-Belgian draft Treaty which appeared three days ago in the *Daily Telegraph*. Paris has been critical because—unlike the proposed Anglo-French Pact—it is not specifically directed against Germany, but can be evoked against any possible violation of the integrity of Belgian territory.

THE stipulations of the treaty between England and Belgium will probably serve as a model for later documents, so that the fact that the present treaty is not directed against Germany establishes the broad principle that domination over Belgium by any Power is intolerable to England, and will probably create a precedent of great international importance.

THE present position of Belgian affairs, according to the Belgian press, which is largely influenced, if not directed, by Paris, makes the discussion of the precise relationship

between England and Belgium a subject of considerable
delicacy and one not without real importance.

THE Belgian Foreign Office is unusually well informed.
By far the best reports from Berlin before the war were
written by Belgian diplomatists, and it is not improbable
that in the future Belgian agents will know more of what
is going on in Germany than even ourselves or the French.

January 12, 1922.—Briand resigned.

January 16, 1922.—Poincaré took office.

January 19, 1922.—Declaration of policy by Poincaré :
" to uphold firmly all France's rights under the Treaty of
Versailles."

CHAPTER XII

SECRET INTRIGUES

Radek in Berlin—Bolshevik ingratitude to England—Wirth's merits—French bid for German support—Rathenau as Foreign Minister—Views on policy—Rathenau seeks Radek.

BERLIN, *January* 20, 1922.—Radek [1] is now in Berlin to discuss with German authorities and business circles the best attitude to adopt at the forthcoming Genoa Conference.

HIS visit is termed secret and has been kept out of the papers.

I GATHER his conversation with the German Government comes under three heads :

(1) WHAT does Germany offer Russia as compared with the French offer to Russia three months ago, which was to assist her in recovering from Germany a war indemnity, with the ultimate idea of taking what Russia obtains from Germany in payment of Russia's debts to France ?   Radek says : " I am against this, but at the same time you must understand that it is rather a tempting basis for us."

(2) REGARDING Poland, what attitude shall Germany and Russia assume towards Poland ?   Russia cannot fight, and is anxious to arrange matters regarding transit through Poland, on a friendly basis.

(3) REGARDING the proposed big Consortium for economic

---

[1] RADEK, Karl Berngardovitch.—Bolshevism owes a great deal of its success to the activities of Karl Radek.   He was imprisoned during the Revolution of 1905, and became later a member of the editorial staffs of several Social Democrat newspapers in Poland and in Leipzig.   Until the war he agitated in Germany on behalf of the German Social Democrats, but was forced to leave in 1914, returning to the country again at the outbreak of the Revolution.   In 1918 he reorganised the German Bolshevik armies, but was imprisoned in 1919.   During his stay in prison he was visited by Talaat Pasha, and as a result of their negotiations, relations between Turkey and Russia were re-established.   Radek was one of the chief Bolshevik delegates in the International Conferences of 1915 and 1916.   In 1917 he took part in the Brest-Litovsk peace negotiations, and in 1925 he was appointed Rector of the Sun Yat Sen University for Orientals in Moscow.

development in Russia.   We at Moscow are rather afraid
of this idea, because we are not China and we do not want
to be exploited or to be compelled to make concessions.
We will give concessions voluntarily to this or that nation,
but not to a general Consortium.   What would anybody
gain by the big Consortium?   Would you have greater
ability to support your rights?   Why bother, since in the
early years we shall certainly carry out our engagements?"
RELATIONS between Moscow and Angora are quite friendly :
the Russians have some kind of an idea that they can
engineer an arrangement between Paris and Angora.   One
of their main reasons for opening direct negotiations with
Paris was the conclusion of the Franklin-Bouillon Agreement.

THEY are also devoting a large amount of attention to
Afghanistan.   Indeed, their present orientation appears
more to the south and south-east than to the west.

EVERYONE who comes into contact with Radek says he is
an extraordinarily clever fellow, though a terrific liar.   He
knows the recent political and diplomatic history of every
country—has rather too many ideas than too few.

THERE is no doubt a good deal going on between Paris
and Moscow.   Poincaré knew about the pourparlers two
months ago and will probably continue them.   The Poles
are getting alarmed, as they fully realise that their somewhat
expensive charms would wane rapidly in French eyes when
contrasted with those of a Moscow heiress.

BERLIN, *January* 28, 1922.—I understand that the Soviet
people are not at all grateful to England about the Genoa
Conference.   They have a very curious and characteristic
argument, viz. that England, desiring to trade with
Russia, for purely empirical and practical reasons, has no
business to mix up theoretical considerations or demand
engagements of a theoretical character, like abstention
from propaganda, in connection with their empirical desire.

Another thing they say is that Lloyd George asks too high a price for England's favours. Everybody knows that England will trade with anyone who will trade with her. It is unjustifiable, therefore, to ask for political concessions in return for what anybody can have if they pay the price.

As they put it, " England is no virgin."

BERLIN, *January* 28, 1922.—A long talk with an intimate friend of the Chancellor's to-day, who described the political situation in Germany in what appeared to me happy terms. He said: " Nobody could have done what Wirth has, whose whole tendency was not republican, and who was not wholly trusted by the Left, at any rate by the moderate Left. To give a musical comparison—the treble in Germany is conservative, but the bass is liberal and republican. The shriller notes come from the Right, but the steady heavy accompaniment proceeds from the working classes, who are firmly anti-monarchical.

THE recent crisis has shown that Wirth now possesses the undivided support both of the Centre and of the Democrats. This he did not have three months ago. The Volkspartei is still divided. They have strong bonds with the Right, but their general tendency is to come over towards us, and this should materialise in the course of a short time."

BERLIN, *January* 28, 1922.—Radek has been multiplying his interviews with German ministers, officials, and party politicians. To all he tells the same story, that France is seeking a secret agreement with Russia, to whom she would promise trade credits, diplomatic support at Angora, economic aid for reconstruction purposes, and the payment by Germany of a war indemnity in accordance with Art. 116 of the Versailles Treaty. Strange to relate, this is not Radek's policy at all, but Tchitcherin's. Radek at heart is against it, but is willing to use it for tactical reasons.

Radek, indeed, says to the German representatives : " Now, if you don't want us to be driven into the arms of France, make us a counter-offer : give us a loan, and agree to resume full diplomatic relations at once, before the Genoa Conference meets. If you wait until it meets, your tardy recognition will not help us. You must also support our efforts in securing the admission of Turkey to the Genoa Conference." The German retort to this appeal, or rather blackmail, is that no satisfaction has yet been forthcoming from Russia in respect of the murder of the late German Envoy, Count Mirbach,[1] that Germany herself is short of money, and could not lend to Russia on any scale, without drawing upon herself increased demands by the Reparation Commission, which would not be slow to point out that, if Germany could lend money to Russia, she must be well able to pay reparations. On the other hand, in their talks with the French, the Soviet agents maintain that the condition of a Franco-Russian understanding is the abandonment of Poland by France. They appear adamant on this point.

[1] MIRBACH, Count.—Count Mirbach was attached to the German Embassy in Petrograd before the war, and there became well known and popular because of his agreeable manner and appearance ; his influence, in fact, was greater than that of the Ambassador, Count de Pourtales, or the Councillor. IT was probably his former popularity which secured his appointment as Ambassador shortly after the advent of the Bolshevist régime. After the Treaty of Brest-Litovsk and the discussion of the transference of prisoners and the resumption of commercial relations between Germany and Russia, Mirbach proceeded as Envoy to Moscow.

AT the time there was distinct unrest among the Bolsheviks against Germany and a great deal of propaganda was being circulated ; rumours were abroad that German pledges to Russia were being violated, and Mirbach had to contend with a great deal of hostility. This reached a climax in July 1918, when two members of the Tcheka, Andreieff and Estumkin, disguised as Soviet officials, obtained entry to the Embassy and there assassinated him.

THE breach of international trust caused strained relations between the two countries, though Germany declared her intention of carrying out her pledges. Mirbach's popularity as a diplomat and his long experience—he was Minister in Athens in 1910—aroused personal, apart from diplomatic, interest in the affair.

REGARDING Turkey, the Bolsheviks assert that they are in a position to help France at Angora, where French influence, they contend, is seriously on the wane.

ON Monday, Radek and Co. are to meet the German Chancellor as well as representatives of Krupps and Stinnes and the A.E.G.

BERLIN, *January* 31, 1922.—England has offered France and Belgium a guarantee of support in the event of a German attack, and I imagine that people in London consider that in return for this we enjoy the deep gratitude of those countries. But we don't always get what we deserve, even from our Allies. I hear from Brussels that the Belgians are quite indifferent about our offer of protection—their press still continue attacks upon us. Apparently the Belgian idea is that their only safeguard lies in a military convention with the one Power in Europe with a large modern army ready for immediate use ; so, though we make our offer with the best intentions, Belgium decides that a guarantee from a non-military power counts for nothing.

BERLIN, *February* 1, 1922.—Rathenau had luncheon here yesterday, just before his appointment as Foreign Minister, and we had a long talk, in which he gave me his impressions about the past and future.

HIS great fear is that the Volkspartei will be brought into the Government too soon, and that the Right Section of the party will hamper the policy of the Wirth Government.

HE says that Stinnes tells all sorts of fairy-tales about what he (Stinnes) said in London and what was said to Stinnes by different personalities. Outwardly Rathenau is on friendly terms with Stinnes and had breakfast with him the other day, but at heart they are bitterly opposed. Stinnes said to Rathenau : " You and I as powerful industrials are too big to take office. Will you promise me not to accept office if it is offered you ? I will do the same." Rathenau declined.

It would seem from Rathenau's conversation—which I believe to be sincere—that he was much impressed both with the moderation and with the ability of the English representatives with whom he has come into contact in London and at Cannes.   Having started by being pro-French, he now thinks the English broader view so sound that it requires to be defended against the French skill in minor tactics and persistency in complaint.

In one thing Rathenau shows his mobile intelligence— that is, he has come back with much less unsound ideas about currency than he started with.   He naturally says that what he now thinks he thought all the time, but as a matter of fact the two conceptions are completely different.

He has taken to International Conferences with passion. He wants them to go on all the time.   There cannot be too many.   Let them be small in point of numbers, but long in point of time : not too many Powers to attend, but plenty of time to discuss.

About Russia he says : " Let private trading corporations go in individually.   When they have got a sufficient number of contracts, the Soviet system will fall."

He is proud to be Foreign Minister of Germany, and will certainly do well, if anti-Semitic fanatics let him.   But I doubt if he gains in authority more than he loses in freedom.

Berlin, *February* 2, 1922.—Wirth was here last night, until two in the morning, and appeared to enjoy the ball at the English Embassy immensely.   Care and responsibility sit lightly on his shoulders, and he is more youthful in manner and outlook than ever.   The French press criticise the ball, remarking ironically that " Le Reich s'amuse."

Wirth does not seem alarmed about the railway strike, thinking it will break down in three or four days ; nor did he seem much perturbed at the Volkspartei's attack on Rathenau : " That damned Volkspartei are not intelligent enough to understand how intelligent Rathenau is, but I shall not give way to them."

BERLIN, *February* 6, 1922.—A long conversation with Rathenau this morning.

HE said he spoke quite unofficially, but was anxious to make me realise the real position in which Germany found herself. The truth was that she was bullied and blackmailed by nearly everybody. There were perpetual incidents which led to recriminations against Germany— one day Wünsdorf, another day a steamer at Stettin, a third day something else. Of course, everyone knew that in life one must be perpetually doing things which, if they were known, would be a legitimate ground of protest from somebody else. It was impossible to avoid this, but in ordinary practice either the person did not know or was not in a position to protest. With Germany they always knew and always protested. This rendered the establishment of a steady policy for Germany, and con- tinuous work for Germany, almost impossible. England was much more reasonable than anybody else, and under- stood the situation far better, but still he found the position very difficult.

AFTER the Genoa Conference he hoped that an Economic Conference of a few Powers (or if not a Conference a discussion between delegates of four or five Powers) would be possible. English statesmen were constantly in touch with French ministers, but had not had any interview with German ministers. Would not a meeting be possible at some time or other ? French ministers might or might not be there ; at any rate, he hoped for American participa- tion in the conversations—America represented by some- body with economic views like Hoover, who understood the world-position.

FRANCE thought politically ; England thought economically. France said : " I don't understand where economic discussion will lead me ; what I do know is that with political alliances and with my military force I can maintain my position. If I go to Genoa, I do not know what will be said nor how far I may be led."

RATHENAU went on to talk about who could be sent as German representative to Washington. The Americans had asked, not for a big name, but for somebody with commercial experience who could talk business. But in the first place very few business men had any diplomatic ability ; and in the second place those who had, wanted to restore their private fortunes rather than enter the Government service. Very few people in Germany had considerable private fortunes left. Cuno, for instance, had very little, and wanted to make his financial position secure, besides which he was no genius. Rosen understood nothing about figures, so he would hardly do. Kühlmann was very clever, and would perhaps do later, but he had against him that he was the man of Brest-Litovsk, besides which he rather personified the old régime. Altogether he did not know where to turn for a suitable representative.

BERLIN, *February* 6, 1922.—We are in the midst of an extensive strike—railways, municipal workers, etc.

BUT the Berliners are beginning to be expert in strike life. Yesterday, before the water was cut off, the consumption of water throughout the town was three times normal, everybody having filled up their baths and every conceivable receptacle so as to provide against short supply.

THE opinion is very widely held that the agitating centre is Moscow, and that the agitating means is money from Moscow, but I have not heard any serious evidence to substantiate this. The net result of the strike has been to set public opinion more than ever against the Communists.

BERLIN, *February* 12, 1922.—Rathenau has had an inter-view with Radek, who is an old friend of his. He did not tell me exactly what passed, but I gather that Radek made a less good impression than before. Rathenau said : " He is, of course, clever and witty, but very dirty. The real type of low Jew-boy."

I DON'T think that Rathenau attaches as much importance to the alleged negotiations between Paris and Moscow as Maltzan does. He considers that the Soviet are merely trying to create trouble between France and England, and to create competition for Soviet friendship.

IN " Petite Entente " circles the move of Moscow towards Paris is considered most important. The Slav view is that Poincaré will do everything to postpone Genoa. If he cannot postpone it indefinitely, he will endeavour to go there with an assured majority of " Petite Entente " and Russians.

CHAPTER XIII

TOWARDS GENOA

France on security—Verses on Paris—Bolshevik leaders in Berlin—Excessive armaments—Indebtedness—Rathenau on the Kaiser—Narrative of events in July 1914—Interview between Lloyd George and Dr. Wiedfeldt—Von Kluck on his attempt on Paris—Germany and war revenge—Rathenau driven wild by French Notes.

BERLIN, *February* 14, 1922.—It seems as if France CHAP. would really like an Anglo-French Pact, but not XIII one based on what we are prepared to undertake, February but on what France says we ought to undertake. 1922

THE fundamental criticism which may be directed against the French draft of January 29 is that England undertakes definite and very extended responsibilities in order to avoid a danger which she believes to be largely imaginary. An armed attack by Germany on France within the next twenty-five years is admittedly improbable, an attack by Germany on England in the same period even more so. The atmosphere of unreality and of non-adjustment to present-day facts which prevails in the clause protecting France is pushed even farther in the reciprocal clause which binds France to protect England against Germany. Here we are in the realm of polite manners rather than of business, and it may well be doubted whether the present value of the contingent assurance given by France is more than infinitesimal. Indeed, the whole contract might conceivably be pronounced invalid on the ground that there was no consideration by one party for obligations undertaken by the other.

THE questions therefore arise : first, is it wise to undertake heavy responsibilities, extending into a distant and unknown future, for so small a positive or potential gain ? Secondly, are the means adopted to allay alarm at the alleged danger such as to produce a maximum calm at a minimum cost ?

ON these points it must be remarked at the outset that the whole tone of the French is to assume that the real danger to the future peace of Europe is military aggression by Germany. To what extent does this assumption agree with the facts and with reasonable expectation ? To what extent does assumption of so incriminating a nature serve the interests of future pacification ?

ONE of two views must be adopted : either Germany must be regarded as a danger and be held in check by military conventions and by overpowering force, or Germany must be regarded as an ex-enemy whom it is desirable to treat with fairness and generosity in order to strengthen the elements of peace and reconciliation within her borders. It appears difficult, if not impossible, to frame a policy reconciling these conflicting conceptions.

ON another point, the French speak of the future war as probably being a chemical war. If this assumption is correct, it is clear that the specific value of the treaty concerning the prohibition of fortification of the Rhine is diminished ; but this is not the only conclusion.

IT follows that the effective safeguard must be supplied rather by continuous pre-attack control than by a promise for subsequent post-attack assistance. On this ground also the French proposal appears to me to lack appropriateness to present conditions. The defence is not suitable to the attack. It may, indeed, be characterised as a scheme devised to meet conditions of three years ago and not those likely to obtain in the future.

THE reception which the report of the conclusion of a defensive pact by England met with in Belgium is strong confirmation of the view that the proposed arrangement as drafted does not effectively guard against any real danger and will not allay any real fear.

THE above criticisms are directed against specific details of a particular draft, and do not involve or imply scepticism regarding the general ideas of a convention so framed as to give France real security on a basis of general pacification and disarmament.

PARNASSUS ON PARIS

England, *loq.*:

> Fair Paris I love, but hourly I prove
> The hazards and doubts of unconsecrate love.
> The wolves are about : there are dangers ahead.
> Let us seek the repose of a treaty-made bed.
>
> Is my fear but polite ? are her fears but chimera ?
> Mine is somewhat assumed : I know well what hers are.
> But neither believes what either may say,
> So neither believing, we neither betray.
>
> Let us comfort the wolf by disarming the lamb ;
> And drink to the Pact though the argument's sham.

BERLIN, *February* 19, 1922.—The Bolsheviks, Rakowsky,[1] Radek, Krassin, and one or two others, have had a conference here and have now left for Moscow, in order to discuss the attitude of Russia at the Genoa Conference. The most influential of those who were here was Rakowsky, who is a kind of Governor-General of the Ukraine, and is said to have great authority with Lenin.

RAKOWSKY talked over the position with a Socialist acquaintance of mine on the following lines :

[1] RAKOWSKY, Christian.—Rakowsky inherited his revolutionary tendencies from his ancestors, who had organised rebellions against Turkish rule from their home in Kotel. Rakowsky's education was interrupted when all the schools of Bulgaria were closed to him because of his seditious influence.

IN 1874 he was expelled from Russia and went to France, where he continued his education by studying law and practising journalism. In 1897 he wrote his famous thesis *The Etiology of Criminology and Degeneration.* After his stay in France, Rakowsky returned to Russia, where he denounced Czardom. In 1907 his civil rights as a Rumanian were taken away, and for five years Rakowsky was an exile, the question of his citizenship becoming a *cause célèbre* in Europe.

AT the outbreak of the Soviet Revolution, Rakowsky at once came into power and favour. He was appointed head of the delegation in the Ukraine peace negotiations, and in 1924 was Chargé d'Affaires in London. In 1926 he was appointed Soviet Ambassador in France, and a member of the Central Soviet Council.

RAKOWSKY's brilliance as a journalist and diplomatist has made him a particularly valuable member of the Soviet Government.

17

" Russia is endeavouring to make friends with France because friendship with England is not enough for her. If we find France obdurate, then we will throw ourselves ' hair and skin ' into the arms of England. At present we consider France important."

" Why ? "

" Because we want to be sure of our western frontier. France can influence Poland, Rumania, and Turkey. We are not quite comfortable about Central Asia and Siberia. If we could spare several corps from our western front we could put things straight in the east and settle with some tiresome fellows there. As long as France is hostile we daren't take troops away from the western frontier, owing to her influence with our Petite Entente neighbours.

" So far, negotiations with France have not gone very far. Millerand is reported to be very hostile to Russia and to be violently against the Quai d'Orsay, who are anxious to come to terms with us.

" Germany, for the moment, we can neglect. If we end by making terms with England, Germany will follow suit.

" We are quite against being made the field of exploitation of a big European syndicate or of an English-German syndicate. We prefer to deal with each Power by itself."

Rakowsky was anxious to know whether anti-Bolshevik declarations would be made at Genoa. " If they are, Russia will, of course, resist. But if we are treated as equals, we shall do what we can to make the Conference a success. Improved commercial relations are an indispensable necessity for us. Without them we shall not last very long. I do not mean what you call ' long ' in Europe—namely, two or three months ; I speak of years."

When asked why the Russians had permitted Radek's interview in the *Matin*, which gave the impression that Moscow was fishing round and anxious to intrigue with everybody, Rakowsky said : " You must not let the English think they have it all their own way. They will appreciate

us all the more if they think there is danger of our going
elsewhere."
WHEN my friend told him that this was a very dangerous
policy and would end by getting the Soviet discredited
elsewhere, Rakowsky would not have it, and said that it was
the only way of getting Russian friendship appreciated.

ON February 25 Mr. Lloyd George, at M. Poincaré's
invitation, agreed to meet the latter at Boulogne in
order to discuss Anglo-French differences regarding
the Genoa Conference, the Near Eastern crisis, and
other matters. So strong was the feeling between
the two Prime Ministers that M. Poincaré lunched
at the Sous-Préfecture, leaving his British colleague
to order his own luncheon at the railway-station.
This discourtesy was resented by Mr. Lloyd George,
and the subsequent conversation but served to accentuate their personal opposition as well as the diverging
standpoints of Great Britain and France. Yet a
misleading communiqué was issued at the close of their
conversation, in which their agreement was recorded
" on the political guarantees to be secured in order
to prevent encroachments either on the rights of the
League of Nations or on the treaties signed in France
after the Peace or on the rights of the Allies to reparation." It was decided to postpone the Genoa Conference from March to April 10, and to hold a preliminary meeting of Allied Economic Experts in
London.

> Were I affrighted—which I'm not—
> France should enjoy this happy lot.
> France should protect—against a fee—
> My insular security,
> And I should buy immunity,
> Instead of arming cap-à-pie.
> Yet if remote the danger be—
> My fear a phantasmagory—
> Were it not wise to wait and see
> Developments of history ?

February 25, 1922.—Meeting at Boulogne between Lloyd
George and Poincaré.

BERLIN, *February* 28, 1922.—There can be no doubt about the direct connection which traces unemployment to bad trade, bad trade to taxation, taxation to excessive expenditure. This abnormal expenditure is due in the main to :

> Excessive armaments, and
> Excessive indebtedness.

Public extravagance might be added, but this is perhaps less an inherent factor of the situation itself than a method of administration. These are undoubtedly the underlying causes of the present distress, and if the Conference at Genoa can devise effective solutions, Europe will be able to face the future with confidence.

GIVEN reasonableness and a sincere desire of the nations to promote the aims of peace, it should be possible, by some method of reciprocal international control and assurance, to create a general atmosphere of confidence, and such atmosphere of confidence would make possible—or, indeed, necessary—a general reduction of expenditure on armaments.

REGARDING excessive indebtedness—between nations or between classes—there are several possible ways of dealing with this. History shows that, in the long run, it generally finds its cure through its own excess. One method—not a very elegant one—is to remove the over-burden by repudiation, but the process is hardly conducive to social contentment or economic restoration. Currency inflation affords another means.

IT is usual to assume that a level of prices is due to the inscrutable designs of providence, working through the wicked intermediary of profiteers. This assumption is erroneous. The general level of prices in each country should rather be considered as determined by legislation or administrative action, and as very largely controllable by intelligent statesmanship. If this is true, the evils resulting

from violent fluctuations of the general price-level are
definitely amenable to human treatment.

ANOTHER error is to talk of over-indebtedness as if it
existed between nations and to ignore the much more
fateful circumstances of over-indebtedness between classes.
HISTORY shows that this condition has been—no less than
wide fluctuation in the current standard of value—one of
the most potent causes of economic disturbance and social
unrest.

BERLIN, *March* 1, 1922.—Stabilise currency—this, in my
judgment, is the one condition precedent to the improvement of the financial position here.
NOTES are issued from the printing press at an alarming
rate, exchange continues to fall rapidly, yet there are
still many who do not appreciate the connection between
inflation and depreciation.
THE Reparation Commission has recently come to an
arrangement with Germany with the object of increasing
deliveries in kind by Germany. But it is obvious that
the net effect of increased deliveries in kind can be as
disastrous as deliveries in cash. The deliveries in kind
will have to be paid for in notes to the German producers,
and, of course, these payments will be met by increased
printing.

BERLIN, *March* 4, 1922.—Rathenau was here yesterday
to luncheon, and was interesting about the Kaiser. One
of the Kaiser's misfortunes was his real superiority to his
entourage both in memory and in argumentative ability.
He had an incorrect instinct, his judgment was usually
wrong, but he could put his case admirably and overwhelm
his antagonists by feats of memory. The latter was exercised in the main on insignificant detail, but it served its
controversial purpose. Rathenau remembered one particular discussion about Kiao-Chou. He had said to the
Emperor : " Your Chinese policy has been very successful,

but I cannot see how you would be able to keep Kiao-Chou if there was a war against either England or Japan." The Emperor however proved, with an abundance of detail, that Kiao-Chou would never be attacked, and produced reasons from the history of India and China since the Flood—all superficially relevant, all essentially unimportant or misleading. Rathenau went home from the conversation with his head in a whirl, and Kiao-Chou went to the enemy as soon as the war started. Rathenau once asked a high official of the Imperial régime : " How do you manage to keep the Kaiser in such a good temper ? " The official replied : " His Majesty delights in explaining mechanical contrivances, such as a clock or a compass or a barometer. I keep a special barometer, and whenever the Emperor comes I ask him to explain how it works, saying that I have forgotten what he told me last time. He gives an admirable exposition ; this puts him in an excellent temper, and he signs the documents I put before him."

As a contrast to the Emperor, who spoke well but judged wrongly, Rathenau mentioned old Bleichroeder, who talked the greatest nonsense in the world but who hardly ever made a mistake. The one big mistake he made was over the crisis in 1887, when Bismarck told him that war between Russia and England was certain. He went a heavy bear and lost millions of marks on Bismarck's advice.

THERE are a great many similar cases in everyone's experience. What is rare is a man who comes to a right decision by instinct and can support it by logic. The French have a saying, " Un bon rédacteur a toujours tort," and most people who have attended international conferences would be inclined to agree.

TALKING about international conferences, somebody said the other day, with regard to Boulogne, " Ils sont d'accord ; ils ne doivent pas se comprendre."

RATHENAU is a little less gloomy than usual about the prospects. He harps on a great deal about the notes which

Nollet [1] sends in from the Commission of Control, particularly one which says that the police organisation has to be decentralised and handed over to local authorities before March 15. He is persuaded that the French scheme is to create an incident, to be able to put the German Government in the wrong, and say : " Since you have not carried out your engagements, we shall take this or that sanction and stop all idea of abolishing or reducing military control."

THE general opinion regarding Nollet is that he is a pacifist by conviction and is as moderate as the military authorities in Paris will allow. Rathenau says that this is all wrong, that Nollet is just a sergeant and tends rather to increase difficulties than to smooth them down.

RATHENAU says that Stinnes is more inclined to disagree than anybody he ever met. When you explain your view to him he always answers : " I entirely differ. It would be impossible to be more wrong than you are." You then seek a compromise and put 50 per cent. water in your wine. Stinnes still says : " You are totally wrong. I cannot understand your view." You add a further 50 per cent. of water. He says still that you are totally wrong and will not budge an inch from his position, so you lose your head and lay down your arms.

THERE are some signs that Stinnes, notwithstanding his habitual attitude, is coming round to a more sensible and moderate policy, but the old instinct of contradicting everybody and everything will probably persist.

---

[1] NOLLET, General Charles Marie Edouard.—General Nollet was appointed President at the Inter-Allied Military Commission of Control in Berlin, for which he had qualified by his successful record during the war. Born at Marseilles in 1865, General Nollet was educated for military service. He was promoted during the war from the command of a corps to a division of chasseurs.
HERRIOT chose Nollet as his Minister for War in the 1925 Government. In the following year, on the collapse of the Herriot Cabinet, General Nollet became a member of the War Council in the Briand Government, and still holds that position.

A CORRESPONDENT of the *Tageblatt*, who has just been to Moscow, is back here and is rather in love with the Russians, although pessimistic concerning the outlook there. He says the principal danger from Russia now is typhus. Its ravages are appalling ; it will certainly spread west. Europe should send doctors rather than food. He says Wrangel and Denikin shook the Soviet much more than anybody knows. This I hear for the first time.

BERLIN, *March* 9, 1922.—Met an exalted personage at luncheon the other day, who was interesting on the subject of the Emperor during the month of July 1914. He had special knowledge about the cruise to Norway—the time when, it is alleged, the Emperor kept away from Berlin to allay suspicion.

THE thesis of the exalted personage was that the Emperor was kept uninformed about the crisis, that during the fortnight or three weeks, from about July 7 to July 25, he had no telegrams, and that when the crisis had become irretrievable he merely received a telegram from Bethmann-Hollweg giving him the position, and urging him to stay away from Berlin. One morning the Emperor came in to luncheon and said : " This is an unheard-of blunder. They tell me nothing for three weeks, and then inform me that the situation is irretrievable. More than that, they urge me to remain away ; but I shall return at once, as it is my duty to my country."

IT appears difficult to explain how, since the crisis had begun before the Emperor left Berlin, he can have been left uninformed during the three weeks. It is also difficult to explain how the Emperor, if he was as friendly to England as his supporters make out, can have not only consented to, but have actively and personally pushed, the naval policy of Germany. It is all very well to say that for him the navy was a plaything. Nobody with the

smallest political sense could have ignored the danger
that it would embroil Germany with England.[1]

ANOTHER view held here is that the Emperor was surrounded by a camarilla of about six persons, and was
allowed to see nobody except with their approval. It is
said that Kühlmann overheard a conversation between two
of the camarilla, on one of his visits to Headquarters
during the war. One camarillist said to another : " That
Kühlmann is here. He can eat with the Emperor, but
must not talk with him. We cannot allow any private
interviews."

BERLIN, *March* 9, 1922.—Rathenau discussed Genoa with
me this morning. He is impressed by what he has heard
from Wiedfeldt,[2] who had an hour's talk with Lloyd
George. The Prime Minister said : " I have no definite
programme for Genoa. They say Russia is my pet child :
well, Russia will be the feature at Genoa." Rathenau says
the Soviets are mainly characterised by " a grandiose
unreliability. It will be easy for the French or anybody
else who wants to upset the Conference to put questions
to the Russians which will make them break out or boil
over."

RATHENAU is evidently very alarmed at L. G. having no
definite programme. " If England has no programme,
who will have one ? The Petite Entente and Italy will
raise all sorts of minor questions, and the Conference will
become a kind of vanity fair in which each will parade his
own particular local affairs." The only safeguard would
be for big theoretical discussions to be initiated, and this
he hopes Germany will help to do. But she wants guidance
and suggestions. Genoa will not have been in vain if,
as a result, permanent commissions are appointed to sit

---

[1] THE view that the Emperor was in constant touch with Berlin is confirmed
by documents published since the above was written.
[2] A DIRECTOR of Krupps, and later German Ambassador to Washington.

on different large questions.   These commissions might take as main subjects (1) Economics, (2) Transport, (3) Currency.

L. G. is further reported to have said to Wiedfeldt : " England cannot help you alone.   You must get other people to assist us in the task.   You must make further friends." Rathenau asks : " Who ?   The French are impossible. As long as this Chamber continues, there is nothing to be done.   In Poincaré the unreasonable section have got a good lawyer who puts their wrongheaded points in such form that they are not quite easy to answer.   The Russians are too unreliable, besides which, for the moment Russia does not exist.   The Italians are also unreliable, and the Japanese will not take a sufficient part.   The Czecho-Slovaks, although energetic, intriguing, and intelligent, are also immensely unreliable and are too much under French domination.   The Belgians are also hopelessly under France."   In his judgment, nothing remains but America.   If he could only get a good German Ambassador at Washington he might be able to bring them in to help Europe.   " It would be worth a great sacrifice to do this." He thinks of Wiedfeldt.

RATHENAU continued : " I wish you would think over the whole subject.   See what can be suggested."

THE P.M. is also reported to have said to Wiedfeldt : " I cannot understand why the industrials do not support the Wirth Government ; it is their duty and their interest to do so."   This made a great impression.   Wiedfeldt replied : " We think Wirth too socialistic."   Rathenau says : " It is nonsense to say we are socialistic : we have converted the Socialists to indirect taxation."

As to the Czechs, Rathenau is already in touch with Masaryk.   The Prague negotiator said to Rathenau : " We can easily arrange a meeting.   Have you got a mother ? "   " Yes."   " Why should she not go to Karls-bad ?   Why can you not visit her there ?   Why cannot

Masaryk and Benes also come to visit her ? " But Rathenau says his mother won't go.

BERLIN, *March* 9, 1922.—" Strengthen the Right ! Strengthen the Right ! " Von Schlieffen, head of the German General Staff till 1906, died murmuring these words. They applied to the plan of campaign which he had elaborated and which was adopted as the basis of the German advance in 1914. Fortunately in 1914 it was " not pure Schlieffen, but Schlieffen and water." This was Hindenburg's criticism of the Moltke plan as it was finally carried out. Schlieffen would have concentrated the whole strength on the right, in a wide turning movement. Von Moltke [1] was more timid, and, fearing a French advance through Lorraine, kept too large a portion of his forces on the left. He was also uneasy about the Russian front, and at the critical moment withdrew divisions to meet the Russian danger.

VON SCHLIEFFEN had deliberately planned to sacrifice East Prussia and to allow the Russians to advance as far as Danzig, counting upon destroying them after he had destroyed the French.

SUCH was the general view of the 1914 campaign given me by General von Kluck, whom I met yesterday. A young-looking man for seventy-five, somewhat depressed

[1] VON MOLTKE, General Helmuth.—Helmuth von Moltke, nephew of Germany's great tactician, succeeded General von Schlieffen as Chief of the German Staff. His own tactics were based on von Schlieffen's, but with some modifications, and to these modifications was attributed the German defeat on the Marne. Von Moltke was deprived of his command and given the consolatory position of Chief of the Home General Staff in Berlin.

VON MOLTKE probably owed his position to his connection with the more famous General ; it was due to the Kaiser's influence and intervention that he was appointed to his command in 1906, and had he been more determined and courageous in enforcing von Schlieffen's methods, he would probably not have been displaced by Falkenhayn in the early days of the war.

HIS death took place quite suddenly in 1916, while he was attending a Reichstag function.

by having been so close to fortune and missed it, but genial and communicative.

As regards his own failure in the advance on Paris, he says—or rather implies (he does not say it directly)—that the miscarriage of the movement was due to von Bülow, the Commander of the 2nd Army, i.e. the army on his immediate left. Von Bülow was constantly in fear of being isolated from the armies on each side of him, and sent countless demands and requests to their commanders to close up and to leave no gaps. Von Bülow, before the war, had a somewhat superior court position to other generals, having more influence, and he probably resented not being left in full command of the entire right wing (as was originally intended). As von Kluck says, " Even if Bülow had not been able to advance as fast as my army, that would have been rather advantageous in that it would have facilitated the encircling of the French forces and accentuated the turning movement."

As regards the reason why von Kluck did not advance from Compiègne direct on Paris, he says that Paris was constantly his objective right up to Compiègne and Creil. He calculates that he could have been in Paris within three days, but German Headquarters forbade the advance on the ground that there was no military objective in it, the first necessity and condition being to defeat the French army in the field. Von Kluck was ordered to allow no gap between himself and Bülow ; as Bülow obliqued to the left, von Kluck had to conform, and did so most reluctantly.

It is a complete misconception to suppose that he was driven eastwards or diverted from the direct line on Paris by the attacks of the French 6th Army under Maunoury. So far from being driven east by these attacks, he had completely overcome them, and at the end of the third day of fighting—when Major Hensch came to him with final orders to retire (September 6) in order to conform to the

movements of Bülow's Army—he was in a position to
dispose of the French under Maunoury completely. If
Hensch's automobile had only had an accident and his
arrival had been delayed six hours, the whole campaign
would have been altered, because by then it would have
been apparent that no retirement by the Germans was
necessary. Hensch had been at his headquarters five
or six days before, but unfortunately had not been seen by
von Kluck. Hensch, as a junior, had some scruples in
disturbing an army commander, and had gone away
through deference, without discussing the general position.
Hensch was a capable officer, and certainly carried out
instructions given him to the best of his ability. Moltke
was also capable, but was ill—a good deal proceeded from
this.

Von Kluck is intensely proud of the marching feat of his
army in the advance from Mons to the Marne. He said:
" They covered distances which were rivalled by no
previous army. They advanced continuously, with no
day of rest. It was incredible what an army could do
under the leadership of a real leader, in the full understanding of the essential necessity for the sake of victory.
The only chance the men had of sleeping was during a
fight. All the rest of the time they were moving on."
This is confirmed by letters I have read, written by cavalry
officers in von Kluck's army. Though not on foot,
they complain of the appalling suffering on account of
want of sleep.

The above rather confirms the criticism that von Kluck
drove his men forward to exhaustion—marched them into
the ground.
It is also good evidence of the wonderful performance of
the English Army, who must have covered equal distances
on the retreat, and who were not, as the Germans, cheered
by success. It was a magnificent achievement for an army

to have retired so rapidly without losing cohesion and discipline.

ON other specific points of special interest von Kluck said : " THE English Army ought never to have gone to Mons in 1914. It lost its freedom of action and its manœuvring capacity, by being muddled up with the French. It should have been sent to Amiens, where it could have exercised a far more powerful influence.

" THE two-days resistance of the Belgians at Liège was not of any great importance. It could hardly have been expected that the Germans would get through quicker. The Belgians had made a great mistake in not defending the narrow pass near Liège. If they had concentrated there, instead of farther back, they might have exercised an important influence. No one realised sufficiently how narrow the pass was at Liège and Aachen, between the hills on the south and the Dutch frontier on the north, nor how difficult it was for the Germans to get their troops through the funnel with sufficient rapidity."

THE views given me by von Kluck regarding the fight between his army and that of Maunoury are very fully confirmed by French officers who were under Maunoury. They endorse the view that on the day before the German Army retired towards the Aisne, in obedience to orders from Headquarters, von Kluck had driven Maunoury back 11 kms., and was master of the situation. The same French officers minimise the importance of the supposed taxi-cab advance from Paris, saying that only one brigade of infantry was sent forward in this manner, and that the means of locomotion was not satisfactory.

VON KLUCK is loud in his praise of the original English Expeditionary Force. I stupidly forgot to ask him about the fighting at Le Cateau.

BERLIN, *March* 13, 1922.—Another talk with von Kluck to-day.

HE impressed me as less good-natured than at our first meeting : more of the Tartar and Kalmuck, but still something of the genial old Oriental who drives his men to death and the enemy to destruction, without any particular malice or animosity.

HIS great requisite for a military commander is " drive." A military commander must have something demoniac about him ; virtue and talent do not suffice. Joffre, whom he has met in Switzerland, he considers a good sensible man, but with nothing demoniac. Foch, on the other hand, has this demoniac " quality "—it serves to explain his victory.

HE further said : " Troops must have big artillery behind them—not that it does so much damage, but it gives moral strength and support. Even if the guns shoot wide, the noise gives the troops confidence. Much the same may be said of tanks—with tanks, troops think they are invincible. Military success is largely a question of ' psychose ' of moral forces—these and training to enable the men to march for ever. Marching capacity won 1866 and 1870."

HE again talked of the mistake made in not marching straight on Paris, and again said that the diversion eastwards was dead against his views.

HE is convinced that the 1st Army could have got to Paris and taken it. It might have caused the Germans heavy losses, but victory was certain, for the French had no heavy artillery.

HE praised Marshal French's strategy in the retirement to the Marne, saying that most commanders, after two fights like Mons and Le Cateau, would have said : " The third time I will stand to the last gasp and not retreat again." If Marshal French had done that, his whole army would have been captured or destroyed. He was wise to retreat behind the Marne. But von Kluck considers that when French decided again to attack, he did not advance rapidly enough. He ought to have thrown in his corps on the left without waiting for the right to wheel up and advance together. In situations of that kind, troops must be thrown into the fight immediately, without waiting for reserves or supports. That was what he himself did at Mons and what French ought to have done on the Marne. The English were too slow in attack.

VON KLUCK has a high opinion of Haig, and said that the handling of his troops during the retreat from Mons was masterly.

HE would not say much about Le Cateau, except that he nearly caught " die Engländer." But he thinks a lot of our First Hundred Thousand.

THE following is typical of the von Kluck mentality : When the troops complained that they were being driven forward too fast and marched to death, he said, " Children, I am only the interpreter of the situation. The situation demands that you should march—and march you shall."

[NOTE BY AN EYE-WITNESS

BERLIN, *March* 14, 1922.—Curiously enough, I happened by pure chance in 1914 to be present when an incident occurred which rather bears out General von Kluck's contention that the Army Commander on his left was constantly in fear of being out of touch with the troops on each side of him, and consequently made a mistake by deflecting eastward instead of continuing on his course. Some day between September 3 and 6 (I am not quite sure of the date, but, speaking from memory, I think it was September 4) I was in the Invalides, General Galliéni's [1] headquarters, and was present when

---

[1] GALLIÉNI, General Joseph Simon.—At the outbreak of war, General Galliéni was entrusted with the defence of Paris, and achieved fame by the speech he made declaring his firm intention of protecting the capital to the last.

ALTHOUGH he had reached the age for retirement, Galliéni's appointment as Governor of Paris was confirmed, though he gave way later to General

the General received reports to the effect that the
German Army on von Kluck's left—von Bülow's—was
marching eastwards. General Galliéni looked very surprised, and kept repeating : " C'est inconcevable qu'ils
obliquent à gauche." He then explained in detail to a
Captain Stewart (since killed) and to some officers of his
staff what a great mistake this movement constituted, since
there was now—as he put it—" un trou." He went on to
say that he had given orders to attack von Kluck's right,
in order to contain him and prevent him following the
eastward movement, and that to complete the success of
the plan and isolate von Kluck's army it would be necessary
for the British Army to push into the space thus created
between the two German armies. I know perfectly well
that he then started dictating a letter to Lord French, in
which was the sentence : " Le Général commandant la
forteresse de Paris invite le Lord French à . . ."—upon
which the officer who was taking this down remarked that
Lord French was a Field-Marshal, and that " invite "
was rather a strong expression to use ; whereupon he said,
" Bien ! Mettez ' Le Général commandant la forteresse de
Paris prie instamment le Maréchal French . . ." I presume this letter was delivered and is preserved somewhere
in our archives. There has been a great controversy in
the British press at various times as to whether the credit
for first seeing what was happening and initiating necessary
measures was to be attributed to General Galliéni or not.
The above incident would appear to go some way to support

Joffre. It was greatly due to Galliéni's presence of mind that the Germans
began to retreat from Paris and the French troops, under the General's
command, were able to occupy a more favourable zone.

IN 1915 Galliéni became Minister of War in the Briand Cabinet and pressed
two measures which contributed to the later French successes. He aimed
at unity of command and attempted to enforce changes in the power given
to General Joffre.

SHORTLY after Galliéni was forced to retire, owing to increasing ill-health.
He died in 1916. On April 12, 1921, the Chamber of Deputies conferred
upon him posthumously the title of Maréchal de France.

18

the contention that General Galliéni played a considerable rôle in the matter, but, of course, he is dead and cannot give his own version now, and others have been only too eager to claim the credit of success.]

BERLIN, *March* 13, 1922.—A war of revenge by Germany is, under present conditions, outside practical politics. Unless she is joined by a military Power who could replace her deficiency in heavy military equipment, success is out of the question. The military sense and understanding of the German people is such that they are the nation in the world least likely to commence a war without adequate preparation and war material. They would rather over-rate than underrate the importance of the equipment factor, and would be thoroughly unsuited by temperament and training to wage an irregular or partisan war with skill and success. Apart from *matériel*, the whole sentiment of the working classes is against war. The sufferings undergone in the Great War were too severe and are too recent. The first condition which would induce the mass of the public to engage in aggressive warfare is confidence in success ; and that confidence they have not, and cannot have, for the reasons developed above.

IT would, therefore, seem that apprehensions regarding a war of revenge in the near future are, so far as can be foretold, unfounded.

WHETHER it is politically desirable to dispel them, in so far as they are real, is a different matter. There are obvious disadvantages in the unrest they create. On the other hand, were they removed, the position of affairs might not be much better. The predominance of France and of her military allies would then not only be a fact—as it is to-day—but would be so clearly realised that it might lead to an aggravated attitude of self-confidence. Over-confidence might be worse than apprehension.

WHATEVER conclusion may be reached on this point,

it appears essential not to commit the error of judgment which would be involved in assuming that a war of revenge during the next few years is possible, on the military facts, with any chance of success.

THIS has to be repeated, because when a cry of " Wolf ! " is constantly raised, one is inclined, through weariness and weakness, finally to attach some credence to it : an attitude of active scepticism requires a considerable effort against the endless iteration of fear, or folly, or design.

I HAVE not mentioned the point, so often raised, of " moral disarmament." I not only doubt the existence of this at the present moment, but its bare possibility at any date.

No one that I have met here would think a successful war morally reprehensible ; nor would anyone advocate a war likely to prove unsuccessful, on the ground that it was morally defensible.

BERLIN, *March* 14, 1922.—Rathenau came to luncheon to-day in a state of some nervous excitement. He said he was driven wild by the perpetual notes of the French Embassy regarding this and that supposed default of the German Government. One day it was Upper Silesia, the next day a French Consul at Leipzig, then again disarmament. He would send me the number of the French notes he had received. I should see that life was impossible under these conditions, as the whole time of the Foreign Office was taken up answering more or less futile accusations. It was quite clear that the deliberate purpose of Poincaré was to multiply instances of supposed failure on the part of the German Government in order to make a case. He would soon say : " We have sent 24 notes to the German Government ; 12 have been left unanswered, 8 have been answered inadequately, and 4 have been answered with impertinence. It is impossible for a victor to stand this."

RATHENAU further said : " If I let the public know about

these notes there will be such a row in the Reichstag that the Ministry will fall.   I therefore keep them quiet ; but it is a great responsibility, and also a great ministerial danger, as attacks are sure to develop as soon as the deputies know the way in which the German Government is being treated after having done so much to meet the wishes of the Entente both in matters of payment and in other things."

RATHENAU appeared to be profoundly irritated, and not far from threatening to resign.

I ASKED him : " What do you suggest should be done ? " He said : " All I ask is that, when they come to you to join in signing notes of protest, you will point out that no German Government can live on such treatment.   Unless the Entente wish the present Government to fall, they must treat them better."

CHAPTER XIV

TOWARDS GENOA (*continued*)

Herr Loebe, the German Speaker—Lloyd George on disarmament—
German experts on Egypt and Turkey—French pin-pricks exasperate
Rathenau—A discerning diplomatist, M. Tusar—Fresh note from
Reparation Commission—Rathenau on Genoa prospects.

Berlin, *March* 14, 1922.—The President of the
Reichstag, Loebe, in his address to a large meeting
in Berlin a few days ago on the foreign political
situation, said :

" News from across the Channel would suggest that
Mr. Lloyd George intends to retire. I would deeply
regret his retirement. The International Economic Conference in Genoa has been already hindered by ministerial
crises in France and Italy. Mr. Lloyd George is the
greatest motive power among the statesmen of the victorious
countries who have realised that Europe cannot be restored
unless German reparation obligations are given another
form. He is the statesman who has pleaded most energetic-
ally for the co-operation of the peoples of Europe upon
economic questions. I sincerely hope that he will succeed,
supported by the confidence of his country, in carrying on
the task which he commenced, the aim of which he realised
so completely."

Professor Hoetzsch,[1] in the *Kreuz Zeitung* (which represents the Right), emphasises " the fatal consequences of
Mr. Lloyd George's retirement. In France they would,
of course, be very glad to see him go."

The *Frankfurter Zeitung* states that " the fall of Mr. Lloyd

CHAP.
XIII
March
1922

---

[1] Hoetzsch.—Dr. Hoetzsch was born in 1876 and was appointed early in
life Professor of European History in the University of Berlin.
In 1920 he was elected a member of the Reichstag, and has held this position
ever since. Dr. Hoetzsch is a specialist in foreign affairs, and has advocated
resistance to the Treaty of Versailles.
He is a strong supporter of monarchy, and rigidly opposed to Socialism in
any form. He is also a believer in denominational education.

George would allow M. Poincaré to exploit the situation at the expense of Germany."

BERLIN, *March* 14, 1922.—I rather gather that Rathenau has recently drawn up a Note on Military Disarmament, in which he suggests that Germany would agree to a permanent scheme of moderate military control provided that such military control was part of a general scheme of disarmament. He sent this privately to Lloyd George, asking that Lloyd George should make an exception to his rule and read it. The reply he got was that the Prime Minister thought publication of the Note premature. He has probably given this advice because he thinks it a mistake for Germany to take the first step.

HOWEVER, Rathenau is much disappointed at not being allowed to fire off his masterpiece, and regrets having consulted Lloyd George about it.

BERLIN, *March* 15, 1922.—A former German acquaintance came to see me this morning, and was interesting in this sense, that his attitude gave the measure of the changes produced by the last twelve months, both in political feeling inside Germany and in Germany's foreign relations. He is a clever, rather jovial, prejudiced business man with strong " Deutsch National " proclivities, an ex-naval officer, now a partner in an engineering firm.

A YEAR ago he made a great fuss about putting a foot inside an ex-enemy Embassy : said that notwithstanding his personal friendship with me he could not think of eating under an ex-enemy roof ; said, further, that Germany was on the path of national humiliation, and was being betrayed by unnational Socialists and timid servile Democrats.

To-DAY his tone was quite different : he said the political situation had greatly improved—even Wirth had some merit, while Rathenau was certainly clever. The next

President of the Republic must not be a General or anybody
too much to the Right, but rather a rich business man with
broad-minded liberal tendencies.   So far from being hostile
to England, he appeared friendly, and regretted that
the enormous fall in the valuta made a journey to London
too expensive.   He held the usual German heresy that only
by a continuously falling valuta could Germany compete in
neutral markets.   If valuta became stabilised, German
competition would lose its advantages, but he had nothing
to say when I suggested that this policy must finally
bring Germany down to the level of Austria and Russia.
" Après nous le déluge " is more true to-day of German
business men than it ever was of France in the eighteenth
century.

HE told me what was very interesting regarding commercial conditions : that an American steel company
had asked his firm to quote for big steamers—vessels of
20,000 tons.   Their price would be approximately £7
a ton, but as the ships would take eighteen months building,
the German company could not quote a firm price on
account of the danger of fluctuations in the valuta.   The
risk was too great.   But the Americans would only deal
on a firm price in gold or dollars.

HIS firm had also sent agents to Russia, but the moment
anything was settled with the Russians the latter broke the
contract.   Their unreliability was intense.   On the other
hand, he had private friends acting for themselves in a
small way who did pretty good business in Russia, taking
electric lamps and so forth and exchanging them for flax
and bringing the flax back to Germany.   One of his personal
friends had been doing this for a couple of years and had
come very well out of it.   This friend did not find conditions
of life in Petrograd so very bad.   Of course, he suffered
from the cold as there was very little heating, but general
conditions of comfort were improving—there were even
to-day a few cabs and sleighs plying for hire.

BERLIN, *March* 21, 1922.—Had a conversation to-day with the Czecho-Slovakian Minister here—M. Tusar.[1] He is perhaps the best-informed of the Diplomatic Corps in Berlin, being in close touch with all sections of German Socialist opinion, as well as with the Government and with President Ebert.

HIS view of the position is much more gloomy than it has been previously. He attaches grave importance to the continued fall of the mark, mainly because it must lead to a further rise in the cost of living, which, in its turn, will necessitate renewed negotiations about salaries. All this means discontent and unrest.

TUSAR tells me he is leaving to-morrow for Prague, where he proposes to put the position very clearly before the Government. He will give it as his opinion that unless rapid measures to relieve the financial situation are introduced, a severe collapse is probable. He considers the French policy absolutely insane, as, if there is a collapse, it will probably lead to some form of Labour Government, and this means the total non-payment of reparations. French arms might compel payment from a monarchical

[1] TUSAR, Vlastimir.—Tusar was the leader of the Social Democrat party in Czecho-Slovakia on the attainment of the independence in 1919, and at this time President Masaryk asked him to form a Cabinet.

THE task was a difficult one ; the Government was faced with the necessity for elaborating the Constitution, at the same time developing its own policy of agrarian reform. Tusar was to a large extent successful ; the country's international position was consolidated and her interests developed at the Peace Conference. The Prime Minister did not lose sight of the agrarian question, and many important reforms were effected.

THE new Government, however, was submitted to hostility from the People's Catholic Party, and in 1920 there was a forced general election which, however, showed a majority in favour of the Social Democrats.

ONCE more Tusar formed his Cabinet, but dissension rose in his own party on questions of policy, and within five months the second Cabinet was dissolved.

TUSAR's success was based on clear-sightedness and recognition of proletarial needs, rather than brilliancy of statesmanship. His independence of character made him particularly suitable as Premier in the initial days of the Republic.

Government ; it is out of the question for them to use
military force against Labour.

I QUOTE these views without expressing any opinion regarding their accuracy, but they have importance as they are held by a shrewd observer who knows the conditions here.

BERLIN, *March* 20, 1922.—I understand that Rathenau has recently made lively protests to the French Ambassador and to the Belgian Minister against the manner in which the German Government is being treated. His line is to say that the position of a German Foreign Minister is impossible if his whole time is occupied in answering notes of complaint regarding the non-execution of minor details.

RATHENAU states that since January 15 the Ministry for Foreign Affairs has received no less than 42 notes of complaint—9 from the French Embassy, 25 from General Nollet, 3 from Admiral Charlton, and 5 from Air Commodore Masterman.

THE working capacity of his subordinates is taken up in preparing answers on these subjects, and his own health is suffering.

THE Belgian Minister, I am told, replied to Rathenau that his Government was animated by friendly sentiments, and that it was quite untrue that Brussels merely followed in the wake of Paris. So little was this the case that Jaspar was being attacked in the French press for his pro-English proclivities. Rathenau appears to have answered with some sharpness—that he did not care for friendly sentiments which found expression in joint notes like that which was sent in by the Ambassadors on March 14.

IN conversation with the French Ambassador, Rathenau appears to have held somewhat similar language. He is reported to have said: " We will talk in three capacities: first, as representatives of our two Governments ; secondly, I as a Minister and you as an Ambassador, both of whom know Germany ; thirdly, we will talk as

old friends who have had extensive business relations."
What was said in the first two capacities may easily be
surmised.   As an old business friend, Rathenau appears
to have told Laurent quite straight that the present position
was intolerable, that no good could come of it, either for
France or for Germany.   Unless there was some change
in the attitude of Paris, he (Rathenau) would resign.

I DO not think that there is much danger of this threat
being carried out, but there is no doubt that the Foreign
Minister is profoundly irritated by constant criticisms and
by constant complaints.   Although I understand some of
the annoyance and irritation, one must not forget there
is another side to the question and that the German Government could undoubtedly have shown greater skill than
they have done in meeting the minor demands of the Commission of Control.

BROADLY speaking, it may be said that disarmament has
been carried out, and carried out very effectively, but
Germany gets little credit for this because shreds and
remnants are left which, while they can be of no possible
benefit to Germany, are profoundly irritating to those who
desire to clean up the situation and to prove that it has been
cleaned up.

IN conversation with Rathenau I have taken several
opportunities of impressing this view upon him and of
urging that Germany should not only carry out disarmament
on broad lines, but should endeavour to remove the above
grounds of complaint, which, if small and not intrinsically
of major importance, constitute, none the less, legitimate
reasons for complaint.

BERLIN, *March* 23, 1922.—The latest demand on Germany
by the Reparation Commission is as follows : Exchange
having fallen from 45 paper marks to 70 paper marks to
1 gold mark, the German Government must put on 60
milliards of new taxes.   Apparently it didn't occur to them

to demand that the level of exchange should be restored. This is probably feasible, and would benefit the whole position. To attempt to make good depreciation by increased taxes is almost certainly impossible, and resembles nothing so much as urging a dog to run after its own tail. To attempt to enforce such a policy by threats would render the Entente at once odious and ridiculous.

BERLIN, *March* 30, 1922.—The main event of the past month has been the receipt of the Note from the Reparation Commission establishing the conditions on which payments due by Germany during 1922 might be temporarily reduced. There was a good deal in the Note of the Reparation Commission which was quite sound, notably the recommendations to reduce expenditure in certain directions, to do away with subsidies, and to improve the railway administration ; but the Note was unfortunately marred by one or two grave blunders. The worst of these was to demand from the German Government—who have just passed a scheme of taxation for the country—a large additional increase of taxation. This demand was so extravagant that no German Government could possibly accede to it. The tone of the Note was also such as to ensure a maximum of opposition.

THIS has unfortunately been the case in a good many of the communications from the Entente—possibly due either to the genius of the French language, which is somewhat dictatorial, or to unconscious hectoring on the part of the French draftsmen. On many occasions the tone in which a demand has been made has gravely diminished its chances of acceptance, and this occurred in the present case. Apart from the above-mentioned very unfortunate demand, the Note did not indicate any clear line for financial improvement ; in particular, it omitted to emphasise the necessity for currency reform as an essential basis of future stability. I have always regarded this as a cardinal and essential feature, without which there is no serious foundation for any future improvement.

THE reception which the Note of the Reparation Commission met with in Germany was extremely unfavourable; all sections of public opinion joined in demanding that the Government should refuse, not only the demand for the increase of taxation by 60 milliards, but also the measures of financial control by some international body.

A DEBATE is now proceeding in the Reichstag and appears likely to end in a formal negative on the above points, joined with an expression of readiness to negotiate and discuss. I do not think any other result could have been expected. It would be at once futile and foolish to regard the Note of the Reparation Commission as an ultimatum for which immediate compliance must be exacted. I hope that the French Government will not be foolish enough to demand this.

REGARDING the establishment of some form of financial control in Germany, I have always considered that this might be done in such a manner as not to be unacceptable to German opinion, and I also hold the view that some kind of exterior financial supervision is often of great assistance to the finances of the country controlled. It gives the Finance Minister the requisite support in refusing this or that foolish measure. Certainly in Turkey, in Egypt, and in Greece and in Serbia, foreign commissions or councils in control of certain revenues and with specified rights over the financial administration have contributed powerfully to financial restoration. They have afforded, in a more permanent form, the kind of assistance derived from the Geddes Committee in England.

THE financial times are so difficult, owing to the burden of the war, that the ordinary apparatus and machinery is inadequate to cope with the task. Something of an extraordinary nature is required.

REGARDING military control, discussions on the continua-

tion of this in Paris are not yet sufficiently advanced for a
Note to be sent to the German Government, but I imagine
that something will be forwarded in the course of a few
days. It is probable that the demand for a continuation
of military control will create excitement and resentment
here. It is unfortunate that these two questions should
have arisen simultaneously. But in this question, as in
financial control, a good deal depends on the form in which
the demand is made. My own view is that the German
Government will not accept any form of permanent control
unless such control is part of a general system of disarmament and pacification. In other words, they will
demand some kind of counter-measure in other countries,
or some reciprocity. They will also certainly demand the
evacuation of the three Rhine ports—a demand which
the English Government has considered justifiable since
the acceptance of the ultimatum of May 1921.

BERLIN, *April* 1, 1922.—Rathenau talks as if a passive
trade balance was a sign of poverty. It is nothing of the
kind. All rich countries had passive trade balances—
Great Britain, France, etc. They did not produce any gold,
yet they were able to meet the position.

THE most heavily indebted countries have had the most
favourable trade balances—e.g. Egypt, because she was
paying her debts and could not, therefore, buy for consumption the full counter-value of her exports.

SIMILARLY, if Germany paid her debts and raised the
necessary sum by taxation, her imports would be less
than her exports, i.e. she would consume less and sell
more.

RATHENAU takes the balance of trade as an unalterable
fact revealing the condition of the patient. He listens
through a stethoscope : " Exports are less than imports ;
the patient's condition is serious." But this condition is
produced by the patient at will, and can be altered as he

chooses. It is the direct result of his diet, and proves, not that he is ill, but that he is living beyond his means.

BERLIN, *April* 4, 1922.—Rathenau does not hope much from Genoa, and fully realises that the whole Conference can be wrecked if one Power chooses to wreck it—either France or Russia or Germany.

HE developed at great length the theme that suffering in Germany is becoming acute in the middle classes through the rise in prices, and that the position is intolerable.

HE also reverted to his old analysis, which explains the absence of unemployment in Germany by the fact that a million men are working for reparation, a million are working to produce goods with which to purchase the necessary food, and another million are working to make up the loss through the eight-hour day.

TALKING of his own work, Rathenau said he had no idea how severe the labour could be. Since he became Minister he has never been to bed before 3 a.m.

RATHENAU says that Tchitcherin is a serious politician and makes a very good impression. Radek, of course, is not serious, and Litvinoff is just a small lawyer.

HE says the Russians are reasonable about the Genoa Conference and evidently intend to do their best to behave well.

BERLIN, *April* 4, 1922.—A private talk with Rathenau this morning.

HE read me a long letter which he is sending to Lloyd George, pointing out that the financial situation of Germany had become incomparably worse during the last three months. The real barometer is the price of exchange, and it has fallen from 500 to 1,500. This measured the incapacity of Germany to pay. Meantime the Reparation Commission sent in severe notes without taking into account Germany's position or German possibilities. It was essen-

tial that the whole question of Germany's ability to pay
should be examined under Art. 234. It was quite obvious
that the Reparation Commission had not yet done this.
The examination must be conducted by the best experts
of neutral countries.

RATHENAU's idea is that the loss caused by the war is too
great to be made good merely by belligerents.

THE whole world must contribute. He would suggest
that a reparation tax should be put on all raw produce—
coal, iron-ore, etc.—and this would form a world-fund for
restoration. World-indebtedness, he said, is symbolised
in the debt to America—namely, £2,000,000,000 sterling.
He would divide this into three parts :

ONE part should be blotted out.

ONE part should be paid by the levy on raw products
throughout the world.

ONE part should be paid by Germany.

CHAPTER XV

GENOA—THE RAPALLO TREATY

Franco-German frontier position—Rapallo Treaty signed—Wilhelmstrasse explains—Germany's secret Memorandum on Rapallo—Treaty badly received in Germany—No military clauses—Why Germany signed—British attitude over Rapallo—Nollet on German disarmament—Lloyd George and Wirth—Collateral causes of Rapallo.

THE GENOA CONFERENCE, APRIL 10—MAY 19, 1922

THE Conference assembled on April 10, under the presidency of the Italian Premier, Signor Facta, who was accompanied by his Foreign Minister, Signor Schanzer. Mr. Lloyd George headed the British Delegation, M. Barthou the French, MM. Jaspar and Theunis the Belgian, MM. Tchitcherin and Rakowsky the Russian, while the Germans were led by Chancellor Wirth and Dr. Rathenau. Twenty-nine European States were represented, including neutrals and ex-enemies. The inaugural session witnessed a breeze between M. Tchitcherin and M. Barthou, who had been peremptorily instructed by M. Poincaré to oppose not only any discussion of the peace treaties and the reparation problem, but any discussion on disarmament. The French Premier had further vetoed both the admission of Germany as a member of the Supreme Council and the appointment of any Commission to treat with the Soviet Government on political issues.

FOLLOWING on the opening session, the Conference set up four Major Commissions, which were to deal with (1) the consolidation of European peace, (2) financial problems, (3) economic and commercial problems, and (4) transport problems. The first Commission inclined to override M. Poincaré's veto, when it proceeded to appoint a Sub-Commission on Russian affairs, to which was referred the report of the Allied Economic Experts who had met in London between March 20 and March 28. This Sub-Commission included representatives of Great Britain, France, Italy, Belgium, Soviet Russia, Sweden,

Poland, Rumania, Switzerland, and Germany. But
at the request of the Soviet Delegation—a request
which, strangely enough, harmonised with M. Poincaré's veto on the participation of Germany on an
equal footing with the Allied Powers—it was decided
that the examination of the report in question should
be carried out informally by Great Britain, France,
Italy, Belgium, and Soviet Russia, Germany being
excluded.   Whether or no the Soviet Delegation, by
this request, had aimed at preventing any reconciliation
between the Allies and Germany, the result was a new
and bitter dispute between them, on the occasion of
the signing by the German and Soviet Delegations of
the Treaty of Rapallo, on April 16.   This act created
a great stir throughout Europe and aroused bitter
resentment among the Allies, who regarded it as the
outcome of a deliberate policy.   It threatened, indeed,
to break up the Conference, of which, in any event,
it was bound to mar the success.   Lord D'Abernon,
however, took a different view of the matter, holding
that it had been brought about by a series of accidents
and blunders.   The Allies, nevertheless, accused
Germany of bad faith for negotiating secretly and
separately with Soviet Russia.   The Germans retorted
by complaining of the Allies' attempt to reach an agreement with Soviet Russia independently of Germany
and to her probable detriment.   Finally, the German
Delegation withdrew from the general conversations
with the Soviet Delegation, while the Allies declared null
and void any clauses in the Russo-German Treaty which
might be held to conflict with the existing peace treaties.
THE Rapallo crisis, however, was only the first and
gravest of a series which deprived the Conference
of all practical fruits.   When the Russian Sub-
Commission (minus its German representative) resumed its labours on the commercial proposals to
be submitted to Russia, M. Jaspar, subsequently
supported by M. Barthou, upon the receipt by the
latter of fresh instructions from M. Poincaré, insisted
on complete restitution being made to foreign owners

19

of their former private property in Russia. The
Sub-Commission's proposals were handed to the
Soviet Delegation on May 3, with the Franco-Belgian
reservations, to which the Russians demurred in
vigorous terms.   On May 13 Mr. Lloyd George,
in order to break down the deadlock, brought forward
a new set of compromise proposals, which were
carried against M. Barthou's opposition.   It was
agreed on May 14 by the principal Allied Powers
and Belgium that a conference should be held at the
Hague in the following June, at which the Russian
problems examined at Genoa should be further
considered by a mixed commission of economic
experts.   The United States was to receive an invitation to this conference (which Washington declined),
but Germany was to be excluded.   The procedure
was elaborated by the British, Italian, and Soviet
delegates, France and Belgium withdrawing from
the discussions, although on the closing day their
representatives on the First Commission expressed
an oral and qualified acceptance of the scheme.
Meanwhile, on April 25, Mr. Lloyd George had put
forward his project of a European Pact of Non-
aggression.   M. Poincaré, however, laid down as
conditions of France's acquiescence in such a Pact
so many and material restrictions and prohibitions
as to impair the scope and value of the suggested all-
round undertaking.   Thus emasculated and reduced
to little more than an academic resolution, the Pact
of Non-aggression was adopted by the Conference on
the closing day, May 19.

THE Vatican was represented at the Genoa Conference
by an unofficial observer, who, nevertheless, on May 9,
addressed to the Conference a note from the Papal
Secretary of State, requesting that, in any agreement
between the Powers and Soviet Russia, guarantees
should be inserted for safeguarding liberty of con-
science, liberty of worship, and providing for the
return to the Roman Catholic Church of all property
owned by it in Russia.

April 10, 1922.—Genoa Conference opened.

BERLIN, *April* 12, 1922.—The frontier problem between Germany and France is of great interest. Military experts may know all about it, but I doubt if the man in the street fully appreciates the position. The map in pocket of cover shows the main features. It will be seen that on both sides of the Rhine large tracts of impassable country very much restrict the possible avenues of advance by a large military force. On the left bank of the Rhine the Vosges and the Ardennes block nearly three-quarters of the line where the French and German frontiers are either close or march together. Obstacles prevent any large advance, except along three clearly defined lines, one of which is extremely cramped. On the right bank, similar conditions confine a possible advance into Germany to three lines, corresponding to those on the French side. The Siegerwald, Westerwald, and Taunus correspond to, and are geographically opposite, the Ardennes and Hunsrück ; the Black Forest lies opposite the Vosges. An aggressive movement from either side is therefore restricted to two (or at most three) possibilities—an advance through the Palatinate, or an advance by the Cologne neck ; the third possible route— the Valley of the Moselle—being too narrow for the operations of a large force. Similar obstacles restrict an eastern move by the French troops into Germany.

THE practical result is that France and Germany have to defend, not a frontier, but two passages or defiles—one 70 miles broad, the other 20 miles broad: the Palatinate ; the Cologne neck.

PRESENT French policy is thus rendered comprehensible. These facts explain the determined efforts made to secure the Palatinate, as well as the persistent occupation of the Rhine ports—Duisburg, Ruhrort, and Düsseldorf. The former is the historical course of invasion, the broadest front available to either side, well adapted to an advance by force ; the latter district separates the Ruhr from the Cologne neck, and at once blocks the German advance via Cologne and facilitates a French entry into the Ruhr.

A FURTHER point clearly brought out is the extreme importance of the Dutch frontier, since the tongue of Dutch territory stretching south towards Cologne restricts the passage between the Ardennes and the Dutch frontier to extremely narrow dimensions. The defence of Belgium and Northern France is thus facilitated.[1]

April 16, 1922.—Treaty between Germany and Russia signed at Rapallo.

BERLIN, *April* 23, 1922.—Had an opportunity this morning of obtaining the German version of the negotiations with Russia which led up to the Treaty of Rapallo. My questions were rather direct than diplomatic, but they elicited a good deal of material for history.

MY first question was :

" WHY, after the full communication which was made privately in January regarding negotiations with the Russian delegates, did not the German Government make equally frank communication regarding more recent conversations with the Soviet on their way to Genoa ? "

THE German reply was :

" THERE was really nothing to report in the matter of progress. We constantly discussed the same questions more or less as we have been discussing since 1918, viz. Art. 116 : Confiscation of German property in Russia ; Assassination of Mirbach ; Diplomatic recognition of the Soviet.

" MANY drafts were prepared, but no real agreement was reached. This was mainly owing to two reasons. We did not want to go faster than England in the matter of

___
[1] In this connection, see conversation with General von Kluck, pp. 271–276.

recognition.   We did not want in any way to compromise our position at Genoa, or tie ourselves up there.   We all recognised that we should eventually come to terms with the Russians, but we were deliberately keeping the negotiations back until after Genoa."

" WAS it not the case that the agreement signed at Genoa was a copy of a similar agreement already initialled in Berlin ? "

" THAT is quite untrue.   Nothing was initialled here. The proof of this is that the negotiations on Sunday at Rapallo were extremely difficult and quite different from the mere ratification of a previous text.   Apart from any question of our right to make an agreement with Russia, it is quite obvious that our whole position at Genoa would have been vitiated by a previous agreement."

" WHEN did you first hear of the intention of the German Delegation at Genoa to make an agreement with the Russians ? "

" THE first news came in a telegram which we received at 2.40 on Sunday, April 16.   In this we were requested to inform the President that the local political situation rendered signature of a special Russian agreement necessary in order to avoid the isolation of Germany.   All the Delegation were unanimous that this was requisite."

IN further talk I learned that private letters received from Genoa told of an extraordinary series of contretemps which occurred on the Saturday and Sunday—meetings had been missed, telephone messages had gone wrong. The Germans had telephoned to the English and had been told on Sunday that they were out for the day.   This was understood as meaning that they did not wish to be consulted.   On the other hand, the Italians had invited Wirth and Rathenau to tea on Sunday to meet Lloyd George, but Rathenau had gone off to Rapallo and had then gone off to luncheon with Mumm at some place beyond.   Wirth could not go without Rathenau, consequently the Germans did not turn up at tea, and this was naturally regarded as deliberate abstention.

BERLIN, *April* 23, 1922.—The signature of the agreement between Germany and Russia, at Rapallo, is not regarded with much favour here. The mode and moment of signature is much criticised, and the fact of a separate contract with the Bolsheviks displeases many people.

IT is generally acknowledged that the German Delegation at Genoa committed a serious blunder.

THE supposed jubilation at an act of independence does not appear to exist, nor does anybody here believe in the possibility of military aid from Russia.

MEANTIME, the German Government deny emphatically any secret clause, military or otherwise.

THE following document purports to be the text of a secret Memorandum written by the German Delegation on events at Genoa in connection with the conclusion of the Rapallo Treaty.

IT is probably authentic, but must be read with due reserve.

GERMAN NOTES ON THE EVENTS LEADING UP TO
THE SIGNING OF THE GERMAN-RUSSIAN TREATY

BERLIN, *Tuesday, April* 11, 1922.—1. At the sitting of the Sub-Commission I., Lloyd George handed in the so-called English Expert Memorandum, remarking that without being binding it would serve as a basis for the various Governments on which to shape relations to Russia. Art. 6 of this Memorandum expressly confirms Russia's right to Art. 116 of the Versailles Treaty. Arts. 11 and 15 of Annexe 2, however, expressly exclude any claim of Germany against Russia.

2. ON Tuesday evening a conversation took place between Mr. Gregory, the head of the Russian Department at the Foreign Office, and Baron Maltzan. Gregory asked about our attitude towards the Memorandum. It was indicated to him that our attitude was

rendered very difficult by the Articles mentioned in (1).   Gregory
showed great surprise, said he did not attach the same importance
to this Article as we did, but had to admit that the text would justify
our assumption.   It was obvious that Germany could not be asked
to commit suicide : he would talk to the English Experts.

Wednesday, April 12, 1922.—3. A conversation took place at
4.30 p.m. in the Hôtel Miramare between the English representatives, Gregory, Sir William Clark, Fountain and Wise, and Maltzan
and Dufour on our side.   Maltzan set out afresh his anxieties as
explained to Mr. Gregory the previous evening   The four gentlemen, especially Sir William Clark, agreed that the Articles contained
in the Memorandum, which by the way did not contain the conditions of the Government, rendered Germany's position very difficult.
The Prime Minister would be spoken to, and it was hoped that they
would let us know as soon as possible.   Baron Maltzan remarked in
this connection that the Russians, with whom he had already negotiated
in Berlin, had shown themselves very accommodating as regards
Article 116.

WE had not closed with them at Berlin in order to have our hands
free at Genoa.   The fact that Art. 116, the effects of which are
represented to us by those present to-day, as well as by Lord D'Abernon, as harmless, has been expressly included in the London Memorandum, forces us to be most cautious.   Furthermore, the experts
and party representatives here, as well as the German press, have
taken up the attitude to the Memorandum described by me, and had
reproached us for having failed to accept the Russian offer.

Thursday, April 13.—4. The sitting of the Sub-Commission I.
announced for to-day has been postponed *sine die*.   Reports are
confirmed that far-reaching conversations are taking place between
the inviting Powers on the one hand and the Russians on the other.

Friday, April 14.—5. The English have so far failed to communicate
with us.   On the other hand, Charlier, the Belgian representative,
asked me how we regarded the London Memorandum, adding that
he hoped we would fall into line with them against the Russians.
I set out the same views to him as I had already done to the English
on the 11th and 12th.

AT 11 p.m. Schanzer's private secretary, Giannini,[1] appeared on behalf of Schanzer and asked to see the Chancellor in order to tell him that since Wednesday conversations had been taking place between the Russians and the inviting Powers, and that they are still going on.   A basis had been reached, by virtue of which the Russians would probably recognise their pre-war debts by the payment of long-term obligations.   As compensation for the socialisation measures, 99-year concessions were being contemplated.   War damage would be calculated as far as possible in conjunction with actual, but not formal, recognition of the Russian counter-charges for damage caused by interventions.   Giannini inquired on behalf of Schanzer respecting Germany's attitude to these proposals and the Memorandum generally.   Minister Rathenau asked if this meant an official request by Schanzer regarding our attitude to the Memorandum.

GIANNINI replied in the affirmative.   Rathenau explained to Giannini at great length, making a visible effect on his hearer, that, with respect to the burdens in the Memorandum set out as above, especially Art. 116 and the stipulations of Art. 260 of Versailles, our attitude to the Memorandum was of necessity very embarrassing. He asked Giannini expressly whether the question of altering these provisions had been suggested or contemplated.   Giannini answered in the negative.   Minister Rathenau stated expressly that we must reserve our attitude and accept alleviation respecting Art. 116 wherever we found it.

Saturday, April 15.—Maltzan met Joffe [2] and Rakowsky at 10 o'clock in the Palazzo Reale and related the events of the preceding day and

---

[1] GIANNINI, Dr.—Formally Financial Councillor to the Italian Embassy in London.   Played a big part down to the end of 1922 in all the reparation discussions and schemes.   Was distinguished by the excellence of his relations with the British Treasury, and can be said to have prepared the way for the subsequent Anglo-Italian Debt-funding Agreement, so favourable to Italy. Strongly supported the efforts of Mr. Lloyd George to re-establish friendly and business relations with Soviet Russia.   Left Italian diplomatic service on the advent to power of Signor Mussolini.   Is now one of the heads of the Bank of Italy.

[2] JOFFE.—M. Joffe was appointed head of the Bolshevik delegates at the Treaty of Brest-Litovsk, and was chiefly instrumental in forming the policy of revolutionising the German forces, since it would be fatal to reject openly the demands of the Central Powers.   This was the beginning of Russian

obtained from them accurate outlines of the negotiations in Lloyd
George's villa.   A prospect of help was held forth to the Russians
by the Germans in case the Russians would grant us guarantees for
Art. 116 and most-favoured-nation terms.   The Russians agreed,
but pointed out that the best course to attain this was to sign the
agreement proposed in Berlin.   They indicated their readiness to
accept this even at this juncture.   It was agreed to exchange views
on this subject later.

MALTZAN immediately tried to find the English, but failed.   In
the afternoon, however, he had a two-hours conversation with
Wise in the garden of the Eden Hotel.   He explained everything
over again to him, and informed him of the renewed Russian offers,
giving him to understand that negotiations respecting Arts. 116,
260, 11, and 15 were now under foot with the Russians, and that
an effort would be made to obtain any alleviations possible in that
quarter.   Wise showed no surprise, but quite realised the difficulty
of our position, indicated that he had placed the points at issue before
the Prime Minister, but it was difficult for England to effect any
improvement in the matter.   He confirmed the fact that the conversations with the Russians were going on at the time in Lloyd
George's villa and were apparently taking a favourable course.

Saturday, April 15, 8 *o'clock.*—Rumours as to a French-Russian-
English understanding thicken.   Telephone call from Wise to
Maltzan, Saturday, 11 p.m., asking him to communicate afresh
German anxieties regarding the four onerous points in the English
Memorandum.   Wise mentioned in this connection that Art. 260
of Versailles no longer came into question, as, in his view, the rights
of the Entente had expired.

Communist propaganda, which was one of the leading causes of the German
military collapse in 1918.
IN 1918 Joffe was sent to Berlin as Ambassador, and continued his seditious
activities there ; large sums were distributed on all sides, and the German
Government became quickly alarmed at the spread of Bolshevik sympathies.
Joffe was forced to leave the country, though he left behind a force of secret
agents and more money.
IN 1922 Joffe was invited to visit Japan to discuss relations between Japan
and Russia, and was chiefly instrumental in carrying out favourable negotia-
tions, which resulted in the resumption of diplomatic relations in 1925.
IN 1925 Joffe was appointed Minister Plenipotentiary in Austria,

Sunday, April 16.—Early, at 1 o'clock, telephone call from Joffe that the Russian Delegation was ready to enter into fresh negotiations with the German Delegation, and would be grateful if we could come to Rapallo for this purpose at 11 o'clock.

Easter Sunday.—Early, at 8 o'clock, Maltzan failed to get Wise on the telephone, and was told that Wise would call up himself later. On trying again at 9 o'clock he was told that the English gentlemen were not in.

AT 11.30, arrival in Rapallo, conversations with Tchitcherin, proposal to re-examine the text, and more especially a demand for a better guarantee that Germany would get equal treatment with other States in case socialisation compensation were granted. Between 3 and 5, conversations between Gaus, Maltzan, and Litvinoff.[1]   Agreement reached on final text after much difficulty. TELEPHONE call from Genoa to say that Lloyd George and Schanzer invited Rathenau and Wirth to come to tea at once.

Seven p.m.—Rathenau arrived in Rapallo again.   Treaty signed after exchange of friendly assurance.

Sunday, 10 *p.m.*—Sir William Blackett is informed of the agreement reached.

Monday, April 17, 7 *a.m.*—Maltzan informs Wise by letter, adding the different points of the agreement.

Ten a.m.—Conversations between the ministers.

---

[1] LITVINOFF, Maxim Maximovitch.—Litvinoff, with Gorky, founded the first legal Social Democrats' newspaper to appear in Russia—*New Life.*   He had been associated with the Bolshevik cause from the age of seventeen, and had been a member of the Central Commission until the 1905 Revolution. He was chosen in that year to attend London as a delegate from the Riga Commission, and visited England several times later; when the reaction against Bolshevism set in, he was deported from England.   During that exile he was not idle, organising the transport of weapons to the revolutionists in the Caucasus.

TOWARDS the end of the war he was appointed diplomatic Soviet agent in England, and was the premier delegate for the Soviets at the Hague; this was followed by his appointment as Commissar for Foreign Affairs and Chief-in-Staff of the Red Army.

Eleven a.m.—Agreement with Russian press to arrange publication of text of treaty.

Twelve o'clock.—German press and German experts are informed.

End of alleged German Documents

BERLIN, *April* 24, 1922.—The conclusion of the Rapallo Treaty between Germany and Russia has not been well received by public opinion here.   No dominant section really desires close co-operation or alliance with the Bolsheviks, who are distrusted and feared by all parties (except a few extreme fanatics).   The general view is that the Germans were stampeded by the Russians at Genoa ; the members of the German Delegation were in a corner (or thought they were), so they signed the treaty in a moment of great despair.   It is quite obvious that the conclusion of the treaty was not part of a deliberate German policy, or the outcome of a deep " plot."

THE conception that as a result the general trend of German policy will be modified is not shared in Berlin.   The treaty is considered to be a mere understanding, getting rid of certain financial menaces, not as giving a new orientation to German policy.   But the position is not immutable ; extreme pressure or extreme distress is likely to convince the Germans that a change in their policy is necessary. If any such change occurs, the main responsibility will rest on French extremists, who are doing their utmost to bring about what they and we have most to fear.

BERLIN, *April* 26, 1922.—An opportunity presented itself this morning to question a German official concerning the current allegations in the Allied press regarding a military agreement with Russia.

AFTER consultation with the head of the Russian Department, I was formally and deliberately assured that the subject of military preparations had never been mentioned between the Germans and the Russians. The Russians had made no proposals of this kind. I observed that a similar clause to that quoted in the *Daily Mail*, prohibiting the transport of arms to Russian border States, had been proposed by the Soviet as a secret addition to other treaties they had made, notably with Czecho-Slovakia. This lent probability to the idea that the Soviet had also proposed it to Germany. The denial was maintained. The official then showed me a statement issued by Krupp, denying any contract with the Soviet for the construction of arms factories in Russia, but I observed to him that this only contradicted a small portion of the *Daily Mail* assertions. In view of the increased distrust of Germany which the Russo-German Agreement had provoked, it would be most desirable that the German Government should deny, not generally, but specifically, the various points in the alleged treaty, if indeed there was no basis to the allegation.

I WAS also informed that von Simson had come back from Genoa to report to the Cabinet regarding the Russo-German Agreement. Von Simson had been surprised to find how cold the reception of this agreement had been, both in Government circles and by the public in Berlin. He told the Cabinet that at Genoa the whole German Delegation had been in favour of it, and had considered it the only means of avoiding a grave danger to Germany. Von Simson gave, generally speaking, the same account of the proceedings as that contained in the German Memorandum. He added little to it.

I GATHER from another source that Ebert,[1] the President of the Reich, was extremely annoyed at the signature

---

[1] EBERT. Born in Baden, 1871. Was a man of humble origin and by trade a saddler. As first President of the German Republic, he performed the feat of earning the approbation of practically all the parties, including even the Monarchists. Ebert, who looked like the mayor of a small town, displayed outstanding qualities of courage and determination in steering the ship of state through the stormy seas of post-war years. More than once he intervened personally in order to arrange a compromise in the formation of

of the treaty, without his being consulted and without
his approval.   He considered that the signature of such a document went beyond the powers given to the ministers when they left for Genoa.

DURING a discussion with a German official as to the real bearing of the agreement, it was emphatically stated that no change in the general trend of German policy was indicated, nor any modification of the policy of fulfilment. The Rapallo Treaty was merely incidental and was resorted to as an expedient to remove certain grave financial dangers which were thought to threaten.   There was no change in the general trend of German policy.   It was absurd to suppose that it indicated a new grouping of Russia and Germany against the Western Powers.   I replied that, if this was so, it was unfortunate that the fact had not been made more clear to public opinion in the West.   It was evident from Poincaré's speeches, and from other sources, that the Russo-German Agreement was widely considered to be a new departure in German policy.

BERLIN, *May* 3, 1922.—Evidence continues to accumulate to the effect that the Germans were " jumped " at Rapallo. Many diplomatists thought and think that Maltzan was working for a signature at any price.   I had also rather suspected one or two other permanent officials of the old school of the same tendency, these officials representing the pre-war anti-Western tradition.   But a good witness, who saw Maltzan and his assistants on the day they left for Genoa, is pretty certain they were *then* against concluding anything.   Indeed, one of them said : " We are leaving

a Government when matters had reached a deadlock.   He and his successor in the Presidency, Field-Marshal von Hindenburg, had a great mutual respect for each other.   Ebert was also on quite good terms with the head of the Reichswehr, General von Seeckt, whose anti-Bolshevik ideas he shared strongly.   Died in 1925, and was succeeded by Field-Marshal von Hindenburg.

without any definite instructions and without any definite plans, but we intend to do our best to bring Genoa to a successful conclusion, and to regain our European status."

ASKED whether anything had been concluded with the Bolsheviks, he said : " No ; there are still many points of difference, and we shall certainly not conclude anything with them without declaring it openly."

MALTZAN, on the same day, said that, while he was anxious to make an agreement with the Bolsheviks, he was altogether against recognising them officially before Genoa. " What do we get by official recognition ? We are already at peace since Brest-Litovsk. Besides which, we shall get no concessions from the Russians for recognition, unless we add cash to the recognition. That is what they are really after. From the German point of view, the only reason for hurry is Art. 116."

BERLIN, *May* 4, 1922.—Met Nollet (the French President of the Military Commission of Control) at dinner last night, and had a long talk with him and with General Barthélemy, who is the ablest of his assistants.

I WAS impressed with the moderate and sensible views which they took. Both fully realise that Germany is to-day incapable of waging war. Barthélemy in particular said that war without all the scientific appliances and heavy guns was absolutely impossible. Against Poland, Germany might conceivably carry on a campaign on the guerilla basis ; against a French army this would be out of the question.

BARTHÉLEMY further said that the idea of suppressing completely secret military organisations in Germany was a Utopia ; one might restrict them, but they were impossible to uproot. History showed that such attempts were futile. They had been tried with the Jesuits and completely failed ; they had been tried in France against the Freemasons

and had failed equally. The only way was to keep as
firm a grip as one could, and trust to the men who had been
in the late war dying off and on their not being replaced by
others.

BOTH Nollet and Barthélemy thoroughly realise that the
real check on Germany's revenge policy is *matériel*, and
not *personnel*.

I DO not know what they report to Paris. Their private
judgment is apparently against the existence of any military
danger from Germany.

NOLLET is further optimistic about a solution. " Vous allez
voir—tout s'arrangera."

BERLIN, *May* 4, 1922.—The Blackett plan for the reduction
of reparations to 45 milliard marks under certain conditions
is again mentioned in telegrams from Genoa.

ALTHOUGH it receives a certain amount of notice, it is
strange how little enthusiasm it evokes in German circles,
when one considers that it is a reduction from 132 to 45
milliards. Six weeks ago, when the plan originally appeared in the European press, I was surprised at the small
notice such a windfall received. When I discussed it with
Rathenau, he said : " Even the reduced amount is more
than Germany can pay." The failure of the German press
to accept with avidity the Blackett proposal arouses suspicion regarding German sincerity in seeking a reasonable
compromise.

BERLIN, *May* 4, 1922.—President Ebert is reported to be
quite unreconciled to the Rapallo Treaty : says it was as
unwise as it was unconstitutional ; he ought to have been
consulted. He is determined to have Maltzan out, and
if Maltzan's fall involves Rathenau, so much the worse.

I DO not think all these threats will materialise, but it is a
symptom of the Majority-Socialist party's annoyance at the
Russian Agreement.

BERLIN, *May 5*, 1922.—Received an account this morning from a German source at Genoa of a recent interview of Lloyd George with Wirth and Rathenau.

THE dominant impression was that Lloyd George only cared for the Russian question, and was absolutely bent on arriving at some agreement with the Russians, either with or without France.

WHEN Wirth said he had to return at once to Berlin, Lloyd George urged him strongly to remain to assist in negotiations and to act to some extent as intermediary.

DURING the whole conversation there was not a word of reproach about the Rapallo Treaty ; the resentment at this appears to have passed off.

BERLIN, *May 8*, 1922.—It may be well to set down the collateral and minor causes which led to the signature of the Russo-German Pact at Genoa.   Personal vanity played a considerable part.

WHEN Rathenau started for Cannes last December he was rather inclined to support what is called a continental policy for Germany, and was undoubtedly much impressed by the desirability of Germany coming to some arrangement with France.   His general view was that although Germany would not have chosen France as a neighbour, and France would not have chosen Germany, they had been placed in such proximity by Providence that it was necessary for them to come to terms.   On his way to Cannes, Rathenau stopped in Paris.   He called on various French authorities, but the visits were not returned.   This offended him deeply.   On arrival at Cannes, the English financial delegates and Lloyd George treated him well, talked over things confidentially with him, the Prime Minister having been greatly attracted by his theoretical views about working hours, balance of trade, etc., etc.

AT any rate, Rathenau returned to Berlin greatly attracted by Lloyd George and believing he had secured a firm friend.

EITHER as a result of his conversations in Cannes or as a
result of his previous visit to London, he established various
private channels of communication between himself and
Downing Street. Working through these in the course of
the spring of 1922, he put forward several ideas and consulted Lloyd George regarding them. The replies received
were generally negative, and Rathenau—who might be
termed, like Behemoth, the King over the Children of
Pride—was offended. His experience in this matter
probably inclined him to go ahead at Genoa without
previous consultation with the P.M.

IN March, before Genoa, Rathenau made a very foolish
speech in the Reichstag, saying that Poincaré had got
the better of Lloyd George at Boulogne, that Lloyd George's
star was on the decline, and that he would probably be
replaced by some other leader. What induced him to
make this blunder cannot be said with certainty. I
attribute it largely to annoyance at his proposals not having
found immediate favour in Downing Street. I do not think
that he desired the fall of Lloyd George or that he expected
more support for Germany from anybody else. However,
he made the speech. Lloyd George saw it, and began to
pay Rathenau out for it by greeting him very coldly at
Genoa, by refusing to receive him at all through the first
week, although Rathenau declares he made three or four
separate attempts. This was another blow to Rathenau's
vanity, and he reacted quickly by taking up the negotiations with the Russians which had been simmering for the
previous three months.

RATHENAU says that he told Wise and others that he
intended to sign the Russo-German Treaty. Perhaps he
did; perhaps Wise did not understand; perhaps Rathenau
was not explicit. Probably what he said was : " If Germany is excluded from the negotiations between the
Powers and Russia, she will have to defend herself as best
she can." In his mind this may have meant that Germany

20

would sign with Russia, but I do not think Wise or anybody else could be expected to gather the precise meaning.[1]

BERLIN, *May* 10, 1922.—Information from Socialist circles indicates that Rathenau will meet with severe criticism on his return, on account of the Rapallo Treaty. Majority Socialists care principally about the reparation question. If Genoa and Rapallo produce no alleviation in this, someone will have to pay the penalty.

MOREOVER, Rathenau has to face the undying hatred of the Right and he receives continually threatening letters from members of the extreme Nationalist organisations. As he is courageous, and indeed contemptuous of danger, he refuses all police protection. But he has often told me that he is sure to be assassinated.

[1] ON December 13, 1928, Mr. Wise, in a letter to the *Daily Telegraph*, stated that, immediately prior to the Easter Sunday on which the Rapallo Treaty was signed, he saw Baron Maltzan at the latter's request on two or three occasions, there being present at one of these meetings certain Foreign Office and other members of the British Delegation. When the Germans expressed alarm on account of the discussions then proceeding between Mr. Lloyd George and the Russian Delegates, they were repeatedly assured that such alarm was entirely unfounded and that the discussions could in no way affect them adversely. On Dr. Rathenau expressing a desire to see Mr. Lloyd George, this request was at once transmitted through the proper channels.

MR. WISE continues by stating that the first he knew of the matter was on the Monday morning after the Treaty was signed, when he received personally a note from Count Maltzan enclosing what was in fact an incomplete copy of the Treaty—the signatory clause and date had been torn off —in which it was indicated, not that the Treaty had been signed, but that it was under consideration. In reply to Press inquiries Baron Maltzan indicated that Mr. Lloyd George, Mr. Wise, and M. Giannini had been informed. In all cases, Mr. Wise states, these allegations were at once denied.

CHAPTER XVI

AFTER RAPALLO

Views from Moscow—General Le Rond—Upper Silesia—Break-up of Genoa
Conference—Lloyd George and Poincaré—Maltzan's own story of
Rapallo.

ERLIN, *May* 10, 1922.—News from Moscow suggests
that the Soviet Government are working towards
closer co-operation with Germany, but how far
this attitude indicates a real change of policy on the part
of the Bolsheviks, or how far it may be considered of
a tactical nature, designed to impress the world with
a sense of impending peril, is doubtful. Personally, I
rather incline to the latter view. My opinion has always
been that the signature of the Rapallo Treaty was not the
result of any serious faith in a policy of lasting co-operation;
it was more of the nature of a provocative demonstration.

A STRANGE element of mockery is often evident in the
proceedings of the Soviet Government ; they delight to
play a trick on capitalistic powers, even though the
trick mars the success of their own policy. I doubt if
they regard the Germans as possible collaborators in their
schemes for reforming the world. It is noteworthy that
since the signature of the Rapallo Treaty, so far from abstain-
ing from propaganda, they have accentuated it and have
already come into conflict with the German Government
on this subject.

I REGARD prolonged and close co-operation between Germany and Russia as improbable—with this reserve : that
the two Governments are not driven together by external
pressure and by exposure to a common danger.

As regards military co-operation between Germany and
Russia, although the German Government deny emphatically the existence of any agreement or understanding of
a military nature, a number of alleged documents have
been produced recently—military conventions, contracts

for sale of arms by Germany to Russia, etc., etc.   Some
may be genuine, but most of them are forgeries.   I am
sceptical of any wide compact involving officially the
German Government, but German firms will be found
ready to enter upon any lucrative commercial deal which
does not involve undue political risk.

DURING the last two years we have heard many tales about
German officers in Russia, but, so far as I know, nobody
has as yet seen a German officer in any position of authority
in the Soviet Army.   During the Bolshevik attack on
Poland in 1920 no German officers were found among
the thousands of Russian troops who surrendered.   The
truth is that the military class in Germany is too violently
anti-communistic to allow much prolonged co-operation.

I AM very sceptical about the existence of official contracts
for the delivery of large quantities of war material by
German firms, if such involve direct violation of Germany's
obligations under the Treaty of Versailles.   There is no
doubt a good deal of smaller trade going on, for it is obvious
that any German, having to choose between the destruction
of old armaments and a possible sale to anybody—in
Russia, Turkey, or anywhere else—will prefer to run a
certain amount of risk in hope of gain rather than lose
his property without compensation.   In my judgment, it
is extraordinary that the Disarmament Commission have
been able to obtain the destruction of such vast quantities
of guns and munitions, and that more of these have not
found their way out of Germany.

APART from ordinary considerations of gain, it must be
constantly remembered that there are in Germany a large
number of small Jewish traders, who are specialists and
experts in second-hand dealing, and who are strongly
attracted by the large profits obtainable on transactions
in arms.   In a certain section of their complicated mentality
these classes have more than a sneaking affection for
the Bolsheviks.   Many of them are inclined to regard their

co-religionaries at Moscow as rather fine fellows, who have done something to avenge the misfortunes of the Jewish race ; they consider Trotsky and the Cheka the apostolic successors to Judith and Deborah.   The conjunction of this idealistic hero-worship with the possibility of a high percentage of gain forms an almost irresistible temptation to such as happen not to be imbued with an exceptional austerity in regard to international obligations.

BERLIN, *May* 12, 1922.—Met the famous General Le Rond[1] yesterday at luncheon at the French Embassy. I had previously seen him at Spa.

HE talks as if he was sincerely anxious to get away from Upper Silesia, and expected to achieve this ambition in the course of six weeks or two months.   He said the Germans and Poles had already settled down to a considerable extent and he did not at all give the alarming picture of conditions there which telegrams usually present. Indeed, he talked of Upper Silesia as a prosperous industrial country rapidly regaining its pre-war activity under his guidance.   He said specifically : " I pay no attention to any facts except the figures of coal production, which is now 85 per cent. of 1913.   March was the best month we have had."   His conversation was that of an enthusiast for economic reconstruction, whose mental horizon excluded all thought of political intrigue.

[1] LE ROND, General.—In 1921 the Korfanty insurrection broke out as a result of the plebiscite in Upper Silesia.   The head of the Inter-Allied Commission appointed to administer and control the region was General Le Rond, whose passive attitude towards the insurgents gave rise to criticism and dissatisfaction.   It was proved that at one time, armistices between the officers of the Commission and the rebels were held, if not with Le Rond's permission, certainly without any objection from him.
THE affair of Upper Silesia caused a crisis in European political circles, menacing as it did the conditions of the Treaty of Versailles.   Polish hostility to German demands was not lessened by Le Rond's objection to the proposed settlement of Silesia by the Commission, though the Italian and British representatives were in full agreement with the terms.

THE Germans regard him as half Machiavelli and half Mephistopheles.

BERLIN, *May* 15, 1922.—Am informed from a second reliable source that President Ebert remains hostile to the Rapallo Treaty.   He says Maltzan must be dismissed. Rathenau deserves to be, but Ebert cannot afford to do without him.

EBERT considers Maltzan much too intimate with Tchitcherin and Bolsheviks generally, and wedded to the one idea of close co-operation with Moscow.

ON the other side, a section of the Volkspartei, including Stinnes, is getting quite excited about the Rapallo Treaty, which many of them now cordially approve, and on which they build many castles in Spain.   Outside the Volkspartei, the tendency in political circles among other groups remains cold to hostile.

SOME people consider that the Rapallo Treaty, which has to be ratified by the Reichstag, will not obtain ratification.

FURTHER, by the constitution, the treaty requires the President's signature, and he is loath to give it.   It is impossible to say what will happen, but exciting debates are probable directly the German Delegation get back from Genoa.

MY own impression is that hostility to Rapallo will not be pushed to an extreme.   But the animosity against Rathenau is bitter.

BERLIN, *May* 17, 1922.—The Genoa Conference comes to an end this week.   It has accomplished extraordinarily little in five weeks of feverish work.   The result is notably a minus in the political sphere, for the relations of the different Powers are worse rather than better.   Certainly this is the case between England and France, and is probably the case between Russia and the Entente.

THE German delegates, after their blundering mistake

in being duped into signing the Rapallo Treaty, have applied themselves to regaining favour, and would appear to have succeeded well. Certainly in the case of Lloyd George, a friendly basis has been established so far as Wirth is concerned. Rathenau, Lloyd George seems to dislike and to suspect—the re-echo of that idiotic speech of Rathenau's six weeks ago.

THE German financial delegates all speak of useful conversations with English technical advisers, and with the technical advisers of other countries. The work of Economic and Financial Sub-Commissions has unquestionably been sound. It may be called theoretical, it may be called elementary school teaching, but I put the Sub-Commission reports on Currency, Credit, etc., as considerable assets.

So far as regards the general outlook, everything seems to turn on the negotiations in Paris for a German loan to pay reparations and to give Germany a breathing space. I remain of the opinion that if Germany has time, she can pay a considerable amount of reparation. The one attitude to avoid is that of a blind, relentless Shylock.

YESTERDAY, a visit from Mr. Tiarks, partner of Messrs. Schroeder, London. He attaches great importance to the meeting called by the Bank of England of the leading State banks in the world. I cordially agree in this view. He says that Norman (Governor of the Bank of England) is the heart and soul of this co-operative movement between the note-issuing banks of the world, and that a better man could not be found for the negotiation. Great benefit may come from the discussion. I warned Tiarks that Havenstein,[1] the President of the German National Bank, although honest and straightforward, is ignorant and

---

[1] HAVENSTEIN.—President of the Reichsbank in 1922. Was long regarded in Germany with tremendous respect by all classes as the very embodiment of sound State finance. Whereas, as a matter of fact, he completely misled both the bank and the Government on the subject of currency, and was one of the chief causes of the inflation which very nearly proved Germany's complete ruin. Died 1923.

obstinate. His speech the other day on German currency pressed into the shortest space the maximum number of fallacies and errors. Havenstein apparently considers that the fall in German exchange is quite unconnected with the gigantic increases of German note issues, and he goes on merrily turning the handle of the printing press, completely unconscious of its disastrous effect. Tiarks was greatly surprised when I told him this and refused to believe that anybody could fail to understand the connection between increase of note issue and exchange depreciation. It was proved by Havenstein's speech and by Rathenau's speech of about the same date that what he considered was impossible was true ; moreover, there was evidence that ninety bankers in Germany out of a hundred express and perhaps hold the same views. He was surprised, and shocked, and startled, and did not believe it, but it is demonstrably true.

THE current opinion that Lloyd George is changeable and unpersistent in his views is the exact opposite of the truth. He is persistent to the verge of obstinacy ; in fact I think it is his fidelity to causes which makes him so apparently changeable in his views of people. The person is sacrificed to the thing. Take his attitude on the Turkish question. In this case he has had all the best opinion against him, including most of his colleagues, almost all the experts, and the large majority of people with local knowledge. It has not made him budge an inch. Genoa was merely a revival of the Prinkipo idea of two years before. Encouragement to the Greeks in Asia Minor was undoubtedly given by him through private channels long after everybody else realised that the Greek cause in Asia Minor was absolutely hopeless, the policy having been fundamentally wrong from the beginning and being no less clearly disastrous for Greece than for England.

An extraordinary instance of his persistency against expert

opinion and of his force was the imposition in England of the tax on imports from Germany. The entire London Conference of 1921 was against this view, not only all the foreign delegates, but all the English experts, except perhaps some unknown person behind the scenes. A Technical Committee met at 3 in the afternoon and unanimously condemned the idea. It was presided over by the Chancellor of the Exchequer. Three hours afterwards a full meeting of the Conference adopted the device. L. G. simply sailed over his opponents.

IT was much the same at Genoa with the Russian question. Very few people either in the foreign Delegations or in the British Delegation believe in the possibility of any serious arrangement with Russia. Russia is entirely ruined, and no trade of considerable moment can be carried on for a good many years to come. The Soviet Government are absolutely and totally unreliable, their main object in negotiation being to make bourgeois delegates appear ridiculous. Their promises are worth less than nothing, as they take a delight and pleasure in breaking them. Their fundamental ambition is expressed in Bela Kun's message to Lenin : " I am proud to be your pupil, but in one thing I excel you, and that is bad faith." And yet for five weeks at Genoa the whole areopagus of Europe has been held at the beck and call of the Russian Delegation and has made itself ridiculous.

THE worst of the present conflict between London and Paris is that in many points the French are right and we are wrong. This is pre-eminently so in regard to Turkey and in regard to Russia. In the case of Germany, on the other hand, I think that the French are wrong and that the destructive policy they have adopted must lead to European disaster. But in the Russian and Turkish questions they have undoubtedly been more sensible and more clever than we.

POINCARÉ is characteristically a man of legal documents

and precise mathematical formulæ. Unskilful in handling men, he is profoundly intolerant of the artistic and rhetorical. Within his own limits, a great force with an uncanny knack of getting his own way by making his opponents appear unprecise, unmethodical, and unpatriotic.

IF one is asked what the faults of Genoa were and what Genoa ought to have done, the answer is not difficult. In the first place, Genoa ought to have avoided the initial blunder of believing too much in the Bolsheviks and making the whole conference pivot on them. They made the Bolshevik game of dividing Europe too easy. In the second place, Genoa required a much broader theoretical view. It needed a general survey of the whole European financial and economic position. This survey must necessarily have included indebtedness, both between nations and between classes. No essential improvement is possible without this. Apart from indebtedness, a second great cause of trouble is excessive expenditure, notably military expenditure. Here, again, a broad survey is requisite. Military expenditure brings attention naturally to guarantees for peace. The suggested pact with its reserves in favour of the Petite Entente, with its reserves in favour of sanctions for non-fulfilment of reparation, and the other reserves made for other specific causes, rendered the net result rather an aggravation of existing dangers than an alleviation of them. The basis of pacification and of reduced military expenditure is to be found in the elimination of the fear of Germany. This might be achieved to a large extent by the establishment of some continuation of military control here. This negotiation would be viewed favourably by Germany in so far as it relieves her of the present Commission. Negotiations with Germany for the continuation of control lead naturally to the demand for reciprocity, and general pacification. Along these lines a general understanding might have been brought about; not easily but possibly. I believe two things—this negotiation would have been

easier than the pact negotiation,[1] and would have been
enormously more effective.   But it was impossible to get
L. G. to take it up.   Rathenau tried six weeks ago.   He
sounded Downing Street.   The reply was : " Inopportune
and premature."

THE Genoa Conference broke up on May 19.   The
most dramatic story of the circumstances in which
the German delegates at Genoa were rushed by the
Soviet into signing the Rapallo Treaty was told over
four years later.
IT is interesting to compare this verbal statement by
Herr Maltzan with the facts related in the memorandum alleged to have been written by the German
Delegation on events at Genoa.   This account goes
a long way to prove the authenticity of the memorandum in question, though there are minor points
of divergence between the two documents.

BERLIN, *October* 2, 1926.— Met Maltzan last night at a
dinner, and took the opportunity of asking him the real
story of the Rapallo Treaty.
HE said the treaty had been practically agreed to with
the Russians as far as regards wording, as early as Christmas,
but Rathenau had been opposed to signature pending
the Genoa Conference.   Rathenau was, indeed, opposed

---

[1] THIS is the pact which was submitted to the Conference by Mr. Lloyd
George on April 25.   It provided for a solemn declaration by the Assembly
that they would not make war upon each other, and was especially designed
to prevent future clashes between Soviet Russia and the border States,
including Poland and Rumania.   The French Delegation, however, as
instructed by M. Poincaré, insisted on altering the original text, which was
simple and straightforward, by the insertion of clauses exempting the Little
Entente Powers from any obligation of Disarmament, and providing for
sanctions in the event of the non-fulfilment by Germany of her reparation
obligations.   These reservations ruined the pacific intent of the pact and
killed any chances it might otherwise have had of winning universal assent.
It is nevertheless of interest to compare it with both the League Assembly's
Pact of Non-Aggression of September 1927 and the Kellogg Pact of 1928.

to the Eastern connection, holding to closer relations with France and England, perhaps more particularly with France.

RAPALLO was signed on a Sunday evening.

THE night before, information from various sources came to the German Delegation at Genoa, from the Dutch, from the Italians, and from others. All reports confirmed the fact that Russia had come to terms with England and France, while Germany was left out in the cold. Rathenau was in despair ; all the schemes he had formed were falling to the ground. The German Delegation talked the position over and eventually decided that nothing was to be done for the moment. So they went to bed. At 2 a.m. Maltzan was awakened by the hotel waiter, who said : " A gentleman with a queer name to speak to you on the telephone." This was Tchitcherin. Maltzan went down to the hotel hall in a black dressing-gown, and commenced a conversation on the telephone which lasted a quarter of an hour. Naturally, everything was heard by the Italian detectives, who kept ceaseless watch in the hall. The upshot of Tchitcherin's conversation was that he wanted the Germans to come to him on Sunday and discuss whether Germany and Russia could not come to terms. He did not say that negotiation with the Western Powers had failed, but Maltzan saw at once that the news given to the German Delegation previously, viz. that agreement was complete between Russia and the Western Powers, was false. Directly Maltzan found that the Russians were running after Germany, he drew back, saying it was very difficult to call on Sunday, the German Delegation had organised a picnic, and that he himself must go to church. Ultimately, however, on the express condition that Tchitcherin would grant most-favoured-nation conditions to Germany, Maltzan agreed to sacrifice his religious duties and make the visit.

HE then, at about 2.30 a.m., went to find Rathenau.

Rathenau was pacing up and down his room in mauvs
pyjamas, with haggard look and eyes starting out of his
head. When Maltzan came in, he said : " I suppose
you bring me the death-warrant ? " Maltzan replied :
" No ; news of quite a different character." When
he told his story to Rathenau, the latter said : " Now
that I realise the true situation, I will go to Lloyd
George and tell him the whole position, and come to
terms with him."

MALTZAN replied : " That would be quite dishonourable.
If you do that, I will at once resign my post as Secretary
of State and retire into private life. It would be behaving
monstrously to Tchitcherin, and I can be no party to such
action."

EVENTUALLY, Rathenau was converted to the Maltzan
point of view and rather reluctantly agreed to meet the
Russians on Sunday. On Sunday morning, a conference
took place between the Russians and Germans. Both sides
were obstinate and little progress was made. The Germans had a luncheon engagement at a village farther away
from Genoa and broke off negotiations at 1 o'clock. They
then went to their luncheon. While this was going on,
a telephone message came from Lloyd George, saying :
" I am most anxious to see Rathenau as soon as possible ;
would it be convenient to him to come either to tea to-day
or to luncheon to-morrow ? " The fact of this message
became known somehow or other to the Russians. The
consequence was that they became at once more conciliatory
and, in the afternoon, the Rapallo Agreement was signed
without further delay.

BEFORE Maltzan could tell me what subsequently took
place between Rathenau and Lloyd George, we were
interrupted. But he confirmed the story that when Lloyd
George was told by Rathenau that the Germans had
explained their position and their predicament fully to
Wise—the official they believed to be specially charged

CHAP.
XVI
——
October
1926

with Russian affairs—Lloyd George said, " Who is Wise ? "

THE German delegation did not realise the purely rhetorical character of this question, being unaware that, in the Welsh vernacular, imprecations and expletives frequently assume an interrogative form.

END OF VOL. I

21